Bound for
Theresienstadt

Bound for Theresienstadt

*Love, Loss and Resistance
in a Nazi Concentration Camp*

VERA SCHIFF
with JEFF MCLAUGHLIN

Foreword by E. Randol Schoenberg

McFarland & Company, Inc., Publishers
Jefferson, North Carolina

Theresienstadt timeline and two maps used with permission from the U.S. Holocaust Memorial Museum.

LIBRARY OF CONGRESS CATALOGUING-IN-PUBLICATION DATA

Names: Schiff, Vera, 1926– author. | McLaughlin, Jeff, 1962– author.
Title: Bound for Theresienstadt : love, loss and resistance in a Nazi concentration camp / Vera Schiff with Jeff McLaughlin ; foreword by E. Randol Schoenberg.
Description: Jefferson, North Carolina : McFarland & Company, Inc., Publishers, 2017 | Includes index.
Identifiers: LCCN 2017013059 | ISBN 9781476669021 (softcover : acid free paper) ∞
Subjects: LCSH: Theresienstadt (Concentration camp)—Biography. | Concentration camp inmates—Czech Republic—Terezín (Ústecký kraj)—Biography. | Jews—Czech Republic—Terezín (Ústecký kraj)—Biography. | Holocaust, Jewish (1939–1945)—Czech Republic—Terezín (Ústecký kraj) | Czech Republic—Ethnic relations.
Classification: LCC D805.5.T54 S34 2017 | DDC 940.53/18092243716—dc23
LC record available at https://lccn.loc.gov/2017013059

BRITISH LIBRARY CATALOGUING DATA ARE AVAILABLE

ISBN (print) 978-1-4766-6902-1
ISBN (ebook) 978-1-4766-2802-8

© 2017 Vera Schiff and Jeff McLaughlin. All rights reserved

No part of this book may be reproduced or transmitted in any form or by any means, electronic or mechanical, including photocopying or recording, or by any information storage and retrieval system, without permission in writing from the publisher.

Front cover image of the inside of the concentration camp Terezín (Theresienstadt) in Czech Republic, Europe © 2017 Shutterstock

Printed in the United States of America

McFarland & Company, Inc., Publishers
  Box 611, Jefferson, North Carolina 28640
  www.mcfarlandpub.com

Table of Contents

Foreword by E. Randol Schoenberg	1
Preface by Vera Schiff	5
Introduction by Jeff McLaughlin	9
Maps of Theresienstadt	15
ONE—Portrait of Lederer	17
TWO—Portrait of the Saddest Star-crossed Lovers	37
THREE—Portrait of Fredy H.	51
FOUR—Portrait of Milada	72
FIVE—Portrait of Arthur	102
SIX—Portrait of Gonda	123
SEVEN—Portrait of Hanna P.	137
EIGHT—Portrait of the Blue Polka-dot Dress	175
Afterword by Vera Schiff	195
Appendix: Theresienstadt Timeline	201
Index	207

Foreword
by E. Randol Schoenberg

Holocaust histories can be told in different ways. For example, one could recount the story of my great-grandfather Siegmund Zeisl, by saying that he was sent from Vienna to Theresienstadt in July 1942 and from there was deported to Treblinka, where he was murdered. This version of his story almost turns him into a passive observer of his own demise, and yet for most victims this is all that we know. But if we could add more details, we might turn Siegmund into a protagonist. For example: After all four of his sons had fled Vienna to safety and his wife Kamilla had succumbed to cancer, the seventy-year-old coffeehouse owner Siegmund Zeisl prepared for his own departure and that of Kamilla's widowed sister Malvine. He obtained four-month transit visas in July 1941, but Siegmund could not find a spot on a ship leaving Lisbon until December 5 and Malvine could only leave on January 9. Siegmund married Malvine and sought an extension of the visas so that he and Malvine could depart together, but after the war broke out on December 7, 1941, there was no escape. In July, they were required to board a transport (designated IV/4) to Theresienstadt, arriving at the time when that ghetto was most overcrowded and the mortality rate reached its peak. Having survived for two months under terrible conditions, Siegmund and Malvine were required to board the crowded second transport (Bp) to Treblinka where along with 2,000 other victims they were gassed to death upon arrival. It is the same story, but with the added details we can see elements of resistance, even an attempt to escape, and also of love, how the widower and widow tried to stay together and help each other.

We are very fortunate that Vera Schiff has been able to share her recollections of her years in Theresienstadt in several books. Schiff is a rare survivor who can tell not only her own story, but the story of others. Through her eyes, we begin to see the victims as real human beings. One cannot help but be impressed with her clinical, unsentimental attention to detail, and her dispassionate, clear-eyed understanding of the various forces at play within the ghetto. Her reminiscences are not free from judgment, but she never fails to sympathize with her subjects, despite their flaws. Schiff does not shy away from the complexity of her subject's stories, realizing as she does, that every nuance adds living flesh to the otherwise bare-boned lists of names and dates that populate our Holocaust victim databases.

The phrase "Let us not go like sheep to the slaughter" was famously used in a speech by the young poet Abba Kovner on New Year's Eve 1941 in support of the resistance group forming in the Vilna ghetto, and became the partisan group's motto. As a rallying cry for the resistance, the phrase made sense, but Kovner, and every other survivor, could only cringe at the term's use after the war to describe the millions of helpless victims of the Nazis. Kovner himself was racked with guilt that he left his own mother behind in the ghetto. His poem *My Little Sister* was inspired by his first love Hadassah who, unlike Kovner, chose to stay with her mother, stoically accompanying her to the site of their murder in the Ponary execution pit. Kovner, the hero of Vilna, feels the sting of reproach in her memory. What then does resistance and heroism look like in the hellish crucible of the Holocaust?

The topic of resistance during the Holocaust is very popular, but I suspect that this popularity stems from a desire to find a traditionally heroic story in what is by and large an unrelenting tragedy. During the war, the dire plight of the Jews of Europe never reached the front pages of newspapers in the United States. The sole exception was the Warsaw Ghetto uprising, which was already then used as an example of heroic resistance. In the end, the rebellion was a failure; the ghetto was liquidated and only a few were able to escape the mass murder. And yet the ghetto uprising never ceases to inspire romanticized retelling, as if we need to imagine that effective resistance to the Nazis was really possible, rather than come to grips with the reality that it was not.

Understanding the Holocaust means recognizing that, when faced with an insurmountable enemy, traditional categories of heroism and resistance do not necessarily apply. Holding a child's hand or comforting a friend in the face of imminent death took as much courage as an escape to the forest to join the partisans, while traditionally heroic acts of resistance

Foreword by E. Randol Schoenberg

and escape very often resulted in terrifying reprisals and the immediate deaths of family members and others. One needs to keep in mind that every Jew, no matter what he or she did in an attempt to survive, was a victim. Even acts that might seem selfish and opportunistic in our *post hoc* judgment were more often just attempts to increase the chances of survival or protect family members. Schiff's complicated stories of love, heroism and resistance are therefore important as reminders that the victims were, all of them, human beings with little or no influence on their ultimate fate. That they nevertheless kept their decency and humanity in spite of their horrific ordeal, and continued to love each other and to struggle against their oppressors, is a testament to the indomitable persistence of hope.

E. Randol Schoenberg (born 1966) is an American attorney who represented Maria Altmann in her successful case against the government of Austria regarding stolen Nazi artwork. This story was later depicted in the film Woman in Gold.

Preface
by Vera Schiff

I thought about writing a compilation of a few exceptionally interesting accounts of people during the Holocaust. I have been mulling who these accounts would come from for quite some time now and wanted them to be from differing walks of life. The question returning to my mind was this: Why? Is it really necessary to revisit again the tragic history of the destruction of European Jewry? Slowly I reached the conclusion that it was not only necessary but also was, and remains, imperative! Let me explain how I came to the conclusion that these intimate portraits fill a dire need for present and future generations.

The Holocaust, as serious students of history agree, was a watershed in mankind's existence. It is not that there have been no other spasms of bloodletting in mankind's quest for rule and domination of this planet; but the fact that the Holocaust took place at all, as it did, should shatter our belief that we are slowly shying away from raw brutality and that civilization is progressing. That belief was but a fading pipedream, as demonstrated by this 20th century tragedy. As it happened, following the First World War—"the war to end war"—a time of high hopes for new beginnings took hold in a country in the heart of Europe. Germany, for a very long time, was perceived as the flagship of men's achievements, yet this country accepted a racist philosophy and adopted brutality and performed horrific acts at a premeditated national level. This tells me that our interpersonal polity has not moved an inch from the dark days of our cave existence. The paper-thin veneer of our civilization crumbled quickly and easily, giving way to the most unimaginable bestiality—and that was at the hands of a nation that styled itself to be a standard-bearer of progress, a master race if you will.

My entire family perished right along with European Jewry. Miraculously I pulled through and have ever since been trying to make sense of how and why I survived. I never unraveled the how but I concluded that it was my personal mission never to allow the world to forget the Nazi era. As a survivor of the tragedy I have dedicated my time to writing and speaking to the younger generations, warning them about prejudice, intolerance and lack of respect for one another.

As time passed the Holocaust seemed to become less relevant, and the shock of the industrial mass murder began to fade, obscured by other daily events. I watched the danger of the Holocaust slipping humanity's memory and being filed into the dustbin of history. I resolved to do my best to bring it back to the forefront at least within the spheres I could influence. To my relief and satisfaction I see noticeable curiosity during my lectures, and while the young generation has multilayered interests, their discernment of the past is amazing.

Today the facts are well known, but it is not the data that penetrates the conscience or heart of students and allow them to identify with times bygone; rather it is the poignant stories of those who fell under the wheels of Nazi hatred. There is a hunger to understand, to learn, the different ways people coped. There is the opportunity to drive the point home: that it could have been them, had they been unfortunate to be born as Jews during the Nazi rule of terror.

I gave a great deal of thought on how to choose the individuals described in this anthology. It is my misfortune that although I knew so many, most are long gone and their stories lost. From my extensive experiences I picked out a cross section of exceptional stories of individuals who would have probably led unremarkable lives had they been allowed to. Some were very young, others were pushing middle age, and a few were just embarking on their life's journey. But I am certain that their destinies will touch the heart of the reader. Their struggles for survival, their hopes, dreams and even love stories, all lived in the shadow of the crematories, are nothing short of amazing. As I talk about these individuals to the students, they follow my words breathlessly, totally enraptured. Their attention is undivided and were a pin to drop in the classroom it would be audible.

As I do realize and accept my own time limitations, I decided to offer to the public a compilation of the narratives my audiences found pertinent and enlightening as well as fascinating, poignant and emotive. Never is an event better understood that when seen through the eyes of those who witnessed it. Among those I picked were individuals, some predestined to leadership who fought valiantly against their oppressors. Some stood tall till the very end, others faltered, unable to sustain the superhuman efforts to the very end. The reader will meet people who understood the exceptionality of the tragedy, retaining their dignity and courage in the most dire of circumstances. Others were less fortunate. Each coped in a unique way. It is intriguing to some that love between man and woman did not die at the gates of this man-made hell; in fact, for some the proximity of the Angel of Death only intensified this eternal emotion. It was a way of feeling human if only for a moment or two.

Though the passage of time dulls the sharp and crushing awareness and already three generations have grown up since the catastrophe came to an end, we can ill afford to allow the lessons of the Holocaust to fade out of our collective memory. It is my experience that the most profound experience is evoked in the student by chronicling the diverse experiences of individuals and their coping skills. This is where they learn well the lessons needed if we are to change our civilization and avoid another Holocaust.

Finally, this book should serve as a memorial to those portrayed here and to all who fell victim during the era of supreme hatred. The six million men, women and children do not have graves. It is my great hope that this book will shine a light for their lasting memory.

Introduction
by Jeff McLaughlin

It is now more than seventy years since the end of World War II and this book may be one of the last written by a survivor of the Holocaust. Works that will come afterwards where the author was physically there and met and spoke to those around her will be but a trickle and then sadly cease. We are fortunate to have here a direct report and not a speculation based upon secondary sources. Vera Schiff knew these people personally and so her telling their stories is not only important but also profoundly moving. We are getting an incredibly rich work directly from those involved told to someone within the very setting and context that binds all these portraits together. They are all different people but with the same destination: Theresienstadt.

Accordingly, this book is meant to do far more than just to inform you. After each portrait I asked Vera a series of questions to help provide more context and clarification or to share more deep philosophical concerns and issues. It is my hope that the combination of all these pieces moves you beyond your justified emotions to become more reflective regarding the impact of what you read on both personal and philosophical levels.

So significant is the Holocaust that it is "outside" of time; that is, its relevance does not and will not diminish with the passing of the years. It remains as relevant today as it was yesterday if not more so. Seventy plus years is a long time in the life of a person, but a very short time in terms of human history and conflicts. It wasn't much later after the war when other forces in the world would commit new acts of mass murder and genocide either because they turned a blind eye to the events from 1933 to 1945 or because of them. Thus we must be ever vigilant as such acts of horror can creep quietly up onto the world stage.

Introduction by Jeff McLaughlin

Merely learning facts and figures about the Holocaust does not do it, or its victims, justice. For what harm can truly come to a number? Millions of human beings were murdered, but you can't murder a number. You can't starve or torture a number. You can't destroy the life of a number. Nor can you save the life of a number. You can only do these things to another human being.

A number like six million dead may give you the historical result but does not tell you any of the story; it does not give you the meaning or the significance as much as the number "one." One individual. If we can put a name to that number one; if we can tell you about the love, the life, the courage of that person; if we can share with you who they were, what they experienced, what they did, what they chose, and what was imposed upon them, then you will better understand the enormity of what happened. Indeed, even the mind-numbing number of "six million" does not include all those who were affected. The victims and the survivors did not live in isolation. They had families, they had friends. If they were murdered, there is no knowing what might have been. And if they survived, they may have married and they may have had children who also continue to feel the ripples and echoes of the Holocaust. The more we learn about the names behind the numbers the more we realize we need to stop talking in abstractions and "big pictures" and start talking about individual lives. Each story tells us more than facts about that person; it opens our eyes to begin to appreciate that there are millions of people who shared nothing and everything in common: the Holocaust. Likewise, here you will read a handful of personal stories that share nothing and everything in common: the Theresienstadt camp.

What is remarkable about this work is of course the people of the narratives and the author. But what is unique in Holocaust literature is that these people told their stories to Vera Schiff—herself a survivor—while they were in the Theresienstadt camp. The significance of this is that we are getting a rich and clear work directly from those involved told to someone in the very context that binds all these divergent stories and people together.

Vera presents the tales in her voice and provides her insight, based on experiences and reflections (either explicitly or "between the lines"), which are drawn from her being both a survivor and an educator. Indeed, since Vera was born in what is now the Czech Republic, her way of speaking and writing reflects her way of thinking and her Eastern European roots. It is for these reasons that although I have edited her phrasing somewhat

Introduction by Jeff McLaughlin

I have tried not to alter her "voice," especially with regard to the portraits she has painted.

Telling stories is a human tradition and a way to pass on information and wisdom, both important functions. Yet oral histories can raise questions about the veracity of information. How do we know that what we are told is true or accurate? Years have passed and memories can fade, change, or be influenced. Indeed, ask a group of eyewitnesses about an event that occurred only last week and you might get many different versions. But with those different versions one hopes to be able to find important things they all agree upon.

History is not a static field. It continues to be rewritten because we continue to verify and make new discoveries. Historians do not merely tell us the past. They use words in a way that may emphasize some events and downplay others. They may ignore important details simply by not mentioning them. Even the very words that are chosen can give us different accounts of an event. Read a conservative newspaper report about a public event and then read a liberal iteration of the same event and you may wonder if they were attending different functions. We must therefore recognize that there are limitations to consider and assumptions to be made when reading memoirs, diaries, biographies and autobiographies. Whether the person is honest and reliable are two important questions to ask of any individual's testimony.

Fortunately, in our case, the stories here are being relayed to us by someone who is a well-respected Holocaust educator and author of numerous books regarding her experiences and those of her family and friends. Vera's memoir *Theresienstadt: The Town the Nazis Gave to the Jews* tells her family's history.

The personal narratives in this work describe unimaginable events that she also experienced and witnessed during the Holocaust. Through her writing, others can give voice to their memories. Vera explains how she met these people, who entrusted her with their stories.

> I met Viteslav aka Slavek Lederer in Theresienstadt, where he was for a while hiding following his escape from Auschwitz. He was a friend of my then boyfriend and later husband, Arthur D. Schiff. Both men served, and were officers, in the Czechoslovak army. After the war both men remained in contact and both lived in Israel. Viteslav was quite open about his exploits and sabotages of the Nazis during World War II.
>
> Fredy H. was youth leader in Prague, where I first met him in Hagibor, the only place Jewish youth could gather. His fate following his punitive deportation from

Theresienstadt, where I again was in touch with him, was shared with me by a mutual friend.

Milada was a cousin of mine. We shared a short time of our incarceration in Theresienstadt. Her fate after deportation to Maly Trostinec, a death camp, was reported to me by the sole survivor of this camp, Mr. Hanus Muntz.

Gonda, alias Egon Redlich, was a youth worker in Theresienstadt, where I knew him and his wife. I was in touch with both of them until their deportation to Auschwitz, whence they did not return.

Hanna P.'s parents and my parents were acquaintances and were in close contact before the war and even after the Nazi occupation of Prague. She was in touch with me in Theresienstadt and her later fate I researched with the help of Jewish friends who were deported to the East at the same time she was.

The sisters in "The Blue Polka-dot Dress" were in Theresienstadt. One worked in the same hospital as I did. She quite openly described to me the family dynamic before and even during the war years. Only one survived the war and she was in touch with me during those later years.

I met Arthur and married him in Theresienstadt. We lived together for 56 years. He was involved in many clandestine actions, sabotaging Nazi ordinances. His heroism and hair-raising underground work were nothing if not astounding, though mostly unknown. Some of it, like his work on falsification documents for those in the crosshairs of the Nazis, was later acknowledged, but his secret plan to smuggle drugs into Theresienstadt remained unknown. He never wanted recognition: he did what he perceived as his duty.

The title of this work is not something that was just selected as a way to attract attention. Let me explain why it is *Bound for Theresienstadt: Love, Loss and Resistance in a Nazi Concentration Camp*. "Bound" is the past tense of bind; it brings up images of being restricted, controlled, and tied up. It also suggests travel to a specific destination, as in "This train is bound for...." The word also has a sense of certainty: "It was bound to happen." Next, you are informed as to the location: Theresienstadt. However, since some people may not know where or what that is "a Nazi Concentration Camp" makes it quite explicit. (It should be noted that some authorities refer to Theresienstadt as a Ghetto, however, unlike in ghettos where families were kept together, here they were separated.)

There are common threads and themes that run throughout the different chapters which involve the role of love and loss in determining what happened or what choices were made. Likewise, there are instances of direct resistance against the Nazis and the mere fact that an individual survived to the next day was a statement of resistance. The title also combines the positive connotations of words such as love, and resistance with

Introduction by Jeff McLaughlin

the negative (that is, loss) as a subtle reminder regarding the complex nature of what you are about to read.

Part of the inherent complexity and limitation of a written work is that it is impossible to tell everything. This is why I use the word "portraits" rather than just "stories." A portrait in the sense of a painting is not intended to be an exact reproduction of what a person looks like. Painted portraits are not photographs. Portraits are interpretations which aim not at just capturing the physical truth of the subject but his or her inner self. Thus, an author by her words or a painter by his brush strokes plays a role in the final outcome.

As a philosopher who teaches ethics I have an interest in the Holocaust that is slightly different than that of the traditional historian. Every day human beings engage in decision-making. Most of the time these decisions are minor and have minor consequences, but at other times, they may change lives. We sometimes are free to make whatever choices we wish and at other times we are forced (by other persons or circumstances) to choose between two bad options. Nevertheless, even if we are forced to choose, we choose; and if we refuse to choose we are also making a choice. Whether and when we may be held morally accountable in addition to (perhaps) being causally responsible is a separate matter best left for another time. Yet we can state in general that how we choose, what we choose, and why we choose are key elements in morality. In order to make the best choice possible (given the circumstances) you need to possess knowledge and have an informed appreciation of what the consequences are regarding the different options. The vast amount of knowledge we have about the Holocaust presents humanity with an untold amount of information regarding ethical motives, intentions, choices and consequences.

Consider when a person is aware of a terrible event and yet willingly acts in a way that repeats it. We would rightly deem them to be far worse than someone who does the same act but lacks knowledge. For example, we might say of a child who did something wrong (for example, pulled on a cat's tail) that they "didn't know any better." But if a person did know better and acted in spite of it, or should have known better and acted inappropriately moral condemnation is rightfully in order. Nevertheless, whether through ignorance or willingness, the consequences are the same. And as human beings we tend to need to be reminded over and over again. This is why we need to learn and appreciate history.

Being in the presence of a survivor who is willing and able to discuss what they and their loved ones went through is one of the most intimate, personal and life-changing experiences one can have. Millions of innocent human beings have become victims due to mass murder and genocide. For the majority of them we will know very little if anything about them. They have become anonymous statistics. We won't know their names, or their loves or their acts of courage or desperation. So when we are given the chance to hear about such individuals—especially from those who personally knew them—we should stop and listen. Their lives matter because ours matters. Our life matters because theirs did. In the way that this book is put together, it is my hope that that message becomes clear.

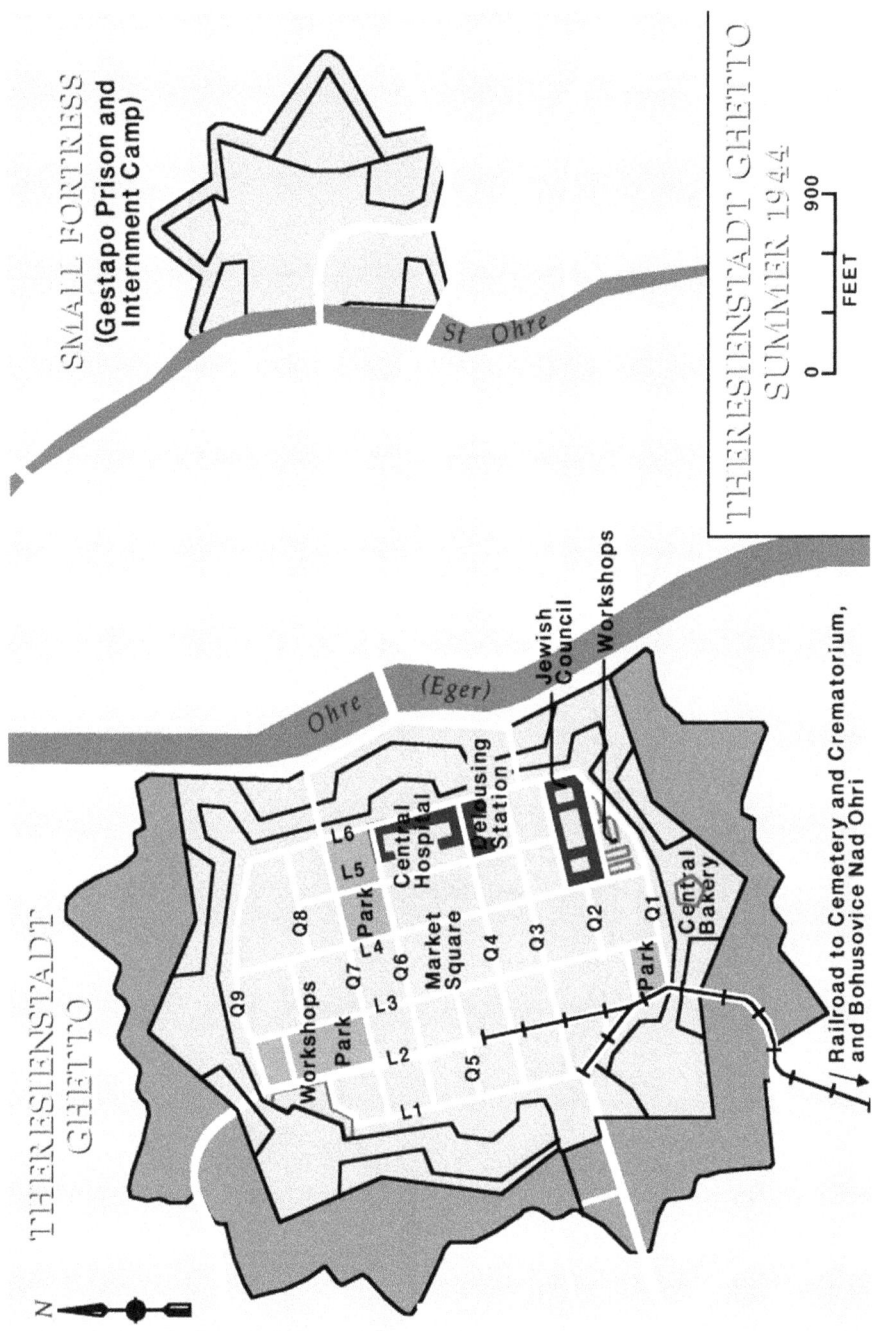

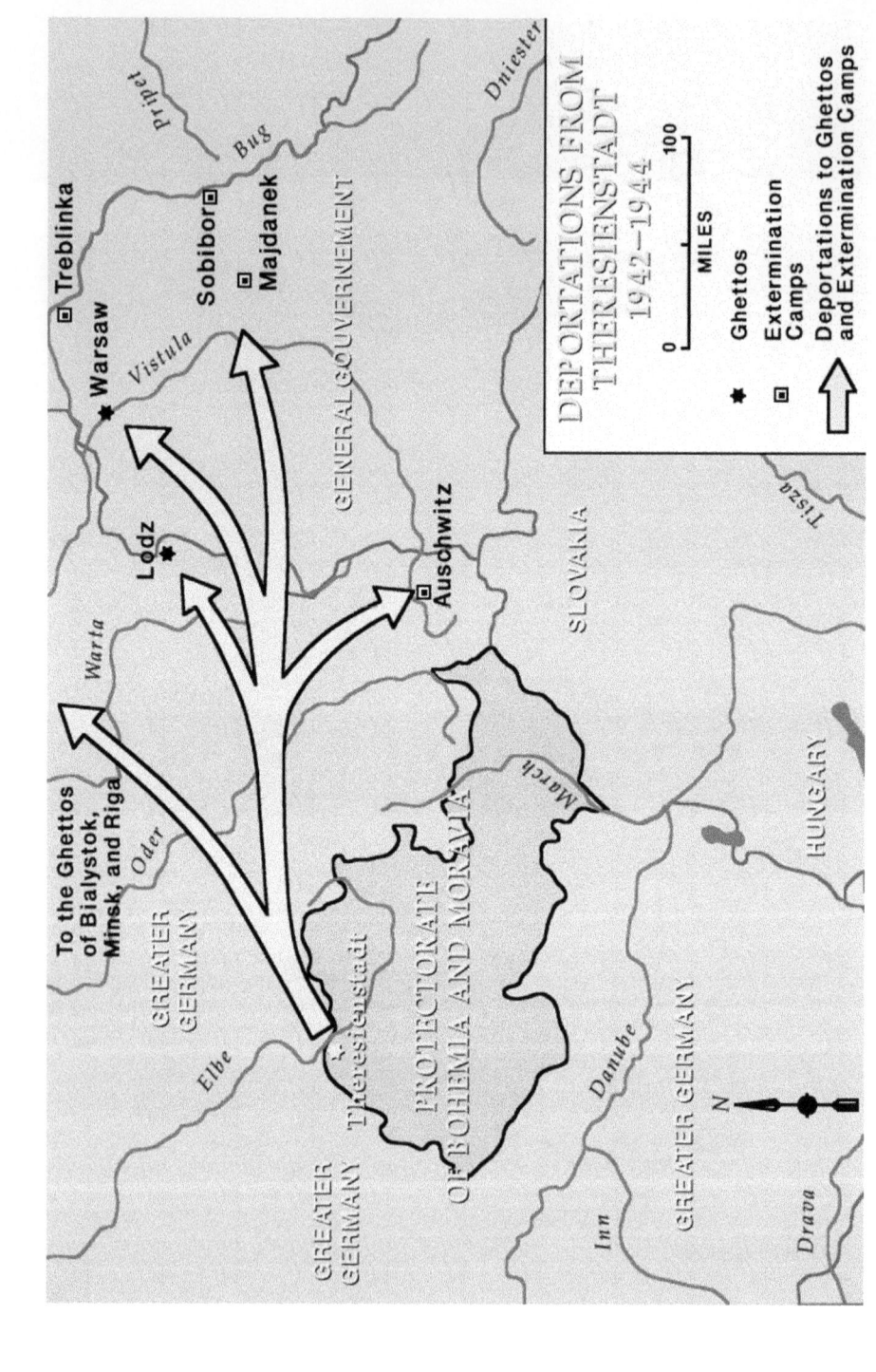

ONE

Portrait of Lederer

I

Strange how I remember that day with such absolute clarity! Perhaps because it had been whispered for a very long time that we stood sentenced, at the precipice of death, and there was no appeal of that verdict. But we refused to believe it. We still could not accept that nothing, absolutely nothing, could alter the judgment passed by the implacable Nazi regime. Still we hesitated to give it credence. Even after a two-year incarceration in Theresienstadt we somehow could not fathom mass slaughter, murder by assembly line executed by modern industrial systems, using chemical means. When I mention this today, most think, I believe, that I am less than honest, posturing or just being plain phony. But that is the honest truth! While we acquiesced that starvation and subhuman conditions would do us in, mass murder by aerosolized poisoning was still not on our radar.

So let me tell you how I learned the bitter, irrevocable truth, one I could not contest or doubt. It was the spring of the year 1944. My mother was ill, suffering with TB, and I was preoccupied in a hectic scramble to find some food she could digest. In my feverish activity, searching high and low for something to help keep my mother alive, I had little interest or time to listen to hearsay that persistently repeated that once we boarded the trains to the East we were doomed, embarking on the last leg of our lives.

My boyfriend at the time, who later became my husband, an inveterate optimist who never gave up his hope that we would survive, came to see me. [Arthur's portrait is presented here as well—ed.] His ordinarily smiling and friendly expression was ashen, dark and grim. I thought that he was physically unwell but he soon disabused me of this assumption. He only insisted that we have a talk and without delay.

I had known for some time that he wanted me to agree to marry him in the only possible way in camp, because rumors had it that if we were indexed as a couple we could be deported together. I hesitated, not because I did not love him. I certainly did, but I was responsible for my ailing mother and for her sake I wanted to stay put, single or otherwise. I knew that in no possible way could she survive the rigors of yet another tortuous journey in a cattle car, jammed with other inmates. I wanted to nurse her in Theresienstadt, hoping that when the slow-grinding war ended I might be able to bring her into a hospital or sanatorium for tubercular patients. I was not willing or able to give up my hope that she might yet recover.

I hated to refuse my boyfriend's repeated proposals, for I knew that he was concerned and wished to stand by me.

On that spring day of 1944 we stood behind a pillar and Arthur began to share with me the following story, sounding grim as he told it. It was as if it had been taken from a horror story but it was, unfortunately, well substantiated. Now, here I am reporting it the way he narrated it.

Arthur talked sotto voce for the din of the jam-packed camp where there was no privacy, and it was dangerous to be overheard or quoted by someone who might misuse the information. Here then is the narrative:

One of Arthur's friends from days bygone escaped from Auschwitz, an almost unheard of feat, and just slipped in to warn the inmates of Theresienstadt. Arthur swore that the escapee's report was not only credible but had the ring of truth, for the man was honorable and brave and took grave risk penetrating the thick walls of the onetime fortress—all in effort of a self-appointed mission to deliver a warning to the inmates and reveal the truth to us. It was high noon to learn that there was no resettlement to the East—no continuation for Jews. Risking his own life, he sneaked into the camp to tip us off to the bitter truth of our impending end. For the time being, he was hiding in one of the multitude of underground passages beneath the one-time fortress.

But let me start at the beginning, so this narrative will make some sense to you.

Arthur, my boyfriend, was drafted into the Czech army right after his graduation from university. University graduates were automatically considered officers in training right after completing their six weeks of basic training with firearms. Sometimes during his military service Arthur met and befriended another Jewish man, a career officer by the name of Viteslav (Slavek) Lederer, who was a few years Arthur's senior. Actually, few Jews chose military service as a life career in those days, as they were

One. Portrait of Lederer

still somewhat unsure about the prospects of life in uniform, for most countries did not bestow officer training eligibility to Jews. Within the ranks of the career officers, prejudice and anti–Semitism reigned. Though the fledgling Czechoslovakian republic attempted to combat this persistent and rabid prejudice, at least officially, this scourge was so widespread in Europe that it was a common malady of the rank and file. To opt for life in uniform was still an exceptional choice for most Jews. Past discrimination was still lingering in the minds of most. By and large most Jewish young men were honorably discharged after their compulsory two years' draft, and then they turned to other goals. Lederer was that exception; he opted for lifelong service in the Czech army.

Viteslav Lederer, called Slavek, was born in the 1904 in Pilsen, a south Bohemian city most renowned for its beer expertise. All went well initially, but in the ominous year of 1938 Czechoslovakia was the country onto which Hitler turned his unwanted attention, choosing to occupy and annex it.

For a long time Czechoslovakia and her allies placed their trust in Hitler's repeated assurances that he was only interested in reuniting all Germans into his Third Reich and not incorporating other nationals. With hindsight this trust seems childish and incredible.

The attack on Czechoslovakian integrity began when demands to relinquish the border regions with Germany were mediated at the international forum. It resulted in protracted negotiations with the British prime minister Neville Chamberlain and his French counterpart, Edouard Daladier. The diplomatic bargaining went from bad to worse. Both Western diplomats, unaccustomed to Hitler's long tirades, endless histrionic monologues and bullying tactics, were bewildered and at a loss in how to deal with a man uninterested in solving a problem but, rather, determined to have his way by hook or by crook. While Hitler was comfortable engaging in screaming and grossly hysterical behavior, the Western politicians were shocked by such uncivilized street-thug outbursts. In Berchtesgaden, also known as the "lion's den" and Hitler's residence, high in the Bavarian Alps, during a conference on Czechoslovakia's future with regards to its Sudeten German minority, Hitler allegedly threw himself to the floor and began to chew the carpet while shouting incessantly about the imperative of their immediate repatriation. Little wonder that in the ominous year of 1938, after yet another abortive meeting with Hitler, the frustrated, frightened and spineless Western leadership wrote off the little country in the heart of Europe and served her on a silver platter to the Nazis. No

Czech representatives participated in either of these high-level conferences; the fate of the country was decided without the presence of even one Czechoslovakian official. In a total breach of all morality and political integrity the allies of Czechoslovakia issued an ultimatum to their own ally to vacate the northern region, the Sudeten, and if they were not in compliance the Western democracies would join the German military, enforcing the implementation of the Munich agreement. Thus betrayed and abandoned by its allies, the Prague government felt that they did not stand a chance of mounting meaningful resistance to the German aggression; and although that small nation was well prepared it did not have the chance of a snowflake in hell of winning the war with the well-equipped and mighty German war machine. The government of Czechoslovakia resigned, the Germans occupied the Sudeten, and the Czechoslovakian army was disbanded. Most Czechs in general, but the younger officers in particular, recoiled with anger and embarrassment. Slavek Lederer was one of them. The officers seethed with shame and impotent rage. All their preparations, training and determination came to naught. It was a humiliating appeasement of a dictator who would not be appeased.

To boot, the British prime minister, Neville Chamberlain, stated on record a shameful utterance proclaiming that England would not go to war for a small country in central Europe, the name of which they could not even pronounce. And thus, waving a piece of paper, Chamberlain exclaimed victoriously that he had saved "peace for our time." Six months later the Second World War broke out.

Slavek, like many other officers, saw the shortsightedness, lack of backbone and plain stupidity of the intimidated and fearful West. During the dark days of the debacle following the Munich conference, the first kernels of the Czech resistance were sowed. These disbanded officers began to organize the anti–Nazi underground resistance movement for the days when the remnant, truncated and indefensible country was overrun. They didn't have a long wait; it took barely five months for the German army to march, unopposed, into the open plains of the renamed Czech republic, which was now known as the Protectorate of Bohemia and Moravia. The eastern part, Slovakia and Sub-Carpathian Ruthenia, were afforded the status of a quasi-independent state, albeit under the leadership of Father Tiso, a Catholic priest and a longtime admirer of Hitler. As matters stood, he was expected to rubberstamp all Nazi orders, under whose tutelage they were granted statehood.

Many a brave and frustrated Czech did not wait for the German army

One. Portrait of Lederer

to march into Prague and the resistance movement was firmly established. They had their work cut out for them though, and they fought diligently preparing for acts of sabotage and smuggling many endangered people out of the country. The underground had to procure false documents for those in dire jeopardy and much more. How do I know this? My boyfriend Arthur was a member of the resistance and it was his main task to create falsified identity cards and other required legal documents. There were many whose lives were in jeopardy: Jews, communists, opposition members of the previous democratic government, and many more.

Another member of the resistance, a girl who worked at the interior ministry, found a way of accessing official blank identity cards, documents she was promptly ordered to pilfer in an unobtrusive manner. She then passed these priceless tickets to life to another member who gave them to Arthur. It was his task to fill in the particulars, often taken from tombstones, affix an appropriate snapshot of the new persona and make all of it look perfectly official and legitimate. Arthur had many other assignments within the resistance, as did most of the previous Czech army officers. But this is not an essay on Arthur's activities, which are also presented in this tome, but rather of Slavek's incredible journey during the Shoah.

It was his rotten luck that his subversive activity for the underground was betrayed to the Nazis soon after occupation. He was arrested and sent to the Small Fortress jail in Theresienstadt. This penal institution served for many decades as a maximum-security jail for predominantly political prisoners. It was a dreadful prison that few survived. Some of its inhumane features consisted of underground dugout cells where prisoners languished in total darkness. It was for all the right reasons perceived as the penultimate station, a place where men lingered, suffering incredible pain, and there most ended their lives.

Slavek had an exceptionally rough course of incarceration in the Small Fortress. Tortured, beaten and incessantly interrogated, he well nigh died right then and there. It was doubtful if and for how long he could last on such a brutal protocol. But somehow the resistance managed to manipulate events. It never became quite clear how it was accomplished, but a near miracle came to pass and he made it out of the fortress alive. Slavek was a Jew and as such the least likely to leave this jail alive, for Jews were marked for the worst of the inhuman treatments. But one day the commandant of the fortress agreed to discharge Slavek to the adjacent concentration camp in Theresienstadt, with the understanding and condition that he would be sent with the first departing transport to the death camps to the East. But the Elder of the Jews, Jakob Edelstein, managed to put a different spin on the matter. He tried at all cost to save Slavek's life, for he realized the value of an experienced military man in their situation. He assigned him work with the camp's fire brigade, as this unit was for a time protected. Slavek arrived in Theresienstadt on January 1942 in a transport labeled with the letter R.

From the get-go he tried to organize resistance through sabotage of all Nazi orders, but this work was greatly hampered by the steady deportations of inmates to the East. There were ongoing efforts by the resistance to smuggle weapons into the camp and radio parts, which would allow contact with the outside world and help coordinate the undermining of the Nazis' plans for the smooth operation of the camp. Unfortunately the Nazis kept sending people to the East at a relentless pace, so little was accomplished by the valiant attempts to sabotage the German efforts.

The attempts to keep Slavek in Theresienstadt ended in December 1943, when he was served with a deportation order. Although he worked in the fire brigade, a protected commando, Slavek was caught smoking, a capital crime in Theresienstadt imposed by the Nazis. He was punished by being enrolled in a transport designated by letters "Dr," which left Theresienstadt on December 18, 1943, for Auschwitz-Birkenau.

There the underground was alerted of the arrival of the transport carrying this highly prized soldier. Few were anxious about an initial selection, for the "Dr" or December transport was immediately bunked with the family camp, which for mysterious reasons was established from a prior transport arriving in September of 1943. Slavek Lederer was assigned work under the watchful eyes of the camp's resistance, which secretly contacted and advised him about their activities of monitoring and undermining the Nazis' atrocities and horrendous crimes.

Within a short time Slavek befriended another resistance member whose deportation from Theresienstadt to Auschwitz was also due to a punitive measure. Fredy Hirsh was his name and his extraordinary story is recited in detail in this book as well. In brief he was a young German Jewish educator in charge of the children in Theresienstadt, and he was appointed to do the same in the shadows of the gas chambers of Auschwitz.

Fredy continued his work in the family camp, inspiring the children to keep clean, shower daily in cold water, exercise and keep their morale high. In recognition of this Herculean effort Fredy was afforded a little corner roomette, a luxury, a private room all to himself that became the center for many secretive encounters. One of the men who dropped by regularly was Slavek Lederer. The two men soon discovered they had a lot in common, first and foremost a shared ambition to sabotage the Nazis' feverish attempts to murder as many Jews as possible. There was still another frequent visitor to Fredy's little roomette. Surprisingly this man was not a Jew. He was a German, a sergeant major who hailed from Romania but was a Volks Deutsche: a person of Germanic descent, and he was none other than group leader Victor Pestek.

II

Now the plot thickens. Who was the Nazi guard who dared to frequent Fredy's cubicle? Enter Victor Pestek, a German national, a group leader in the Wehrmacht, a noncommissioned officer who fought on the Russian front. There he suffered serious injuries and after recovering was transferred to the death camp Auschwitz to less dangerous duty as a reward for his service to the Fatherland.

No one knew if he was a violent anti–Semite before he assumed his duties in Auschwitz, but what we do know is that amongst his duties he was responsible for the daily census in the family camp. There he met an inmate, Renee, a young Czech girl, barely 20 years old, who in spite of conditions prevailing in the camp retained some of her radiant beauty. In addition, she was flirtatious and knew how to utilize her feminine powers. She was also very hungry and frightened of the ever-present threat of death. The obvious admiration of the SS man who inspected the inmates daily was not only flattering but also offered the possibility of saving her life as well her mother's. He began to augment her starvation-size food rations and provided her with all manner of amenities, the kind an inmate could only dream of. Renee and Victor developed a romantic relationship and spent time together in Fredy's roomette. This German noncommissioned officer could help avert starvation rampant in the camp where Renee and her mother shared a bunk under terribly unhygienic conditions. Perhaps he could help ease their starvation and a slew of other deprivations.

Renee Neumann, the exceptionally lovely girl, hailed from the capital of Moravia, Brno, and was deported in December of 1941 in a transport labeled "K" during the early days of the forcible expulsion of all Jews. She and her mother were very closely knit and remained in Theresienstadt for almost two years. Though life there was fraught with shortages and dangers of all sorts, both women remained in reasonably good physical condition. But Theresienstadt was just a transit camp and both women were hit by deportation orders in December 1943. Enrollment in a transport to Auschwitz was a heavy, if not unexpected, blow. Renee and her mother left on a transport designated with the letters "Di." Both women had heard copious rumors about the horrors ongoing in the camps to the East, and, like most people, dreaded deportation. But they were not fully resigned to the notion that they were destined to die upon arrival.

Much to their surprise they were not subject to the selection process. Usually an arriving transport was met by Nazi officers, one of them a physician, and right then and there on the "Jewish Ramp" the medical doctor separated the inmates. He chose those who seemed too weak, old, young or sick to die the same day, while those who still carried the promise of delivering a pound of flesh for the German war machine were destined to hard labor. Instead of undergoing selection, Renee and her mother and their entire transport were sent to the family camp, separate from but within Auschwitz and this is where the Czech inmates were incarcerated. That was a very unusual development and many tried to decipher the inscrutable mind of the Nazis. Why were these Jews treated differently? They were allowed to keep their clothes, their hair was not shorn, and families were not torn asunder. Did the Nazis come down with a sudden case of compassion? Impossible, was the universal consensus. So what did this inscrutable scenario mean? Was this sinister and dangerous or not? What was afoot? The other inmates, in their pinstriped garb and housed in adjacent blocks, watched in disbelief the freshly minted, highly privileged Czech inmates.

The underground was obsessed with this riddle. In addition, the transport had a cryptic addendum of "6 BSSB" after its initial "Di" letter identification. It took weeks if not longer for the underground to solve the riddle. Their conclusion spelled catastrophe, for they agreed with a heavy heart that the 6 BS stood for 6 months, followed by SB, which stood for *Sonder Behandlung*, or special treatment, which in the camp's parlance meant death by gassing. Why the Nazis wanted to keep the Czech family camp intact remained a hotly contested question.

Meanwhile, life in the family camp unfolded in much the same pattern as in Theresienstadt. Fredy H. took care of the children, and all hoped they would escape death in the gas chambers. As time passed they worriedly observed the tall chimneys incessantly belching wreaths of black smoke lit by darting orange flames illuminating the night skies. They knew what was going to happen but somehow they hoped and believed they had an incomprehensibly privileged situation.

With time the resistance construed the Germans' ominous plot. The Nazis were concerned about resistance to deportations from the transit camp, Theresienstadt, where the rumors of extermination took hold. Accordingly, they distributed postcards to the inmates of the family camp and ordered all prisoners to write their relatives and friends in Prague as well as in Theresienstadt. They were allowed 30 words and they had to indicate that they were healthy, living together as families and hoped to reunite with the rest of the families. All postcards had to be postdated April 1944. The Nazis even offered a reason: the wartime censorship caused delays of all postal deliveries and therefore the later date was required. This was the reason for the family camp, the resistance concluded, and its destruction was ordained to occur in six months.

III

Love is a many splendored thing, say the poets. And it can blossom in the most bizarre of places, where no one would dream love could take root. Inexplicably *Rottenfuehrer* Pestek was smitten, heads over heels, with Rénee at first sight. Admittedly she was beautiful but he knew better than most that he was playing with fire. After all, he was a Gentile and an SS officer who swore unquestioning obedience to Nazi laws, which forbade any sexual contact between Gentile and Jew. He was well aware that violation of this edict would net him a bullet to the nape of the neck or worse and of course would also bring about the execution of the Jewess. Perhaps Renee lived on borrowed time in any case; but Pestek had a future, and if you believed in a Nazi victory, a long and glorious one to boot. But Pestek was totally spellbound. He made it his business to crisscross the family camp as often he could when one day he happened to meet the friendly and engaging Fredy. Fredy volunteered to show him some of his work and as they entered his roomette they engaged in amicable chitchat. Fredy was on the lookout for anyone who could ease the restrictions and suffering of the kids and Pestek in turn searched for ways to meet Renee safely and with some privacy. The two quickly saw eye to eye. In time, Renee would show up at the appointed hour, after which Pestek would stroll casually into Fredy's roomette. After a few unobtrusive moments Fredy would make an excuse, leaving the two lovers alone.

Meanwhile, the enamored Pestek worked hard on securing a future life with Renee, whom he loved with all his heart. He amassed jewelry and hard currency, all of which he stashed and buried on the property of Polish friends in the nearby village of Mislovitz. Many SS men did the same, enriching themselves beyond belief; building a nest egg for after the war while keeping an eye on the shaky situation on the battlefields, where the once powerful Wehrmacht were suffering bloody defeats at the hands of the Soviet army.

Still, danger loomed near and no one knew it better than the man who worked both sides of the hierarchy, the SS officer Victor Pestek. He was painfully aware that time was running out and he pressed Renee to agree to follow his plan of escape. He would take care of everything; all she had to do was follow his instructions. Pestek was painfully aware that Renee's transport carried the ominous 6SB and that time would run out in June of 1944. He knew that only two transports had left Theresienstadt with this dark 6SB lettering, one in September 1943—and all of its members were gassed in March 1944, exactly 6 months after arrival—and Renee's, which left Theresienstadt on December 1943 marked for gassing in June 1944. Pestek was growing frantic; time was getting short and Renee adamantly refused to accept his plan for escape for she did not believe that such a venture could ever succeed.

Overwhelmed with worry and aware of the fact that, barring a miracle, Renee would soon die, Pestek confided to another casual visitor to the little clandestine roomette and this was none other than our Slavek Lederer. Slavek had been deported to Auschwitz in December 1943 for his violation of the German rule banning smoking. Although he was protected by his work at the fire brigade and his boss, Mr. Holzer, tried desperately to shelter him, such a serious "crime" was out of reach for revocation of a deportation order. Once in Auschwitz, Slavek realized that this horrible pit would be his last place on earth, and he worked feverishly on a potential escape.

Pestek knew of Slavek's past and, in desperation and aware that he was dealing with an exceptionally brave and intelligent man, was not afraid to confide in him. Though they were enemies from opposing sides they shared a common goal, both wishing to disappear from Auschwitz. Of course, in Pestek's mind the burning issue was that not his but Renee's life was at stake. It is not exactly clear how the plan was hatched, but it was decided that if Pestek could take Slavek out of Auschwitz then Renee could be persuaded that such a plan might be feasible. Renee agreed to wait and see: should Pestek's plan succeed she might follow his advice and allow him to take her and her mother out.

Now what followed might have been considered a hair-raising project, but in reality it was a very clever plan that had great potential of success. All preparations and planning were more or less in Pestek's hands. All he asked in return for taking Slavek out of Auschwitz was Slavek's help in subsequently doing the same for Renee and her mother, for he was determined to free them from the clutches of the Nazis. Slavek agreed he would have probably struck a bargain with the devil—spirit, evil or otherwise—if it helped him escape.

Pestek's plan for the two women was also well thought through and had a great chance of success. But he needed Slavek to assist him. In general, Pestek proposed to forge a letter summoning both women under his supervision for interrogation at Gestapo headquarters in Katowitz and once there he would arrange a hiding place for them, which he would finance from the fortune he had amassed during his tenure in Auschwitz. But first things first, for he had to prove to Renee that it was a viable plan and his arrangements sound. This was to be accomplished by getting Slavek out of Auschwitz, and Slavek quickly agreed to be the guinea pig. Then, Renee in turn promised to join Pestek if Slavek's escape was successful. Pestek was convinced that he could pull it off.

IV

Now we will describe in detail one of the few successful escapes from Auschwitz and the quite ingenious strategy devised by Pestek and bravely executed by both Pestek and Slavek. Slavek burned with desire to get out of the murderous hell called Auschwitz, and, being a brave and intelligent ex-officer in the army, he was well equipped to handle danger and deal with unexpected contingencies that were bound to develop on such a risky undertaking.

The plan called for Slavek to wear the uniform of no less than a Wehrmacht colonel, a uniform Pestek would provide. Pestek disclosed to him the day's password of *tintefass* (inkstand) and instructed him not to say a word during the escape, for Slavek's fluent German had a distinct Czech accent. Slavek was a fair-colored man, slim and with perfect military posture and gait. As long as he did not speak, Slavek fulfilled the image of a Nazi officer to a T. According to the plan, Victor's role was to be the colonel's adjutant. He therefore was to handle all details, including the talking and handling of military documents for his senior officer should they be accosted by an unexpected patrol.

The date considered most propitious was April 5, 1944, exactly three weeks after the gassing of the September transport. As prearranged, Slavek marched through the gate as Victor's shift ended. All went like clockwork. Victor unlocked the gate of the family camp, and Slavek walked out without a hitch. Moments later the shift change arrived, replacing Victor and allowing him to leave his post. At that point Slavek donned the colonel's uniform and with Pestek acting as his adjutant they both walked unscathed out of Auschwitz. Both men bicycled to the Auschwitz railway station and caught a train just as it was leaving for Prague. Obviously, timing of the various phases of the escape was meticulous, for success depended on following the plan precisely, as rapid escape from the region was mandatory.

As soon as the daily and accurate roll call disclosed that a prisoner was missing, the entire expanse of the camp was filled with the uninterrupted shrieking sirens alerting the camp that prisoners had escaped. Members of the family camp stood for hours at a never-ending roll call as punishment for the flight of one of their co-religionists. Many fainted and a few even perished but most rejoiced and prayed in silence for the man who had fled, hoping that he would reach the free world and inform them about the ongoing horrors at Auschwitz.

The intense searches lasted for up to three weeks, during which the Nazis, assisted by highly trained dogs, scoured the region high and low for the escapee. This time they soon realized it was not only an inmate but also one of them who had thrown his lot with the Jews. Victor Pestek became a major embarrassment to the Nazis. Not only was he missing but he obviously had aided the missing prisoner, Lederer. Pestek now was considered a felon and a traitor. The minute-by-minute, detailed planning paid off handsomely, for as the most feverish search began the two men were well on their way to Prague in a train they caught at the very last minute. Had they tarried in the region the dogs would have sniffed them out within a very short time or someone might have caught a glimpse of them.

The two men reached Prague and contacted Slavek's friend, a member of the underground, who found them a safe house in Pilsen, Slavek's hometown. Once there, Slavek secured help from one of his friends, a local barber who spirited him secretly to Theresienstadt. There he hid in the many underground passages and catacombs and secret shelters he knew so well, for after all he had been a prisoner and member of the resistance there for a number of months before his punitive deportation to Auschwitz. Once ensconced in the catacombs, he contacted his prior boss, Leo Holzer, the man in charge of the fire brigade, a few of his closest friends and also the highly revered spiritual leader of Theresienstadt, Rabbi Dr. Leo Beck. One of those was also my boyfriend, as the two men were not only friends but also fellow underground conspirators.

That very day my ashen-faced boyfriend asked me to listen carefully to what he had to share with me. I had to swear not to breathe a word to anyone but to quietly accept and prepare for what was coming up. In no uncertain terms he told me that we were doomed, that all of us would eventually follow the same path and, barring a miracle or an early end of the war, we all would perish. Arthur was surprised that I was not at all so very shocked. I simply told him that I suspected such an outcome was planned for our ordeal. The way the Nazis treated us was surely the prelude to their plan of murdering every single one of us.

After talking with Slavek, Arthur insisted on teaching me how to behave during selection in order to avoid being sent to be gassed during the first screening on the Jewish ramp. He told me that upon arrival I was to behave as follows:

1. Not linger around old people or small children;
2. When asked by Dr. Mengele about my age declare that I was 18;
3. When asked about my skill claim to be an artisan with a practical vocation;
4. Look neat and profess to be in the best of health;
5. Not hold eye contact for long;
6. Stand as ramrod straight as I could.

Having exhausted the tips for selection, Arthur made me promise to stay mum about all I had learned that day. I would have remained so irrespective of his admonishments, for it was perilous to talk about such matters. In the case of this latest information, it could not be doubted, authenticated as it was by a man of the highest reputation now hiding in the catacombs after escaping Auschwitz. If the Nazis caught the slightest hint of this situation, it would spell doomsday for the camp, for the Nazis would not hesitate to blow up the entire Theresienstadt fortress into smithereens to hide the secrets of Auschwitz.

As Arthur walked away that day his customary jaunty gait was gone; he walked like an old, tired man, bent by the weight of his impending judgment day, a man sentenced to death. I, for one, now left alone, began to shake and shiver. What about my mother? Would she have to die suffocating on noxious gas? How could I save her and myself? I was not as composed as I pretended to be by far. I was petrified of dying by asphyxiation and of seeing my poor mom suffering the same fate.

V

Now allow me to finish the narrative of the fate of the two men who tried to inform the West about the mass genocide perpetrated by the Nazis and prevent the murder of the remaining Jews.

Slavek and Pestek were holed up in Pilsen. The resistance forged false identity papers for Slavek that declared him to be a mechanical engineer named Fredrick Walker, assigned to work in Germany. With these brazenly fake documents he travelled through enemy territory until he came to the Swiss border at Constance. There he contacted a family of a friend of Pestek who was killed fighting on the Russian front and with their help he succeeded in forwarding a report on the situation in Theresienstadt and Auschwitz to the Red Cross in Geneva. His was not probably the second such report by an escaping prisoner but its effect or usefulness remains unknown. We can only admire his impudence, for Slavek returned several more times to Theresienstadt, bringing letters, radio parts and some light weapons. Eventually he was asked not to return to Theresienstadt, as the Council of the Elders, pressured by Rabbi Leo Beck, feared that somehow the word would leak out and the Nazis would blow up the camp into eternity with all its inhabitants.

Before Slavek could return to his Gentile girlfriend in Prague, where he hoped to wait out the end of the war, he had to fulfill the promise he gave Pestek, who was waiting impatiently in Pilsen. Now he began seriously to pressure Slavek to live up to his pledge and help him with Renee and her mother's escape from Auschwitz, as time was running out and the date of the December transport's planned gassing was only weeks away.

In spite of the dangers, the two men embarked upon the last part of the elaborate scheme to free Renee and her mom. The two men traveled on the same train but separately and arranged to meet at the Auschwitz railway station. They were wanted fugitives, yet they returned to implement their plan, the details of which were never known to me.

When they reached their destination, but before they could reconnect, suddenly and seemingly out of nowhere, an armed SS unit appeared

One. Portrait of Lederer

on the platform and surrounded one of the train cars. Sounds of gunfire and the explosion of a grenade filled the railway station and amidst the confusion and panic the SS men surrounded Pestek, who was bleeding profusely, and quickly escorted him out of the station.

Slavek watched in utter disbelief and shock at the unfolding scenario. Taking advantage of the commotion with his razor-sharp cool-mindedness, he pinched a nearby motorbike and for two uninterrupted hours rode at top speed to the Czech border. There he caught a train and sneaked back into Theresienstadt again. One more time he attempted to convince the Council of the Elders of the need to prepare for a rebellion in the event the camp was to be destroyed. The Elders rejected his plea, believing that the Nazis would keep Theresienstadt intact if for no other reason than as an alibi for their postwar defense; they wouldn't be so foolish as to set it ablaze.

Now the less-than-helpful council began to be seriously concerned. Slavek's presence, though he was well hidden in the underground passages of the fortress, was an enormous risk. The consensus was that Slavek had to leave Theresienstadt. With every passing hour the danger of his discovery grew in their minds, perhaps out of proportion; but they were convinced that his presence was a huge liability. Rumors of his presence would spread and the punitive measures taken by the Nazis would obliterate the camp.

Slavek, disappointed but undaunted, fled from Theresienstadt, reaching the borders of the Protectorate and Slovakia. Once out of the immediate reach of the Nazis, he joined the partisans, who were fighting against the Nazis mostly from hidden positions high in the Tatra Mountains. There he spent the rest of the war, fighting with firearms the archenemy of the Jewish people. He immigrated to Israel after liberation.

As for Victor Pestek, he was not so fortunate. Profusely bleeding from his injury at the railway station, he was led from the station to Auschwitz and locked in block 11, the infamous punishment block dreaded by all inmates. There, after a month of relentless torture, endless interrogations and unimaginable agonies, Victor was shot, executed by firing squad. To his everlasting honor, we have to recall his bravery and decency. We must stress and remember that in spite of the harrowing agonies his interrogators put him through, he never disclosed the names of the members of the Czech resistance who helped him and Lederer while both men were in hiding.

Renee and her mother survived the war and immigrated to Israel.

The family camp was not gassed as initially planned and those able to work were sent to slave labor camps to feed the hungry German war machine.

Pestek might have started his career as a Nazi, but at some point in time he must have had a change of heart, for he was well aware of the risks he took on and still he followed through. Last but not least, he saved the life of Slavek Lederer. Does the Torah not teach us that to save one life is akin to saving all humanity?

Questions and Answers

Is a marriage based upon just trying to survive any less ethical than a marriage that is entered into out of love?

While normally we choose our unions with those people we love, in abnormal times there may have been other than just affectionate reasons to do so. But I don't think that if a man and a woman are guided by the principle that they will try to survive at all costs that it would be ethically wrong. I think the first commandment of our existence on this earth is to defend our life and try to survive. And while perhaps in normal life people marry for different reasons than pure love, in camps the prisoners were stripped of all the attributes of titles and clothing and anything we might have used to try to impress another person. There you saw persons, so to speak, naked, with all their deficits and if you still loved a person then certainly that seemed to have been a right reason to join two lives together.

In normal times, one marries for love. Were there other normal events that were carried out not for the original purpose but in order to survive longer? Are these justified if the reasons are not as "pure"?

In one's entire life in the camps very few things were done on the basis of a normal motivation. Life was that abnormal. Whatever motives existed, such as looking for friendship or looking for support, I would qualify as pure because people were motivated by the sheer will to live a little longer, trying to fight the odds of the overwhelming power that was trying to murder us all.

Is appeasement ever a good solution?

No, it's hardly ever possible to appease somebody who is pushing for something beyond a normal exchange between people. Appeasers usually are bullies. They are people who want to push their way. And appeasing them only shows weakness; it only invites an acceleration and intensification of even more demands. Politics, the world, and history have taught us that countries in their dealings with neighbors were hardly ever able to appease the aggressor.

What was the view of the ordinary Czech regarding the German Appeasement?

The Czechs were frustrated by the appeasement forced on them by the allies England and France and by those countries' unwillingness to comply or stand by their promise and signed treaty of mutual help. And of course the Czechs did not feel their army was significant in size. Equipment was standing in contest with the Germans, who were at that time supposedly armed to the teeth. So the appeasement caused frustration, anger, and disappointment. Of course there was some relief that perhaps the Germans would not attack or affect the country but it was at the price of national humiliation and a great deal of pain to the ordinary Czech.

Should a country that believes it cannot win a war still try to fight it or should it "give in" and try to save as many citizens' lives and way of life as possible?

My experience as far as Czechoslovakia was concerned was that Czechoslovakia gave in to pressure by allies to yield to the demands of Nazi Germany to give up the Sudeten part of the country, where of course all the fortifications were built into the mountain range. It certainly saved lives, because Czechoslovakia would have not been able over the long term to win the war against a much larger and better-equipped Germany, as I mentioned. Yet it left lasting traces on the Czech character. Czechs always felt they fell short of expectations and they had profiled themselves as more or less cowardly. Also, there was the prototype of the "Good Soldier Švejk," which somehow is a Czech national character and which entailed that was one more time to give in and wait for better days to come. I think the Czechs would have salvaged national pride and dignity, and so too would many other countries, if when attacked without provocation by a neighbor or any other country they had put up a fight and defended what was precious and important to them.

What makes a person come back to tell others about the fate they will face when that person is risking his life to do so?

In the case of Slavek Lederer, whom we are talking about, I think it was his desire to warn people to not be bamboozled and to warn them what was at the end of the last train ride they would be forced to take from Theresienstadt to the East (i.e., Auschwitz). And I think he was prompted to by the possibility that someone could try to escape or try to rebel, because it is better to die in defending your own lifestyle and dignity and your own nationality than to give in and die a victim from an aggression of a vicious dictator. I think he was prompted by his desire to warn people to plan other actions and not to go on these trains, and if they did go to them to know what to anticipate. I don't think there was anything in it for him but to warn his co-religionists—the Jews in Theresienstadt—about the truth of their fate.

Was the act of Pestek from self-interest? Did he do more than just prove to Renee that escape was possible?

Pestek was motivated by self-interest because, for some reason, he fell in love with this beautiful girl he wanted to save at all costs, fully aware that she would be gassed within a few weeks.

Every person in her transport, which arrived in Auschwitz in December 1943, was designated to be gassed within six months. It didn't really come to pass completely, because she wasn't gassed in March. But Pestek knew this was in the plans. So, yes, he was motivated by self-interest and he was hoping that he could get Renee out. As it happens, he died and Renee survived.

Did the Jewish council of Theresienstadt debate or discuss the options presented in this chapter? Was there unanimous agreement?

I was not privy to every discussion of the Council of the Elders. For reasons of self-preservation and security they didn't keep any protocols. However, I do know there were dissenting views among the members of the council concerning how to deal with the information and impose the will of Rabbi Dr. Beck, who had hoped that some in Theresienstadt would survive if we laid low and Lederer was forced to leave, which he was. Some of us did survive, at a great cost, and it is still debatable as to who was right and who was wrong. There was certainly no unanimous view of how to handle this ongoing process, because members of the *Judenrat* (Jewish council) knew that there was a race for time and that we would die sooner rather than later. So there was this hope that some might outlast the Nazis, that the

One. Portrait of Lederer

war might come to its end earlier and some might have the luck to see their freedom again.

Slavek's escape meant that people died (because they perished during roll call). Was this something that was acceptable?

Slavek's escape was of course an enormously risky and courageous undertaking by Pestek and him. In Theresienstadt or in Auschwitz or for any Jews in captivity of the Nazis there were always brutal repercussions. And if there had been eyes on (possibly negative) consequences then one wouldn't even do anything against it because the Germans ruled with an iron fist and crushed brutally any sign of dissent. So collateral losses of victims were a known consequence. But Lederer had the ambition to bring out to the West the information about the conditions as they unfolded in Nazi concentration camps. He believed the world didn't know about the mass gassing of Jews in many camps, namely Majdanek, Belzec, Chelmno, Sobibor, and Auschwitz-Birkenau. So, yes, there could be tragic losses of life due to the wrong course taken and punishment measures for his escape, but these were calculated into the equation and it was hoped that perhaps the world would come to help if they only knew how horribly the Nazis were treating us.

How do we evaluate the actions of a Nazi who does things that seem to help those persecuted?

If he were genuinely trying to help the victims as much as it would have been in his power, it would be a brave act of defiance, understanding that the Nazis are on the wrong side of history. But in Pestek's case there was this enormous strong emotion he felt for Renee and that was his guiding star. He wanted to prove to her it was feasible, as she denied and couldn't believe it could be done. So he took out Lederer to prove to her that this could be done and he would do it for her and her mother. It ended up in tragedy because Pestek was caught eventually and murdered by the Nazis. But to his credit I would say that to his last moment he never disclosed the names of those people who were helpful to him and Lederer during their escape.

Is there a hypocrisy about viewing Jews as subhuman and yet still fall in love with them?

I don't think that all Germans, or even all Nazis, perceived Jews as subhumans and I think some of them might have been taught by Jewish talent, intellect, and past achievements Jews had done for Europe and also for humanity at large. And as we might know, perhaps love is not always, even hardly ever, governed by reason or consideration. I do not know where Pestek stood with his evaluation of Jews at large; but since love is not always, or hardly ever, governed by reason, I don't think there is a large contradiction in that.

How might a Nazi resolve this inner conflict—loving one, but hating that one's race?

Well, I don't know how you resolve that you hate the race of the person you love the best. You have got to come to revise and review your belief of who these people are that you hate so much and whether that hate has a base or foundation or if it has just been fomented by a crazed party or power hungry dictator or demented man.

Two

Portrait of the Saddest Star-crossed Lovers

The saddest star-crossed lovers of the twentieth century had to be Hilda and Avraham. He was brilliant and she was beautiful. According to this fairy-tale beginning, if all went according in the script, they should have met, fallen in love and lived happily ever after. Fate granted them the first two but denied them the last opportunity.

Their love became all-consuming, burning with incandescent brilliancy. Their love story could be likened to a meteoric flash: dazzling but short-lived. They weren't destined to spend much time together but that was a foregone conclusion, for they were Jews born into the first decades of the ill-fated twentieth century.

Let me begin by making a sketch of Avraham Fixler for you. He was an exceptionally talented man, with flair and an exuberant charm. His looks were unimpressive except for the burning eyes that illuminated his face. He had strange, almost Asiatic, features; his cheekbones were high-set, in sharp contrast to his fair hair. He was tall, slim, vibrant and always tense and on the go. He seemed like a thoroughbred ready for a steeplechase. He radiated strength and self-confidence and had the unmistakable aura of a winner. The only inconsistency was his somewhat skeptical, deprecating, sardonic smile that often flashed briefly, as if uninvited, on his face.

Avraham was born in Sub-Carpathian Ruthenia, in the inauspicious year 1911. The First World War was still in the nebulous future but the Jews of Ruthenia could hardly afford to have much interest or involvement in the convoluted politics of the stultified and moribund Austro-Hungarian Empire even though they were subjects of the Hapsburg monarchy that had ruled this part of the world for several centuries. The entire region lagged behind in all aspects of the development taking place elsewhere in

Europe. It was the backwater of the Eastern-most corner of the empire. As was often the case in the stagnant regions in Europe, the uneducated and superstitious population often used the Jews as scapegoats for their own misery, poverty, and misfortune.

Avraham's father was a pushcart peddler who trudged with his wares (pots, pans scarves, thread, needles, brushes and other assorted items the villagers could buy from him) from one hamlet to another, hoping to bring a few coins to his burgeoning family each week. He rarely did. On occasion he made some sales but often some rascals would attack him, topple his cart, and steal his merchandise and the money he made. And the old man had to be glad that they only beat him up. He could have easily been killed. Such were the conditions of Jews in Ruthenia, circumstances young Avraham loathed and worked assiduously to escape. Few had achieved that goal.

Avraham became the best student of the first graduating class of the Hebrew high school in Munkacs. He was exceptionally clever, talented and skillful. He was a fine orator and master of many languages, all of which he learned on his own and spoke with aplomb. He was truly a self-made man, an autodidact. He hustled constantly searching for work, took even the dirtiest and most humiliating jobs as long as they promised some pay. He skimped on everything and saved all his coins for his education. He hated the abject humiliating penury that forced the Jews of Ruthenia into a constant struggle for the next meal and other basics. If his later years were admirable, his young years were just as impressive.

In high school in Munkacs, Avraham became acquainted with the ideas of Zionism and other political movements mostly rooted in the left socialist ideas of those days. He became an ardent Zionist, wishing to be a man who could walk tall and be proud and successful in his chosen calling. Zionism reinforced his desire to leave that God-forsaken corner of Eastern Europe, preferably for the Middle East. He longed to establish himself in a country that was not drowning in darkness, superstitions and poverty.

As soon as he had finished his high school studies, he fled his Carpathian home and enrolled in law school in Prague. He had to make it on his own; no help would be coming from his destitute family. Avraham hated the humiliating hardship of privation so common among the pious Jews of Ruthenia. He also hated that they meekly accepted their fate as if it were God's will to become the lightning rod of every disgruntled peasant.

It was not easy to make a living and pursue his studies. To make ends

Two. Portrait of the Saddest Star-crossed Lovers

meet, Avraham found employment in the then Palestine office of the Jewish community. After the Nazis occupied Czechoslovakia in 1939, he was transferred to the Nazi-run office, the so-called *"Zentralstelle."* This office established by the Germans dealt with the laws governing Jewish life in the Protectorate, mainly the expulsion and emigration of Jews. Eventually its command expanded to include the appropriation of Jewish possessions.

In the Zentralstelle office, the Nazis noticed Avraham's exceptional memory and ability to cut through complicated matters swiftly and with adroitness. He gained their begrudging admiration for his organizational skills and he was soon promoted. He became a liaison between the Nazis' head offices, located in a nice suburb of Prague, and the Jewish community situated in the city's downtown area. And wonder of wonders, the impatient Nazis supplied Avraham with a motorbike. He was the only Jew in Prague who was given permission to drive a motorbike and who didn't have to wear the yellow Star of David attached to his outer clothing. They even paid him a living wage, something no other Jew could boast of, or even dream of, at the time.

Avraham was no fool. Though he was glad that he was spared some of the hardships of the Jews of Prague, he soon became aware that his privileged position would not save his life. In fact, just the opposite might be the case. He was one of the most visible symbols of the Jewish presence in the occupied Protectorate; he was also painfully aware that the Nazis were unpredictable, never allowing any Jew who was privy to inside secrets to live for very long.

For the time being, he was a very powerful man, if only within the confines of the Jewish community in Prague. He also had some limited influence with his Nazi masters. He was able to persuade them to change, delay, or even mitigate some of their brutal rules, which were ultimately aimed at the annihilation of the Jews. On occasion Avraham could intercede on behalf of a friend to arrange some favor but in most cases it only delayed the inevitable. But the fact that he was able to move around Prague, unencumbered and unmarked by the telltale yellow star, zooming through the streets on his motorbike singled him out as an exceptional man.

Avraham had no illusions about his longevity. In fact, he may well have been one of the first Jews to understand that deportation usually meant death. He never spoke about it openly, as he was not suicidal, but on occasion he was overheard dropping none-too-subtle hints. I overheard a conversation between men who were speculating what to take with them for the upcoming deportation. As only 50 kg was permitted, it was a topic of grave concern. Avraham made this caustic remark: "For the first leg of my journey to the transit camp in Theresienstadt, I would take some clothing, but for the next journey to the East I would not take a thing." It did not take a rocket scientist to understand the dark meaning of his words. Aware that he lived on borrowed time, Avraham lived by the doctrine "Carpe Diem." And it was at this juncture that he met Hilda.

Now allow me to recount a brief narrative about the beautiful girl who became the love of his life.

Hilda and Avraham hailed from completely divergent backgrounds, a disparity that was rooted in the economic chasm between the west and the east of the republic. Although both of them were young Jews living in the same state, they might as well have been on different planets. Hilda was born in the border city Moravska Ostrava, an unappealing mining town that lies right on the Polish and Moravian border. Although the town was not opulent, Hilda was born into an affluent family. Her father owned a prosperous business that sold construction materials. Hilda was an only child and her parents viewed her as a miraculous gift. She had come into their lives when they were middle-aged, when they had all but given up on their long futile hope of having a child. What's more, she was a truly enchanting girl.

She arrived in August 1914, at the beginning of World War I. From that day on, she resembled a delightful doll. She was petite, almost diminutive, with exquisite looks. This beautiful baby would later blossom into an irresistible adolescent. It almost seemed as if fate sought to compensate her middle-aged parents for the many frustrating years when they all but resigned themselves to live and die childless. Hilda's fine features were dominated by her almond-shaped, dark, almost velvety eyes, which were shaded by long lashes. Her eyes gleamed, shining, radiating warmth and joy of life. Her face seemed to have been chiseled from fine china; no blemishes or youthful acne ever disfigured her complexion. It was not only her face and slender, elegant body that attracted attention; Hilda had a pleasant disposition and was friendly and polite to all. While a girl with so many attributes might well have been conceited, such character flaws did not mar Hilda. Aware that she was the apple of her aging parents' eyes, Hilda always seemed to conduct herself in an exemplary manner. She became a star student in school, played piano, danced and mustered all the skills a young Jewish girl was expected to learn before entering into a respectable marriage.

Two. Portrait of the Saddest Star-crossed Lovers

When Hilda came of age, she was in no hurry to tie the knot. She graduated from a business school that prepared young girls for a career. The next step was to accept a position as a secretary to some CEO. It was customary then to either seek marriage or continue to scale the corporate ladder. Hilda worked as a secretary for the head of the Jewish community in her town, dated some young men, and generally seemed to enjoy her freedom.

While she was attending one of the frequent dances, she met Karel, the very definition of a "nice Jewish boy." He was handsome, clean-cut and a scion of a respectable family. Karel was every mother's dream as a suitor to her daughter: This prospective groom would be a very suitable lifelong companion. Hilda's parents watched the courtship with delight. Until then Hilda never "crossed the line" for proper girls of the era, but then people began to question the importance of old values in the wake of events in the mid–1930s when Europe began its slide into a man-made hell. Suddenly everything that had been accepted as prim and proper yesterday was now questioned or discredited. Before long, the more disenchanted individuals adopted a nihilistic life philosophy.

Karel and Hilda were also caught up in the turbulent times. They saw no reason to delay their physical pleasures and the young couple consummated their passion before making up their minds about whether they would marry. Karel thought that he knew the intricacies of lovemaking but, as events would show, he was not as savvy as he believed himself to be. Initially Hilda was not alarmed by the fact that she missed her monthly cycle. But the overall feeling of physical malaise came as a rude surprise to her. Although she was in her twenties, her practical knowledge of the "facts of life" was minimal. All she knew was what the servant girls whispered, sharing a few details with her. It might sound incomprehensible to the present-day generation, but in the first half of the 1920s there was a great silence among the middle class in central Europe on the subject of physical love. Sex before marriage was taboo and parents refused to believe their offspring would cross the inviolable boundary. A mother might share some information with her daughter but only near the time of her wedding.

The working class was not so delusional. Youths were not expected to exercise as much restraint. There was many a girl who paid a high price for engaging in risky activities they barely knew how to control. Even so, such girls knew more than Hilda.

In her predicament, Hilda confided in her mentor, the cook of her family home, but the many pieces of advice she received proved to be useless. Hilda was advised to jump from high benches, swallow pills that made her sick to her stomach, and take seething hot baths that nearly scorched her skin. She followed the guidance of the more experienced girls, all without the hoped-for results. With every passing day, Hilda's anxiety was ratcheted up a notch higher.

Karel proposed marriage but even that did not assuage Hilda's worries. She could not elope without scandal and proper plans for a wedding would take months and months of preparations. Hilda was well aware that her parents looked forward to her future nuptials: her wedding day would be the pinnacle of their lives. Hilda was not willing to deprive her doting parents of that occasion. Whatever the solution to her dilemma, it had to happen fast, for time was at a premium.

The only solution seemed to be a back-street abortion. Unfortunately, Hilda did not have enough knowledge to realize why she should dread the outlawed butchery. She knew little about what it might entail or the risks involved. Furthermore, no reputable physician would even consider such an intervention in the medium-size town, where gossip and news traveled with the speed of light. That would have been professional suicide. Hilda decided to follow the guidance of the servant girl who knew of an abortionist who, for an astronomical sum of money, would terminate the pregnancy.

Hilda shared her worries and ultimately, her decision, with Karel, who also was unable to resolve this problem. Karel scraped together the money, which seemed more like extortion than a fee for services rendered. On the prearranged evening they ventured to a part of the town they had never set foot in before this. It was the home of prostitutes, pimps, and other criminal elements. The woman's home was in one of the dark, neglected streets of the seedy part of the town. Hilda and Karel were downcast and frightened by the run-down, ugly face of poverty and neglect they encountered. They were met with an all-pervasive stench of sweat and unkempt dwellings, along with cooked onions and cabbage, the hallmarks of poverty. What they found in the sleazy underbelly of Ostrava was economic poverty as well as moral decrepitude. But our couple knew better than to give in to their first impulse and run away. They gnashed her teeth, determined to soldier on and bring the sordid situation under control.

They found the address quickly. When they knocked upon the smudged door a woman of unidentifiable age opened it, telling them to

Two. Portrait of the Saddest Star-crossed Lovers

come in fast and be silent. Not only did they not talk, they also attempted not to breathe the flat stink of bad cooking, excrement and blood. At first the woman stretched out her upturned palm in the international gesture indicating she wanted to be paid. Karel quickly pulled out the envelope and handed it over. The woman opened it and greedily counted the 3000 crown bills. Obviously satisfied by the payment of the exorbitant fee, she motioned Karel to wait and ordered Hilda, who was ready to faint, to continue through to the kitchen. Hilda was to strip her clothes off from the waist down and lie on the table covered by a rubber sheet.

From this moment on everything proceeded quickly, as if a nightmare was unfolding in double time. Hilda was given a gag, a towel that was to muffle her screams or any sounds she might emit. The smell was so offensive that Hilda retched, but the abortionist ordered her to shut up and lie still. The abortion did not last long although it seemed endless to Hilda, who was convinced she was dying. In her entire life she never knew that there could be a pain so severe. She feared that the woman was bursting her belly open during this mysterious procedure to terminate her unwanted pregnancy. Then all of a sudden it came to an end. The woman ordered Hilda to get off the table, put her clothes on and leave. At the door she said, "If you become ill, go to a doctor. Remember you do not know me, no medical intercession was done to you and ask only for treatment for pain and bleeding if and when any complications set in."

Karel summoned a cab, an outrageous luxury in the mining town of those days. At home he gently put Hilda to bed and went to inform her parents that she suddenly fell ill and was in need of rest. Hilda succumbed to illness. Her belly pains were severe and were accompanied by fever and general malaise. She eventually had to seek out a physician for advice. He diagnosed her with pelvic inflammatory disease and hospitalized her. By then the inflammation was widely spread and Hilda's condition was deemed grave. In those days before the advent of antibiotics Hilda's condition landed her at death's door. The only treatment that could save her life was a radical surgery that removed her reproductive organs. All the unfolding drama meant she could not conceive a child, but in the year 1939 Jews were most worried about their day-by-day survival. With every passing day Jewish women viewed pregnancy as something they would not contemplate or wish for.

Soon after Hilda recovered she married Karel in a religious ceremony, officiated by the local rabbi and blessed by both sides of the family. Neither her parents nor her in-laws ever knew that she was unable to bear them grandchildren. Hilda and Karel's married life was short. Within days the Nazis rounded up the able-bodied men and sent them to Nisko, a camp near the city of Lublin, in Poland. The Germans had intended that this camp be part of their plan to remove Jews to the East so they could bring in the Volks Deutschen. The Nazis wanted to restructure the demographics of their conquered lands by bringing in German minorities as overlords.

Karel was one of the first to be called for deportation. In October 1939 he, right along with a thousand other men, was on his way east. Hilda, his newlywed wife, was left behind, forlorn and dejected. She had no idea that it would take seven long years before they would meet again and by then nothing would ever be the same.

The Jews of Ostrava were among the first to experience the deportations. Wanting to escape the fate of Karel and the others, many of the Ostrava Jews fled to Prague or any other city where they might have connections. Hilda was sent to Prague and her parents found a temporary haven with relatives in another small town. Soon Hilda decided that she had to find some occupation, not only to augment the stipend her parents provided but also as a way to fill the long empty days. As it was, she was often deeply depressed, aimlessly wondering through the streets of Prague.

On one day she walked into the offices of the Jewish community, asking for any type of work to keep her occupied. She was told to wait. As she sat there, she noticed a young man leaning against the wall, obviously expecting someone. He looked at her with burning eyes and great interest. Hilda was always aware that she was beautiful and she was used to being noticed and admired. The man's eyes were intense—almost commandeering—and passionate. Hilda suddenly felt as if flares of heat pulsated in her body. What a strange encounter! Within moments the man flashed a smile, approached Hilda and said, "Hi, my name is Avraham and I am working here. What is your business in this shabby office? I can't recall that we've met here and by now I've met everyone who works here."

Although normally Hilda was self-assured and had presence of mind, she was suddenly lost for words. She stammered something to the effect that she had only recently arrived in Prague and needed to find some work. Avraham bent down and said, "Let's get out of here and I will show you a nice, quiet coffee house, one that lends itself to tackling the problem of finding a job for you." Hilda stood up as if mesmerized. All of a sudden she felt as if all depression and hopelessness fell away and that this magnetic stranger had answers to all her problems. He looked at her half amused and half in awe. He felt as if he had never met a more beautiful and desirable woman.

They spent the next few hours in a quaint coffee shop and while they sat there they fell hopelessly in love. Avraham told her about his younger years, his legal career he had to abandon because of the Nazi persecution, his siblings and much more about his life. Hilda could not take it all in but she was certain that she felt as if a heavy dark cloud was lifted from her shoulders. This man's intense, deep, compelling voice transcended any other encounter she ever experienced before. Within days their lives had changed beyond recognition. His Nazi superiors gave Avraham permission to move in with Hilda, continue to use his motorbike, receive augmented food rations, and draw an adequate salary. The Nazis were willing to be quite accommodating because they needed his services as a liaison between their offices and the Jewish community in Prague. His insights, efficiencies and input about how to deal with the doomed Jewish community were invaluable.

From the moment Hilda met this enigmatic stranger she lived in a trance. Belatedly she understood that what she felt for Karel was only puppy love. It was Avraham who awoke passion and fiery love in her. He was suddenly an indispensable part of her life. When they were apart, she spent her time dreaming of him, and although the Jews in Europe found themselves in dire jeopardy Hilda was limitlessly and ecstatically happy. Hilda and Avraham's passionate burst of intense, overwhelming fascination with each other bordered on obsession. Their romantic insatiability was heightened by the impending demise of Jewish existence: it was intensified beyond imagination. They spent their nights and their few free moments making love in a never ending embrace, hoping to stop time. They wished to dissolve and merge into one, hopefully till eternity. But the clock ticked mercilessly.

As totally consumed as they were with each other, Avraham had not lost touch with reality. His handlers at the Zentralstelle, the Nazi office, at first hinted and later almost admitted that the concentration camps in the East were not for "resettlement." Moreover, he knew that once the Nazis no longer perceived him as useful his life would come to an abrupt end. He had no illusions. His days were numbered, but Avraham faced the verdict with cool resignation. His bliss with Hilda was likewise terminal. He decided that if his life could not be spared, he would do everything in his power to protect Hilda.

Systematically and methodically, he constructed a courageous plan.

Avraham worked on a complex web of protective measures that would safeguard Hilda. To this end he needed the help of one of the SS men with whom he was engaged in black market transactions. Avraham promised that he could make the SS man's black market dealings even more profitable. He would help the Nazi to amass riches through different bribes. He wanted only one thing in return: the powerful German had to spare Hilda's life. In order to safeguard this arrangement even after his death, Avraham locked compromising papers in an undisclosed location. The Nazi would be toppled if they were to see the light of day. And there was only one other individual who was privy to the scheme and the location of the documents. Avraham would never divulge the identity of that person. If his boss was scared for his own skin, Hilda might have a chance at life.

Avraham was deported from Prague to Theresienstadt on January 28, 1943. Before he was parted from Hilda, he had convinced her that they would meet again in that Nazi transit camp.

His prediction came to pass.

Hilda was deported to Theresienstadt in transport designated as "CV" on March 6, 1943. There she was reunited with Avraham, only to be torn away from him permanently in the fall of 1944. Avraham was sent to Auschwitz on October 12, 1944, and was gassed there.

Hilda survived the Holocaust because of the forced assistance of the SS man. Because of Avraham's connivance, the Nazi was sufficiently petrified to keep up his end of the bargain. Her husband, Karel, survived as well. Karel had fought alongside the Soviet army and was hardened by the horrors of the war. The war had changed both of them almost beyond recognition. Few could hope to surmount the experience of years of bitter struggles to survive and battlefields soaked in blood and death. It was humankind's worst and lowest hour.

Hilda never found happiness thereafter. To her death she continued to mourn Avraham and their lost passion. His death in the gas chambers of Auschwitz left her bereft: it broke her heart and burned out her soul for the remainder of her life. She went about her daily duties and chores, but only her body functioned and she lived like an automaton. From her outward appearance, few would have guessed the true state of her inner turmoil, for she was an accomplished actress.

Hilda was not alone. Even among those who physically survived those years, there were many casualties: people who were little more than the walking dead, whose hearts and souls did not withstand the brutal losses of the war's devastation.

Two. Portrait of the Saddest Star-crossed Lovers

QUESTIONS AND ANSWERS

How was Avraham viewed by others for working with the Nazis?

This was a man who was exceptionally bright and exceptionally sharp witted and had organizational skills that could cut through any Gordian knot and make things work. The Germans quickly picked him out as he worked for the Jewish community. I think that everybody on the outside viewed him, perhaps judged him for doing it, but there was also a lot of envy of his privileged position. The man had a motorbike, something no Jews owned in any country occupied by Nazis. He had privileges of income and mobility. So a lot of people would have perhaps liked to have had these privileges. On the other hand, few would have qualified to do the work he did and few would have liked to have known that this was a very short assignment. He knew that his life was at stake and that he will not outlive the Nazis, because the Nazis had a policy that anybody who worked for them who was not German was sooner or later executed, and in his case sooner rather than later.

Did he do this purely out of self-interest? What might have been his motive? Could he have had both good motives and bad ones?

He had the only possible motive, for once you had been picked out by Germans for some assignment you were not at liberty to refuse. If you refused, the next thing you had was a bullet in your nape, so he knew very well that once he was assigned to this task he couldn't question the German order. So it was not that he did it out of self-interest. His motive perhaps was to have that short time of life assigned to him at a better level than the struggling Jews who teetered on the brink of poverty and misery and who had no access to their own money and shops and food. So maybe it was a combination of motives; maybe he did think it was good for him and that it was good for the Jewish community, which needed badly to have a representative there to make a connection between the Nazis and the Jewish community. Thus, in his heart of hearts, it might have been a combination of good and bad motives.

How was he viewed for benefitting—not having to wear a star, getting things others did not?

He was viewed with some disdain and a lot of envy, because at that point you have to understand that all Jews knew that they stood on the brink of death and had been stripped of all possibilities to escape. So it was carpe diem: today we live, tomorrow we might not. His benefits, or privileges, gave him a special position. For this reason, I say it was a mixture of judgment and envy.

What is the Jewish faith view on sex before marriage?

The conservative Jewish position on sex is that there is no premarital sex. Marriages are believed to be sacrosanct. Sex is not only recommended but also expected after the vows have been given and after the couple have been perceived as married. Sex is perceived by the Jewish faith as God's gift, a joy offered to men but not before the man has decided who is going to be his steady life companion.

What is the Jewish faith view of abortion?

The conservative position is that abortion is permitted and perhaps recommended when the life of the mother is at stake, when her well-being—physical, emotional, or any other way—would not allow her to survive if her pregnancy were to proceed. But abortion as such is not considered at all for any other reasons but to save the life of the pregnant woman.

After the war Hilda was "an automaton ... walking dead." How did different people react to their own experiences of the Holocaust immediately after the war?

Well, this is a multilayered question. In her particular case, the loss of Avraham, the love of her life, broke her heart. She did continue her physical existence but I think she didn't try to get herself out of this heartbreak. She was going through the chores and daily needs, but I think the light went out in her life the day she lost the man she perceived to be the only partner she would be happy with.

The differences of other Holocaust survivors in their reactions to their ordeals is by and large that after the war, when the physical devastation of the few survivors had been healed in different hospitals and institutions and the full awareness of the damages and the ravages that had been done to us as a people, were realized—that we had lost everything: our families, our youth, our health, our education, our chances to build a decent life, and, worse yet, many lost their faith in God and man—it took many long years of individual coping with the pains and the shocks of the Holocaust. Most of us eventually decided that there is purpose, that there's an aim, that we should go on fighting for a better world in which Nazis and mis-creations of that sort would never be possible to come to rule.

Did survivors talk among themselves or did you shun each other?

No, we did not shun each other, just the opposite. But we tried to avoid the suffering we had endured through those years in Nazi concentration camps. We tried to force normality as we perceived it then. Only years later did we come to realize that you have got to come to terms with something like that. You cannot pretend it did not happen. You have to understand. And you have to work through it. It is a long, clashing process of painful thinking about what has happened and how to go on. But in the initial stages after our liberation we tried desperately to pretend that we were just as the other people and what had happened we would not talk about. And if we did not talk about it, if we did not think about it, it would go away. We could control not talking about it but you couldn't control not thinking about it—and it never went away. So eventually I think that every survivor realized that they needed to go through this painful process of accepting and reviewing what had happened and started to build a new foundation and platform for a different life, one as good as we were able to do.

How were the Nazis who helped Jews perceived and treated by the survivors immediately after the war and in subsequent years?

I didn't know any Nazis who helped Jews personally, so I am not really qualified to answer. I know of Oskar Schindler and I know there were perhaps Nazis who had a change of heart and in some situations helped Jews and I know Pestek tried to help Renée and eventually got Slavek Lederer out (see "Portrait of Lederer"). But one of the initial emotions of the survivors was mistrust, because for long years nobody offered anything to us but watched the concentration camp and knew that we were probably facing death there and it didn't break anybody's heart. So I don't know personally any Nazis who helped Jews, and I was fortunate enough not to meet any Nazis after the war or have any exchanges with them or testify against them.

How did people who were not directly involved respond to the survivors immediately after the war?

This question is loaded with pain for me because when I returned after the war I thought that we would be accepted with open arms, that people would know we had been tortured, tormented, murdered, and annihilated through no fault of our own. I thought everyone saw it clearly. That really wasn't the case, because for most of the Gentiles I saw in Prague, and later in other places, acceptance was cold and sometimes even hostile. Anti-Semitism was always latent in Europe before the Nazi ascendancy. For centuries Jews were tormented through the Middle Ages by different anti-Semitic factions of the church or governments. The rule of the Nazis, who were in Czechoslovakia for six long years, relentlessly sowed these seeds of anti-Semitism, demonizing Jews in the worse possible way, and brought about a harvest of increased anti-Semitism. A lot of people believed that perhaps there was something wrong with the Jews and there were others who took possession of what we had owned and who wanted to be hostile to us because the last thing they wanted was for us to return for what they took.

Three

Portrait of Fredy H.

Fredy's story is truly a tragic one, yet at the same time deeply inspiring, demonstrating mankind's elevating potential of acting selflessly even when the die is cast. Fredy's life was short but devoted to our youth, a cause he believed in and was dedicated to. Had he been born in different times he probably would have become a school principal or a reformer of youth education, for the young ones were his passion and main concern. He was convinced that humanity's future hinged on improving the quality of education and entrusting it to better-schooled and better-remunerated professionals. Fredy was also an outstanding athlete and gymnast. He believed that the individual should seek intellectual and physical perfection. Like the ancient Greeks, Fredy thought that a healthy mind has to reside in a healthy body and he was the living example of what he preached.

Fredy had unique leadership skills and qualities. People took to him and bought into his doctrines with great enthusiasm and admiration. Children loved and trailed after him like the proverbial Pied Piper. In his company they were happy, felt safe, and listened to his every word. Fredy exuded a powerful charm few could resist. He was an accomplished motivator and a genuinely enthusiastic person. He always projected the image of an upbeat, optimistic winner. He loved to share with his young charges, who were always his captive audience.

Fredy was born 1916 in the city of Aachen, Germany. He studied there and planned to embark upon a career as a youth counselor, majoring in physical education. All his bold hopes and dreams were thwarted by the ascension of the Nazi party to rule in Germany in 1933. Their vitriolic anti–Semitism trampled over all he aspired to. For Fredy was a Jew, and to the National Socialists thugs this represented an unforgivable, capital crime. Fredy fled Germany to save his life, leaving behind his family, friends, some assets and his ruined plans for a creative future.

The Nazis embarked upon a course of annihilation of Jewish life in Germany and eventually in all of Europe, at least the part they conquered. But if Fredy knew one thing it was that he would devote his energies and time to the innocent, wronged, Jewish youth no matter the path he took.

In 1935 Fredy arrived in Czechoslovakia. It was the first stopover on his journey, which brought him to Prague. Unbeknownst to him, it would turn out to be the place where he would leave an indelible mark, for he single-handedly diminished some of the misery of his young charges and became a shining example of man's altruism in helping the weakest among us. It took nobility of heart and courage of mind to set one's own concerns on the back burner and invest all one's resources into assisting and guiding the local youth. Fredy, the born educator, was engaged in teaching his wards, preparing them for their future, which many were about to lose. Only an unusual individual could suppress worries about his own endangerment and the overwhelming gloom and doom and bring some sunshine into the drab and dreary existence of the suffering jailed kids. But that came later.

Once Fredy embarked upon escaping from the Nazi putrefaction, he tried to restart his life in Prague. There he made a few friends, and before long he was recruited to organize teaching and recreational facilities for the youngsters. The winds of Nazi hatred began to affect Jewish youth when they were initially expelled from many clubs and sporting activities and subsequently from all schools. Soon the children were barred from using parks, gyms, swimming pools, and skating rinks. Almost all walks of life—occupational as well as recreational—became inaccessible to Jews. The only place the Jewish youth could gather was on a plateau-like field called Hagibor, which was a meadow-like play area where countless young boys and girls met to exercise or socialize. There they found comfort in sharing their worries, trying not to think about the looming threats, and avoiding loneliness and despair. And there they found their hero. He came in the person of a young man in his early twenties, handsome, impeccably groomed, athletic: a young man called Fredy Hirsh. Fredy became their guiding star, their knight in shining armor.

Practically within days he organized them into compatible groups, taught them games and insisted on a regimen of exercises, hardening their bodies, toughening them into resilient, sinewy fighters. He convinced them that these complex times demanded that they have the minds and bodies of the biblical King David, who could keep his cool while confronting the powerfully strong giant Goliath. And when times get tough the tough get going, right? And the kids believed him; they took it all in.

Three. Portrait of Fredy H.

Under Fredy's wings they blossomed, felt safe and protected. Many a mamma's podgy darling underwent a quick metamorphosis, doing his utmost, if often just to please the charismatic Fredy. The order of the day was to strengthen the body and mind and few doubted Fredy's judgment on this matter. They trusted Fredy implicitly, firmly convinced that he was a paragon of all virtues; they tried to emulate him, hardening their bodies and steeling their resolve.

There was only one group of youth deeply disappointed with Fredy. These were the girls, the young ladies of Prague. Fredy was a tall, slim, muscular chap, with a perfect physique and a handsome face. His black hair was combed back, and his features reminded the beholder of Tyrone Power with a grace close to Fred Astaire's and the eloquence of any modern-day Demosthenes. The young women tried desperately to flaunt their assets in front of his dark, magnetic eyes, all to no avail. The enigmatic indifference only fed the frantic interest in him; his coolness was interpreted as choosiness—most likely he was particular and very selective—and the hunt went on and on. Some speculated that he left his heartthrob back in Germany. Perhaps he was engaged or in love with some very special girl there? What kind of a femme fatale would it take to seduce the one-of-a-kind Fredy? As matters stood, none had a chance.

Few suspected, but no one knew for sure, that even a perfect woman could not stir emotions in Fredy's heart. Fredy had a secret all of his own. He did not like women as sex partners, his priority was men. In those days homosexuality was considered an aberration and was kept a dark secret; it wasn't like it is today. Therefore nobody knew about Fredy's preferences; we never learned the puzzling information. Even today I do not know how Fredy managed to keep his sexual priorities away from the snooping public or how this aspect of his life remained in his private domain, tightly under wraps.

Fredy was also the object of prolific gratitude from the fretful parents who had little to offer their kids. They trusted him implicitly and it is fair to say that he took a great load off their shoulders, at least as far their offspring were concerned. The exercises, games, and social gatherings organized by Fredy were full of fun and good cheer and, considering the dark times, infused with incredible optimism. While at play he would keep an eye on their physical fitness, upgrading it to the highest attainable degree, and his message to the youngsters was "chin up, better days are to come, be tough, unyielding and tenacious."

Fredy's sojourn in Prague came to an abrupt end when he received a deportation order to Theresienstadt, a concentration camp in the heart of the Czech lands. There the charismatic Fredy carried on. He devoted his time and energies to the youngsters of Theresienstadt with the same vigor and enthusiasm as he had in Prague. Within weeks of his arrival Fredy was assigned the task of deputy to the head of children's care under another passionate teacher, the indomitable Egon Redlich. Though they often clashed about some detail of their custodial care, they always kept the interests of the children as the sole priority. Both men put their own well-being out of their thoughts, as they were consumed with their arduous task. So devoted was Fredy that nobody ever heard him complaining of being hungry or miserable about the meager, substandard rations and vermin-infested military barracks that were crammed with a huge mass of jailed Jews.

Fredy was endowed by the exceptional power of conviction. He charmed his charges into believing that even the lack of food could be conquered by self-discipline. For example, he said it was to their advantage to be so very lean! He insisted that better times were around the corner and they could survive the tough, boot camp lifestyle the young detainees endured in Theresienstadt.

Fredy was a great believer in cleanliness and he insisted that the youngsters wash thoroughly even when the water was ice cold. For the time being they were taught to sing, draw, write poems and other subjects, though Fredy knew full well that all that lay ahead was the almost certain summary execution of his blameless pupils. Only Fredy did not have a presentiment as to what was in cards for him. It was commonly known that Jewish children were the special targets of German hatred, for they represented the future and were the lifeblood of Judaism. The fate of the adults, at least in the beginning, was less clear. The German war machine needed every pair of hands and therefore the incarcerated Jews represented a potential shot in the arm of the labor-starved war industry of the Nazis.

At one point Fredy escaped a close brush with death. Some 800 children who were orphans were brought to Theresienstadt from Bialystok. They were housed in separate quarters and according to the rumors they were to be used as ransom in a swap for German prisoners of war. They were kept apart from the camp proper and Fredy, faithful to his solicitude and concern for the young ones, tried to establish some connection. This flew in the face of Nazi orders and Fredy got caught and punished. He maintained an unusually friendly relationship with one of the Nazi officers,

Three. Portrait of Fredy H.

SS Bergel. Rumor had it that even the commandant was so impressed by the explanation given that he let Fredy go, a feat unheard of in Theresienstadt.

Just outside the perimeter of the camp stood the newly erected barracks filled with the terrified children of Bialystok. Fredy, worried, wanted to learn more about these mysterious children at the "Kreta" barracks. In spite of the prohibition to stay away and his capture just three days earlier, he sneaked out of the camp and found out the full truth about the children of Bialystok. Only this time Fredy's luck ran out. He was caught and even his friend SS Bergel could not save him. His punishment was instant and cruel: he had to leave Theresienstadt on a transport eastward.

It happened in September 1943. Fredy and many of his youngsters were ordered into an eastbound transport numbering five thousand people destined for the dreaded death camp of Auschwitz-Birkenau. Fredy packed few basics, doubting the wisdom of taking anything; but on the face of it, he retained an upbeat attitude, encouraging the kids to be brave and keep their hope and faith up.

The nightmarish journey found Fredy and the rest of the inmates expelled from Theresienstadt packed like sardines in dark cattle cars and slowly chugging to their death in the east. The horror lasted for three days and that many nights. Conditions quickly deteriorated, since the travelers did not get any food or water and there was no place to relieve oneself except for one pail that overflowed even before the locomotive was put into first gear. Soon the nervous people began to cry. Some screamed and others took leave of their senses. Already on day two many were dead or dying, and some were semiconscious. Eventually the insane screams and even the lamentable raucousness subsided and lowered to a monotonous whimper. The dreadful plight drained all the energies from the people jammed into the airless, dark wagons. Fredy tried to comfort some of them and encourage the kids, but soon he too gave up and fell silent because he understood that this was the voyage that would end by everyone being dumped into hell. He just whispered—more to himself than to the Supreme Being—"Please, O Lord, make it quick and let us never return to this torturous existence."

Finally, when none of those who still breathed nursed any hope, the train jerked to an abrupt stop. The unloading began quickly. It was accompanied by deafening clamor and brutish violence. The locks of the heavy wooden doors of the cars were ripped open and those still alive and conscious squinted out onto a brightly lit platform. What struck their squinting eyes was a reflection of the worst possible hell on earth. For a moment the bright floodlights that swept the train ramp blinded most. Their eyes had become accustomed to shadowy darkness for the entire duration of the journey. Exposed to the sudden glare, the staggering deportees began to tear up and had to squint in order to accommodate such a sudden brilliance of lights. No time was given to adjust. The scene in front of them was incredibly grim and brutal.

The train was cordoned off by armed units of SS men who held their cocked guns pointed at the people who were hurried out of the car at top speed. Never mind that they were half dead, having been cooped up for three days without food or water in crowded wagons, now the Nazis prodded them with ever-rising swiftness. Nothing seemed fast enough for the murderers. The view on the platform was bad enough and yet the human cargo was not sure what to fear more: the drawn firearms or the snarling dogs rearing, ready to tear the incoming Jews apart, straining on leashes loosely held by cruel SS men.

Fredy was one of the first to regain his presence of mind. In the nick of time he sensed that the sooner they got far away from the ramp the better for all involved. One strangely clad inmate, obviously a veteran of Auschwitz, who had been assisting with the unloading and was dressed in a striped jail uniform, cozied up against Fredy's side. He whispered, "Help to speed it up, get them out on the double—the SS men are irate, they shoot to kill anyone who falls behind." Though nothing seemed expeditious enough to please the SS, Fredy did his best to prod and propel the staggering people toward the large trucks that stood at the end of the ramp. The man who whispered the urgent demand to Fredy pushed and screamed, shouting profanities and swinging his stick with a great deal of violence. Except Fredy noticed that he mostly missed his victims. All too often the blows landed in mid-air, thus demonstrating the efficiency of the Kapo to the supervising SS men, yet rarely harming the newly arrived.

The sight of the night sky transfixed Fredy's eyes. Never before had he seen the firmament illuminated by orange-red flames shooting so high, piercing into the dark night's obscurity. Fredy watched with growing uneasiness the curled wreath of black smoke as it rose from the tall chimneys that belched the heavy haze nightly into the sky. To make matters worse, he could not help breathing in gulps of air filled with the stench of burned flesh and hair. But prudently Fredy concentrated on the moment at hand, resolving to try to unravel the mystery of the bizarre scenario at some later time—should that ever come to pass.

Three. Portrait of Fredy H.

Finally, amidst great ear-shattering noise, the Theresienstadt transport was herded into something singular in the history of Auschwitz. They were taken into a block called the "family camp," which was secluded from the rest of the inmates. That was in itself a deviation from the norm. Most transports arriving in Auschwitz–Birkenau were subject to "selection," in which very young and old, sick and weak-looking individuals were set aside and immediately dispatched to their deaths in nearby gas chambers. Only the few strong and sturdy-looking men and women were allowed to enter the camp proper, destined for backbreaking slave labor.

This transport that arrived in September 1943 became known as the exceptional one that landed the inmates in a Czech family camp. Here, the conditions were similar to those in Theresienstadt: the inmates were allowed to keep their clothes and their heads were not shaven clean. In time, Fredy resumed the teaching and caring for the young ones.

Again they were taught to keep clean, draw, sing, exercise and recite poems, ignore the hunger pangs and be as tough as possible. Of course, many of the youngsters succumbed to malnutrition and illness. The day-to-day scenario was surreal. Fredy doggedly persevered in his efforts to keep the children in a family-like unit. Against a backdrop of the crematories that incessantly darted bright flames and puffed clouds of smoke into the skies, the kids recited poems of love, drew pictures of flowers and butterflies and remembered home-cooked meals. And the agnostic Fredy prayed for their miraculous rescue, and if that was not in cards, then at least for a quick and painless deliverance.

Weeks went by, then months and Fredy began to hope that his prayers were answered. Would the Almighty God grant them mercy? Perhaps the Nazis made an exception; perhaps they would take pity on those few hundred Czech Jews huddled in the family camp? Fredy plodded on, hoping against hope, counting the days while taking in all the rumors that spread through the grapevine. He was also frantically trying to interpret the news from the battlefields. Some of the hearsay gave reason for guarded optimism. Was there perhaps a real possibility for an early German defeat? While some timid optimism began to sprout in Fredy's mind, the unadorned truth was far from reassuring.

When the five thousand men and women arrived in Auschwitz-Birkenau in September 1943, the men and women did not undergo selection, their hair was not shorn, they retained their own clothes, and amazingly enough they were brought into a family camp, where they remained together, fully confined. Some very resourceful, brilliant, old-timer inmates headed the underground resistance. They tried to decipher the purpose behind this different handling of the newly arrived. It did not take a rocket scientist to understand that this special deal was granted to enable a hidden agenda of the Nazis.

This sudden benevolence was to be short-lived and served a sinister purpose. The Nazis had bifurcated intentions. They would—with one stone—kill a few important birds. First, the inmates would be ordered to write to their relatives or friends outside, reporting their well-being. This would assure the world that the news of mass killings of Jews was a malevolent slander. They would also send postcards to Theresienstadt so the inmates who were soon to follow upon the same painful odyssey would not resist. This second purpose was, if possible, even more important. Theresienstadt's population of many thousands of inmates was getting anxious as hearsay reached the camp reporting inevitable doom. The Nazis wished for smooth and efficient operations for the "Final Solution of the Jewish Question." For this reason alone it was important and worthwhile to lull the remainder of the death-sentenced inmates of Theresienstadt into a state of hopefulness for the continuation of their lives. They surely did not want scenes of insurrection or despair. The Nazis, schemers and maxi-manipulators, worked feverishly and unceasingly with tremendous cost and attentiveness to detail to have a smooth eradication of European Jews.

There was actually a third reason for the special status of the Czech transport. Unconfirmed rumor had it that the Nazis set aside the five thousand Czech Jews while they negotiated with the Allies for a prisoners-of-war exchange. The underground received credible information that such negotiations were indeed in progress. Those who knew hardly dared to hope for such a swap and none breathed a word to the outside camp. The talks were highly sensitive and delicate, for the war raged in full fury and officially the two sides were locked in mortal combat, not engaged in wheeling and dealing.

No sooner had the September transport from Theresienstadt entered the family compound than the men of the underground resistance movement huddled together looking at the accompanying documentation and trying to decipher what the one number and the three letters behind the transport designation meant. For behind the letters "DI" that designated the transport that had left Theresienstadt in September was the individual's number and then came the strange connotation: "6M SB." What was the meaning of this new enigmatic compilation of letters? Within hours the resistance fighters had decoded the conundrum. It meant 6 months and then *Sonder-Behandlung* or "special treatment." And that, in Auschwitz parlance, translated into six months of life and then a summary death by gassing, without selection. What a dreadful sentence for the Czech family camp inmates, whose suspicions had been calmed by their exceptional treatment. Most were lulled into the belief that they were being treated with special consideration for unknown reasons and would be allowed to live.

The freedom fighters of Auschwitz pondered at great length about what to do with the news of this six-month doomsday scenario and reached two conclusions. First, there would be no purpose in letting the Czech Jews know of their inescapable fate. They could not elude their sentence, so what good would be served by disrupting their fools' paradise? Let them live with hope, for it would all be shattered soon in any case.

The underground also understood that the Nazis used the family compound as a decoy for the outside world. It was "proof" to the doubters that Jews in Auschwitz lived and were not gassed and burned upon arrival. Once the genie was out of the bottle it was difficult to put the rumors back, to dislodge the suspicion and subsequent acts of desperation from the thousands who were about to follow into the death camps. Hence the six-month respite for the Czechs, who were forced to write letters and postdate their postcards. The senders would be dead before the postcards arrived, "proving" otherwise. The Germans even offered an explanation for the future dating: the wartime censorship delayed much of the mail delivery, making the postdating more credible. There was no doubt that the Czechs would comply, as the order sounded innocent enough.

The top brass of the Auschwitz resistance heard of the negotiations that would lead to an exchange of the prisoners for German POWs. They placed little credence in the probability of success of such potentially fragile mediations. And they were proven correct. If such a deal were ever seriously considered it did not pan out and soon the fate of the Czech family camp was sealed; there would be no mercy or exemption for the Czechs. The inmates of the family camp were doomed, except for a few sets of twins protected by the special interest of the notorious Dr. Josef Mengele. Still, it was concluded that the Czechs should not die in vain; their deaths should serve a purpose.

The members of the underground resistance movement, the freedom fighters of Auschwitz, had been engaged in the hoarding of explosives, guns and ammunition for a long time. It was a laborious, step-by-step procurement of weapons, which usually involved the stealing of guns and sneaking them into the camp. These, it was planned, would be used at a propitious moment for an uprising and the destruction of the gas chambers and crematories. As well, in minute amounts, the women who slugged it out as slave laborers in the munitions factory smuggled the dynamite. They did it under the pain of death, for they were also initiated into the plan to blow the hellish camp into smithereens. Now the resistance movement decided that the time was ripe to swing into action. The decision was made. The hoarded armaments would be smuggled to the *Sonderkommando* (the special unit of men who worked in the crematories removing corpses from the gas chambers, stoking the ovens and burning the dead). These men would stage a rebellion and destroy the murderous installations used for gassing the Jews.

The men of the Sonderkommando were doomed in any case, for every few months the commandant would order them murdered to avoid potential witnesses and install a new crew. After a few months, in a macabre merry-go-round, the same events would repeat themselves. Unlike the ignorant family camp inmates, the men of Sonderkommando knew their fate and were ready for action, hoping to take a few Nazis with them and reduce their killing machines to piles of rubble. The leaders of the resistance movement decided that the gassing of the family camp would serve as an excellent staging location, the flash point for the revolt. To begin with, there would be a large presence of the Germans around the gas chambers and therefore the Sonderkommando could kill a significant number. The Nazis would be taken by surprise, giving the edge to the insurrection. In the wake of the revolt, great chaos would ensue, thus enabling the Sonderkommando to inflict maximum damage.

The plan was feasible and would, at least partially, redeem the deaths of the thousands of Czech Jews from the family camp. The men in charge of the resistance chose Fredy as the leader of the rebellion; he would be the man who would signal the Czechs to rise against being herded into the gas chambers. He was the best man to lead the revolt. He was a born leader, the anointed prince, revered, respected, trusted and followed, no questions asked.

The resistance leaders had it on good authority that the Germans planned on deploying a strong force of soldiers armed to their teeth expecting that the Czechs would fight back. Unlike most of the people rushed from newly arrived transports, still dazed from the long journey and unaware of what was in store, the Czechs lived for six months in the shadows of the crematories, seeing daily the incessant red-orange flames, and knew all too well what came to pass behind the walls of the crematories.

The underground leaders had no illusions; they knew the plan would result in a massacre. The underground received a coded message that the gassing of the family camp was slated for March 7, 1944. Painfully aware of the need for secrecy and the advantage of surprise, they decided to inform Fredy only on the afternoon of the sixth.

A young registrar, Rudolf Vrba, who had the rare privilege of moving almost unencumbered between the blocks, was dispatched to inform Fredy about his historic assignment. The courier found Fredy in the camp, surrounded by his young charges, teaching calisthenics. After an urgent request Fredy relinquished his post to a young assistant and left with the messenger for a secluded corner of the barrack. Without wasting a second the bearer shared with Fredy the shocking facts. Then he quickly familiarized Fredy with his last assignment and demanded consent. He would then report to the men in charge that all necessary preparations were in place.

Fredy's initial reaction was earth-shattering shock. For a moment or two he seemed frozen like the biblical pillar of salt. The registrar did not like what he saw. Fredy's cheeks were ashen-gray, his lips quivered and he seemed unable to get a hold of himself. "Poor sucker," thought the young courier, Fredy had probably deluded himself to believe that the family camps would be spared and his young charges would cheat the executioner. Following some urgent and none-too-gentle coaxing, Fredy begged for two hours of reprieve; he would be ready to receive orders then. He needed the time to adjust his thinking and focus on the upcoming ordeal. The messenger had no choice but to agree, albeit grudgingly.

The men of the underground were also unimpressed. They never gave a fleeting thought to the possibility that Fredy would not be equal to the daunting task. Moreover, it was potentially perilous for the registrar to tread to the family camp one more time. The SS men were also on high alert, for they had been informed about a possible upcoming contingency. But there was no alternative and the resistance leadership settled for the two-hour wait.

Meanwhile, in the crematories the men of the Sonderkommando went about their grim, customary routine. They conducted themselves as usual: all men had to report to work in the early morning hours and all ovens stoked to capacity but the air was filled with urgency. Beneath the hectic compliance with the Nazi orders, the men of the Sonderkommando prepared for their own ominous, final stand. They had the smuggled explosives at the ready. The hidden guns and ammunitions had been rebuilt piece-by-piece. Plans were reviewed and reinforced: As soon as the Czechs started to shout and refuse to proceed into the gas chambers the men of the Sonderkommando would trigger the chain reaction of events. The explosives already placed in strategic positions would be detonated, followed by an attack on the SS formation with the aim of killing as many Germans as possible. Then the rebels would try to escape, even though few really believed that this eventuality would come to pass. In all likelihood all of them would be killed right after the crematories exploded. Most preferred to die in this manner rather than wait another few weeks and follow in the footsteps of the family camp.

All the men were tense and filled with anticipation. The adrenaline ran high and most were tense and highly strung. They understood that they had a rendezvous with destiny. There was little to discuss; the time for action and the end of their earthly time was rapidly approaching.

In the meantime the members of the underground sat on pins and needles. They could not send the final approval to the crematories until they had secured Fredy's cooperation. So they waited.

Two hours later, the young emissary was on his way back. Leisurely threading his way to the family camp, pretending that nothing was amiss, he was all too keen not to awaken the suspicion of some loitering SS man who might have remembered seeing him already once on the same route. Even when the courier reached the family camp, he did not speed up his steps. The inmates were mingling, getting ready to pick up their evening rations of soup. The atmosphere was not changed; clearly the Czechs did not have the faintest idea that they were about to collect their last meal. The heart of the young man gave an extra jolt. In the camp was a young girl he admired and befriended on "Auschwitz terms." They smiled at each other when he had purposefully strolled through the camp, pretending to carry out his duties of collecting evidence and statistics for the Germans, who had a penchant for accurate bookkeeping. They even exchanged a word or two; she seemed to like the young Slovak courier, who was a powerful figure in the camp. And to him she represented a beautiful, dreamlike girl, one who even in the dreary and filthy camp looked well-groomed and classy. He did not even kiss her once.

A shattering thought crossed his mind: by this time tomorrow she would be dead, her loveliness reduced to a small heap of gray ashes that covered the entire expanse of Auschwitz. Her attractiveness and charm would vanish, her body burned into fine dust that filled the air and the nostrils of the inmates. What a heart-wrenching pain!

The young man recoiled with pain and sorrow. But then he straightened, his back ramrod straight, gnashed his teeth and pushed on. If he knew one thing it was that he could not afford the luxury of tears; feelings of doom weakened his resolve. He could hardly escape the grotesque irony of fate. He felt like the biblical Job, a man who suffered a great torment. Or was he, rather, filling the role of the prophet Jeremiah, aware of the dark, merciless verdict of those around him?

The registrar, conjuring up such devastating visions, reached Fredy's barrack. Fredy's cot was squeezed into a tiny crevice on one far corner of the bleak hall. Already from some distance the registrar noticed that Fredy had pulled the sheets close, something he usually did only for a few hours of rest at night, affording some distance and privacy from the crowded barrack.

The young man hurriedly approached the far end of the barrack, now openly rushing to complete his assignment. He quickly pulled the raggedy sheets and looked in disbelief at the sight in front him. Fredy lay on his cot, gasping for air, blue in the face, his rattling breaths sounding as if reverberating from some deep, hollow pit. His handsome face occasionally twitched, the arteries on his neck bulged and his lips were covered with dried up spittle. What had happened to Fredy?

The registrar urgently summoned a physician. He dispatched a young boy to the infirmary with a request for immediate medical help. Then he pulled the curtains closed again and began to strip search Fredy's unconscious body. The rustling of some paper caught his attention and following the sound, he extracted a letter from Fredy's pocket. It was addressed to the men in charge of the Auschwitz resistance movement. It was short.

Fredy shared with the men his agony of not being able to acquit himself of the task they entrusted to him. He begged their forgiveness and understanding. He could not do what they asked because to initiate the massacre would increase the pain the children would have to suffer. They would be better off dying of the poisonous fumes of Zyklon B than perishing in the shootout between the mutinous Sonderkommando and the SS soldiers. Such violence would be far worse than suffocating on toxic vapors in the gas chambers. As he imagined the torment of the children—his little, innocent charges he cared so much about—he had to opt for the least suffering, the death less horrible. If they could not live and all their hopes and dreams were to be shattered, the least they could be afforded was death with less pain and distress. As for himself, Fredy begged for exoneration of his weakness, for he chose death by an overdose of barbiturates instead of making a final stand.

The registrar read and reread the short note. He was deeply disturbed, disappointed and almost sickened to a point of revulsion by the message from the man he believed to be a brave leader and fighter. As he tried to organize his thoughts, looking for an alternate plan for the now-disrupted scenario for the next day's mutiny, the summoned physician arrived. He cast one cursory look at the deeply unconscious man, for a moment listened to his rattling breath and then turned to the registrar: "What about it, what do you want me to do?" The hissed reply was, "Can you revive him, can you bring him back?" The terse answer came on the heel of the question. "Perhaps I could, but it would take at least a week before he would be functional and even if he didn't remain a zombie, he still would be destined for the gas chamber. So why not let him slip away, the way he wished. He already took his leave from this life, let us spare him the agony of another indescribable torment. He is already in the merciful embrace of our Creator; let us not bring him back for more pain and a useless ordeal." The registrar nodded and the young physician pulled the sheet over the face of Fredy, preventing curious people from seeing his disfigured face. "I will stay here to his end and may God have mercy on his soul," whispered the doctor as the ill-fated messenger turned away, leaving the barrack.

The emissary made his way back to the barrack of the *Blockaelteste* (block foreman), where the members of the resistance keenly waited. One look at the ashen face of the courier spoke volumes. The men in charge knew that their well-prepared conspiracy had fallen through. What had gone awry? The only uttered word was "barbiturates." The men shuddered with disgust but it was much too late to find another man and revamp the plot. The Sonderkommando was informed to shelve the scheme for a future day. The rebellion was off.

There was a tragic subplot to the extinction of the Czech family camp. The young registrar who found the dying Fredy was a Slovak boy who was extremely sharp, indeed brilliant. As already alluded to, he had fallen in love, albeit from a distance, with a beautiful Czech girl. In Auschwitz, courting was not a game of two in love. Even those who wielded power had to be very cautious and circumspect. The most the young registrar could do to show his growing infatuation was a smile as he walked through the family camp. But at the moment he understood that the mutiny had

Three. Portrait of Fredy H.

fallen apart, he resolved to give their love a chance. As it sank in that his lovely flame had only few hours to live he threw all caution to the wind, plucked his courage up and under the cover of darkness crept back into the family camp. Soon he found her and for the first time began to talk to her. "Alice, listen, by nightfall I will fetch you. I have to talk with you." Such a telegraphic invitation would have been unthinkable in normal times but Alice understood, and besides, she liked the boy. Worse yet, she had her own foreboding about the dark gloom hanging overhead. An hour of bliss would be God's gift. And so strangely enough the two young people, who until the night of March 6 had never touched each other, spent the night together. Both were virgins. They spent the predawn hours before the upcoming execution in absolute joy of insatiable lovemaking. For a few short hours they reached the pinnacle of happiness only to suffer the incredible grief of parting, for Alice had to die and Rudolf had to live with the pain till the last day of his long life.

The morning came only too soon. Under cold, gray skies in the early hours of a new dawn the Germans began loading the inmates. In early March the Nazis circulated rumors that the SS commandant received orders to relocate the entire family camp to another location called Heidebreck, which offered more food and better living conditions. The members of the family camp were skeptical. They had lived almost six months in the shadows of the billowing chimneys and nursed few illusions, although a few believed that they were somehow privileged. On that fateful March 7 the inmates were ordered onto the trucks. The rest of the inmates watched the departure anxiously; the huge trucks looked like grand monsters, the shadows of the twilight hours making them appear like demons. The cacophony of orders, the barrack closure and the cocked guns were all too real. The snarling dogs straining on their leashes, the noise of weeping infants and women and the despondent shouting, all of this would have shaken heaven or hell if they existed.

At the total closure of the family camp, *Sperre* (the roundup), pandemonium began. The SS beat down on the inmates with their cudgels or the butts of their guns, and blood was everywhere, for no matter how much the inmates tried to comply, they were never fast enough for the crazed sadists in Nazi uniforms in mounting the trucks.

Many eyes frantically scanned the yard looking for Fredy, hoping against hope that he would be able to lead them out of their anguish and misery. But he was nowhere in sight. Few knew that he had met his maker already in the gloomy hours of the preceding evening. His lifeless body, his handsome face was covered and secretly loaded onto one of the trucks. The decisive moment arrived quickly just as they approached the highway. Rather than turn towards Heidebreck, the inmates saw the motorcade in the shadows of the early morning turn instead in the direction of the gas chambers. Most shed tears and recited a silent Kaddish.

Fredy's remains were cremated along with his many friends and the children whom he loved and had hoped to guide out of the darkest hell into a better tomorrow. Their ashes would commingle; they would share the eternal rest scattered on the plains of the Polish countryside. What a fate for a man who loved children, an educator without peer, and what does his fate say about humanity?

The entire family camp perished. The Czechs went to their deaths singing the national anthem, "Kde domov muj?" (Where Is My Home?), followed by "Hatikvah," the anthem of the as yet non-existent home of the Jews, the one they did not live to see.

The attempt to stage a rebellion in Auschwitz, although not led by Fredy, was revived in October of 1944 by the Sonderkommando on duty. These men who were forced to cremate the gassed bodies of their co-religionists were well aware that their stint in the crematories was nearing an end and it was mandatory that they soon be gassed. It was the irrevocable fate for every group of the Sonderkommando men that their life expectancy was a handful of months. For a long time the Sonderkommando had plotted and amassed explosives, smuggled in by women inmates working in a munitions factory. In addition they had sidearms that were used for the mutiny. Crematory #4 was damaged beyond repair in the revolt but all the men perished.

For those wondering about the fate of the 800 children from Bialystok who were kept apart from the other prisoners in Theresienstadt, they continued to be better fed and clad. But on August 1943 they abruptly left the Kreta barracks, where they had lived for some time. Two physicians and fifty-two nurses who took care of them accompanied the transport hoping to save the kids in the promised swap for German POWs. It was not to be. The rumors were that the Grand Mufti of Jerusalem intervened with the Nazis to prevent such an exchange as these kids might later immigrate to what was then Palestine. Instead, the entire transport of the orphans from Bialystok and their attendants was dispatched to Auschwitz, where they went together with their attendants to the gas chamber and, as we said in those days, "through the chimney."

In honor of Fredy I would like to ask if anyone ever has paused long enough to think how much talent and intelligence perished in the death camps and (here being purposely repetitive) went up "through the chimneys"? We must ask ourselves a painful question: How much would Fredy and his beloved children and so many others have contributed to this world if they had just been allowed to live?

QUESTIONS AND ANSWERS

Would Fredy have been treated differently by the Nazis if he had been found out to be gay?

Homosexuals were prosecuted in Nazi Germany. When they were brought to concentration camps they had to wear pink triangles, unlike Jews, who wore yellow stars. They were treated miserably, brutally, and many died by the hands of Nazis who perceived their "deviation" as something that could be controlled by the individual. In those days very few gay people had openly confessed their status to anybody. Had Fredy defiantly done so, he would have had a very short life expectancy even before he was deported to Theresienstadt.

Would he have been treated differently by his own people?

We cannot generalize. There were people who were prejudicial and who had biases against homosexuals. But Prague, I think, was an open-minded metropolis where we knew a lot of people who had different sexual orientations. I think there was by and large a great deal of tolerance. I am sure there would be people who would have judged him because there was this division of opinion. Namely, at the time people would question whether it was just a deviant aberration of a sexual orientation or an inborn inclination and such a person was not in control of his sexual priorities.

Fredy had leadership qualities, but did he lose these qualities at the end? Why? Why not?

Fredy certainly had leadership qualities and he was an inspirational teacher in the occupied protectorate of Bohemia and Moravia, exercising hope, instigating games, inspiring us, and structuring a lifestyle of physical cleanliness and diligent study. He was always stressing that better days would come and the day would come when we would be free people able to develop our talents to the best of our abilities. So certainly he had qualities of a leader who inspired hundreds if not thousands in the concentration camp of Theresienstadt. It was the same in Auschwitz-Birkenau. At the end, he could not do what was expected of him by the underground of Auschwitz-Birkenau.

As to the question "Why or why not?," well, perhaps it's true that he said he could not see the torment of the children and those who would be shot at and beaten to death if there had been an uprising at the entry of the gas chambers, one he was supposed to instigate and lead. Or perhaps he wasn't physically strong enough to visualize himself being tortured. The Germans would probably not have shot him; instead they might have taken him into custody to the punishment block and torn out his nails or his teeth. He knew the brutality of the Nazi investigation. And maybe he just didn't want to put himself through that; and maybe he said if I have to die then let me do it my way, as pain-free as possible, and let me take the barbiturate and let me slip out of this horror as quietly as I can.

Fredy fled, leaving behind his family and friends. Was this leadership?

Fredy fled from Aachen Germany and from then on he was trying to get to what was then Palestine, where the Zionist movement was trying to save Jewish lives. He wasn't successful in reaching there but you have to understand that the situation of the Jew under Nazi rule was that everybody was on his own. He was a single man on the run from the Nazis and tragically he did not succeed.

Is there a difference between being a leader and a moral leader?

Oh, there is a great deal of difference between these two types of individuals. But it does not dictate whether a leader can or cannot be a moral leader as well. There are leaders who are base, from the gutters, and Hitler was one of them. There have always been leaders who are tyrants and who have lacked humanity since its inception. But there are of course the leaders who have morality and who have high standards and expect their followers to fall into the same lifestyle. But, unfortunately, quite often humanity falls into the claws of the leaders who are anything but moral.

What might have been the outcome if Fredy had participated in the rebellion?

Well, with tears in my eyes I can tell you nothing. If he had participated in the rebellion it likely would have brought about the destruction

Three. Portrait of Fredy H.

of one of the crematories, which was the aim of the rebellion. The prisoners had dynamite, and they had explosives to destroy it, and that would have slowed down somehow the day-by-day harvest of death, which amounted to thousands and thousands of gassed Jews.

Fredy's special fate was sealed. He would have died whatever happened and there would have been no mercy for him. If he had participated in the rebellion, it would have made a difference: the explosion of the crematories had to be postponed for a later day and every single day these crematories swallowed thousands of people and murdered transport after transport. Though it could have perhaps resulted in a pause in the function of one of the crematories, of course the Germans would have repaired it and continued with their frantic and frenzied murdering of Jews.

What might have been possible reasons for Fredy's choice about doing what was best for him, the children, the others?

Well, I think that by 1944 Fredy might have been tired enough through all those years. Don't forget the Nazis came to power in Germany in 1933. By 1944 there had been eleven years of rule by a violent tyrant who focused himself and fixated on Jews. There comes a certain time when fatigue sets in and you say there is nothing you can do about it. So perhaps it was best for Fredy to give up and he knew he could not save the children or anybody else, so he ran out of options. He ran out of chances for what to do and he refused to die under Nazi torment they always inflicted on prisoners they perceived as rebellious.

Fredy clashed with Egon Redlich, another leader. What were their differences of vision? Was one vision better than the other? Why? Why not?

Egon Redlich was a Czech educator, a man who was passionately dedicated to children. He hoped to save some in Theresienstadt and he had a child of his own born in Theresienstadt, and his method was a softer approach. Fredy believed in self-discipline and cleanliness. And you know he forced the children take showers in cold water to strengthen their bodies and he believed their salvation could be achieved, or at least some of them could achieve it, by discipline and hardening their bodies. It was not a soft or cushioning approach. He promoted discipline, exercise, supreme cleanliness, and a continuous Spartan-like lifestyle. But Redlich believed that if anything would save those children it would help them to occupy their minds in different ways: singing and writing novels or poems.

This was a different, more intellectual approach on how to promote survival, whereas Fredy wanted to discipline the body to withstand onslaught, to be hardened and strong. So I don't know what studies would say with regards to proving one approach wrong. The whole tragedy is that all those children were murdered anyway, so we have no way to say if Fredy was right or Egon was right. Unfortunately, the murderers succeeded in killing them all.

Fredy had a friendship with SS Bergel. How was this ethically possible?

Well, it wasn't really ethically possible. But a Jew in a concentration camp in which, let's say, an SS officer wanted to be his friend was the rarest of all possibilities. And I don't know what the basis of that friendship was. It may be that Fredy was of course speaking a flawless, accent-free German, or maybe it was their lifestyle. I don't know. There was a friendship between the two men and it was a big ethical contradiction, probably for both men. But it was to the advantage of Fredy, who had been always kept abreast and well-informed by Bergel of what the Nazis had planned to inflict on Theresienstadt. And from this you could up the strength to protect the children and most of the people around you because if you knew what was coming up and who they were rounding up and you could avoid the difficulties, you might have a better chance of survival. So you might have thought it was really unethical for a Jew in a concentration camp but you had to bend a lot of principles in order to try to live another day.

What are "Auschwitz terms"? How and what sorts of relations were possible in the camp between men and women?

Relationships between men and women in camps were of course ongoing. Camps had a division between men huts and women huts. But men and women did interact. "Auschwitz terms" were sometimes brutally pragmatic. But some of these people have been able to help or find someone who was near them to offer comfort or even physical help. But the "Auschwitz terms" were like everything there: they were brutal, stripped of all beauty and softness from the normal day-by-day interaction that we normally do practice.

What lifelong lessons might Fredy have taught the children?

Fredy taught them courage, bravery, Zionism. He taught them that the Jew will develop himself successfully in his own homeland (then Palestine in the Middle East under British mandate rule). He taught them to walk tall, walk proud, and to try to be strong as possible and to hope for a better future and to educate oneself. His prevailing motto was "Discipline. Never to your weakness. Try to plan the day with strength and aim."

Is there any reason to teach lessons to children who are most likely going to die when teaching them is so dangerous?

The life of a child in camp was really a bleak day, with no family, no pets, and no siblings. They were thrust into these barracks where only children lived. They would have been very hungry, cold, and sickly, and they were inadequately clothed. They would have been very bad off. So teaching was salvation for them. They looked forward to being taught: how to write songs, sing, memorize poems. For them it was a substitution of the content for the day. It was heroic to have it offered to them by people like Fredy and Gonda [whose story is also included here], who selflessly cared for them.

Four

Portrait of Milada

Milada was my first cousin. To say that my sister, Eva, and I loved her is a vast understatement of our deep attachment. She was some ten years older than we were, and to us she was the epitome of worldly sophistication and elegance. We monitored her comings and goings and took personal pride in her every success. She was exceptionally beautiful and smart, an overachiever at work, and always dressed to the hilt, yet in subdued and understated sophistication.

She had a throng of male admirers who followed her in droves, clustering around her, hoping for any hint of affection in her dark, almond-shaped eyes. But Milada was in no hurry to choose any of them as she enjoyed being a social butterfly. While she relished their admiration, she generally toyed with them as a cat might with a mouse. And they came back for more, always trusting that one of these days she might become serious about one of them.

But I am jumping the gun. I must go back to her early years for the reader to fully comprehend the experiences that formed Milada's colorful personality. What made her so deliberate in making up her mind, all in her own good time?

Milada's parents, my paternal aunt Miriam and her husband, Charles, were married shortly before the outbreak of the First World War. By all accounts it was a love match. Perhaps there was a matchmaker at work, for in those days, in the early years of the twentieth century, young people were often introduced to socially compatible counterparts by a helpful facilitator. Miriam and Charles were like-minded individuals who made a striking couple indeed. My aunt was tall and slim, her finely chiseled face, in later years, set in a serious, almost sad expression. But her wedding picture reveals the radiant smile of a happy bride whose eyes gaze lovingly at her handsome groom. My aunt looked like a princess marrying her prince charming and indeed my uncle wore the uniform of an Austro-Hungarian army officer. Even the yellowish, brittle, old photograph cannot conceal their bliss in the moments following their vows exchanged so long ago. But perhaps it was much-too-much happiness for the fates to grant one couple, for it seems they sought to recoup it thereafter.

Not long after their honeymoon, fate struck them a blow. Europe was engulfed in a conflict of epic proportions. The Great War scorched much of Europe, leaving it in ashes. Not long after their wedding my uncle was called up to his unit to fight for the old emperor, who started the First World War with little causes and even less responsibility. As the senile emperor slowly tottered into his grave, he dragged an entire generation of young men along with him. Europe was bled white; the battlefields in the West and East were drenched with the blood of millions of innocent lives, all essentially lost for no rhyme or reason.

My handsome uncle was amongst those who made the supreme sacrifice. His much adoring young wife, expecting their first and only baby, hoped and prayed for his safe return. One day the local notables notified her that her husband died for emperor and country and she should be very proud of his heroism. His unit was wiped out during the battle of Mazursky Lakes, where the Austrian army suffered a humiliating defeat. My poor Aunt Miriam was anything but proud of his sacrifice. When the initial shock wore off she was beyond consolation. Her happiness and marriage lasted only for a few hours. How could fate tear him out of her arms so soon? But bad news seems to have more durability than happiness.

She drew comfort from the fact that she was carrying Charles's child; she was about seven months pregnant when the fateful news about his death reached her. And this child, the only positive reality remaining after Charles's death, was my first cousin Milada. Milada never knew her handsome father; she had only the photo of the dashing young man whose death broke my aunt's heart into a thousand irreparable pieces. Miriam hardly ever smiled and, while she adored her daughter, she seemed to live in a world without sunshine and in irremediable pain.

Their household consisted of three women of three generations; our grandmother shared the residence with her daughter and granddaughter. My grandmother, the Grande Dame of our family, looked after Milada in her quiet, unobtrusive way, trying to fill in for her deceased father and her heartbroken, working mother. Somewhere amidst the years of her adolescence Milada made up her mind that a man could destroy you if you love and embrace him fully, and a woman might not recover from such loss. She liked to toy with men, however, to be the lady who never loses her cool or gives her heart away. Unlike my widowed grandmother and widowed aunt, who rarely laughed or raised their voices, Milada's peels of silvery laughter were always at hand, readily spilling into the silent, elegant apartment.

Both my grandmother and my aunt were widowed young, never marrying again. Young Milada moved among them, filled with life and energy, optimism and ambitious plans for her career. While most girls in those days dreamed of marrying the right man, Milada refused even to consider marriage; she planned on ascending high into the business world, to become financially successful and independent.

Milada was also a brilliant student, which greatly pleased my father, who also was her official guardian. She was as dear to him as own two daughters. She was his little girl before he even married and had a family of his own and he never ceased to fret about her decisive ways, resoluteness and stunning beauty. She was still a teenager when boys began swarming around her. She dated few and teased them all. Later when my sister and I became slightly older, she would regale us with stories about her admirers, and the two of us were an enraptured audience. Our greatest wish was to emulate our vivacious cousin.

Following her senior matriculation, Milada enrolled in the business program offered at the Charles University of Prague, where 99 percent of the students were male. If girls decided on a business career, most of them turned to less strenuous programs that were also of shorter duration. The usual road was to enroll in the school of business, at the age of fifteen or so, which prepared girls for secretarial or routine accounting positions. It took four years to complete this program and then the graduate would be ready for a secretarial position or basic bookkeeping and other routine office duties. Milada would not even consider this option; she would scale the highest peak of academe in her chosen field. She would not become someone's secretary; rather she would have one or more of her own one day. My father supported her ambitions; he felt that she should not shortchange herself and should indeed fly as far as her dreams carried her. Her gentle mother and grandmother smiled kindly and Milada, as always, had her way. Our cousin studied, surrounded by men, and graduated with flying colors.

Milada was tall, slim and extremely well built. All her curves were in the right places, perhaps somewhat understated but there nonetheless.

Four. Portrait of Milada

She had a pair of long, slim legs that would have been an asset to a professional dancer. She had a long, slim neck and her face was framed with a shock of dark brown hair. Her hair had a natural tendency to form gentle waves, so that she always looked as if she had just stepped out of the hairdresser's chair. Her face was one of a kind. I have some beautiful photos of her but none caught the essence of Milada. Her features were refined with a touch of sensuality and she had an expression that promised intelligence. We all expected her to have an illustrious future.

As Milada was growing up in a fatherless home she had to make do without many luxuries others took for granted. Although my father helped his mother and sister as best he could, Milada had to forego many frills a young teenager would wish to have. As a widow, my grandmother found work as a seamstress and because of her skills she never lacked customers. Her daughter, my Aunt Miriam, a widow with a dependent daughter, was eligible for government help.

Czechoslovakia was born after the First World War as a consequence of the disintegration of the Austro-Hungarian Empire. The new republic had to shoulder the responsibility of the many war invalids and widows resulting from the Great War. One way the government tackled the huge problem was to allow such recipients to operate tobacconist's shops or warehouses, as tobacco was controlled as a state monopoly.

As it turned out, my father became one of the lawyers responsible for the distribution of this commodity and he arranged that his sister could operate one of the best stores, located in the heart of Prague. Still, it was not an easy way to make a living. My poor aunt kept her tobacconist store open for long hours, and I think that had the three depended exclusively on the store, they might have gone hungry. But my father always stood by, working in two different capacities to supplement my aunt's income and provide all of us a good life. And then there was my granny with her sewing skills, which also brought in a pretty penny. But as the years went by, her eyesight dimmed and she found it increasingly difficult to continue efficiently and gainfully. Her perfectionism required time and precision and she found it harder to uphold her high standard of work. Granny called on Milada to help her and while they worked together, she taught her the trade and also imparted to her granddaughter her exquisite taste and sense of elegance. Milada thus became an accomplished dressmaker, a craft she never wanted to pursue professionally but one that helped her dress elegantly at a fraction of the cost of another person. And Milada loved to dress according to the latest fashions.

During her teens she would spend time with us, accompanying us to the theater, concerts and museums. As an older cousin she also filled in as an occasional governess. My father insisted on paying her for it, a transaction we kids never witnessed. Milada was great fun to be with. She was full of good cheer, somewhat on the mischievous side, and she knew countless jokes that she related with a serious face until the punch line, which she delivered with great gusto and timing. She dispelled for us the mystery of dance classes, which every girl then attended when 16 years of age; she even taught us some extra steps so that we should not feel uptight or insecure.

We also felt free to talk with Milada about sex. While we were enlightened by our mother about the facts of life, we did not dare ask too many questions, though she encouraged us to do so. We knew that we could always pick Milada's brain. When we first discussed the topic, Milada was a university student and we were still little girls. I believe that she was still a virgin but not totally void of experiences. She probably took some liberties, engaged in kissing and fondling, but she did not "cross the line." But she loved to impress us and I think she sounded worldlier than she was. With Milada we felt comfortable and unencumbered to ask the most intimate and perhaps bizarre questions. She, in turn, never made us feel stupid or salaciously curious.

Milada was in her third year in university when she first met the man she fell in love with. It was during the mid-1930s. Life in Czechoslovakia was good but we were much troubled by the police state in neighboring Nazi Germany. There were ugly rumors about the persecution of all Jews, the indignities they were exposed to, the deprivations and threats to their lives. All of us became more serious, Milada included. She became more subdued, and her near spontaneous peals of laughter became rare and less exuberant. Life lost its innocence and we began to anticipate dark days in the offing.

During those times Milada became a less frequent visitor to our house, which was really hard on us. She explained her absences by citing a heavy load of schoolwork and other commitments. We knew that it was not only her academic courses: it had to be something else that kept her away and somehow changed her. She seemed more pensive, softer and mellower. We conjectured that she was in love. Our scenarios were reinforced when we overheard a conversation between our parents that we were not supposed to hear. But, of course, we strained our ears, skulking in the hallway, not to miss a word from a serious debate, which clearly

Four. Portrait of Milada

was of great concern to our elders. The topic of discussion was Milada, our favorite cousin and mentor. Soon we put together the missing pieces of the puzzle: the roots of the deep and almost palpable change in our dear cousin's behavior.

The fact that Milada had become serious about a man would normally have been welcomed news. She was about 23 years old, a perfect beauty by anyone's standard, beleaguered by swarms of admirers. The only part of her life she took with utmost seriousness was her education and her ambitious plans to climb to the top of the corporate world. At that time it was the exclusive domain of men, and few women would even think of attempting to break that glass ceiling.

To my father's chagrin, she always dismissed the thought of marriage as an institution she would not consider, not as yet anyway. Somehow Milada came to the conclusion that marriage would shackle a woman's career. My father, conservative and perhaps old-fashioned, could not imagine his charge spending her entire life scaling the corporate ladder and living this life alone, without a family of her own. Neither my father nor Milada's mother thought much of Milada's plan to have a life bereft of a happy marriage and harmonious family. But Milada laughed and dismissed the thought of her marital future as if it were a bothersome fly returning to annoy her. But it too vanished, as if dispelled by a magic wand.

Though we knew that her penultimate year in the business administration program was not an easy one, we sensed that it was not the main reason for her sudden transformation. And because we loved her so much, we worried and wanted to know what was afoot with Milada. For that and other reasons we hid and listened in silence to the hushed conversation between our parents, Milada's mother and our grandmother. We risked getting caught and punished for our indiscretion but we burned with curiosity. Before long we understood that not only was Milada in love with a fellow student, she was also considering marriage, right after their shared graduation. So why was there a dramatic summit when we all knew that all our elders wanted her to marry in the first place?

Every time Milada dropped by she would be ushered into my father's study and we girls would try to catch a glimpse or two as she was about to leave. I remember that evening when she had no time to share our dinner and seemed evasive, although radiating happiness and looking absolutely gorgeous. So what could be so terribly wrong when she seemed so exhilarated and joyous?

Actually it was simple enough: She was infatuated with a colleague who—according to our family's consensus—was the wrong man. For starters he was not Jewish, and although our family did not adhere to the orthodox version of our faith we still considered intermarriage to be absolutely unacceptable. Perhaps it seems inconsistent and difficult to understand why the Jews of central Europe, almost completely absorbed into the mainstream of society, thought of intermarriage as an absolute disaster and tragic loss. Although in the 1930s quite a few Jewish men married gentile women and that was considered bad enough, these cases were still deemed to be exceptions and the men who selected this path were often perceived as the losers who could not find a Jewish spouse. Families whose members intermarried were often deeply ashamed that one of their own had gone astray and married outside the faith. In those days this certainly cast a dark blot on a family.

The reasons for such upheaval in families were multifarious; religion was only one part of it. For the more pragmatic individuals, experience had shown that intermarriage often added another unwanted hurdle for a couple trying to create a harmonious and lasting union. Children of these couples were often torn between loyalties to different traditions. This struggle complicated daily life and forced kids to take sides. The children often drifted into Christianity, as it was more difficult to belong to a small minority like Judaism. Accordingly, the Jewish partner would often end up in a position of belonging to the minority religion, even in his own home. Given the prospect for a successful intermarriage was deemed so minute that few couples were even willing to try to take on such a feat. Both sides of the newlyweds' families were usually disappointed and sometimes even heartbroken. Therefore, intermarriage was frowned upon as having next to no prospect of success.

Perhaps the Gentiles worried that their new Jewish relative had some of the characteristics ascribed to Jews in the anti–Semitic myths so popular at the time. Jews could be redeemed in the eyes of the Christian world only if they converted, but this meant a great deal of self-denial and self-rejection by the new convert.

On the Jewish side of the equation, things were even more complicated. Since their dispersion from the land of Israel two millennia ago, Jews had seen their ranks decimated by various tragedies, pogroms and forcible expulsions. Intermarriage, though, was considered the worst calamity. Indeed, orthodox Jews considered marriage outside of the faith to be equivalent to the death of the child. They would refuse all future contact and go through the rituals of mourning. They would tear the lapel on

Four. Portrait of Milada

their clothes, strew ashes over their heads and sit Shiva (the seven days when family sit together mourning the deceased). The grieving family would never even utter the name of the one symbolically buried.

Although most secular Jews did not follow these rituals, intermarriage still represented a painful loss. It was as if there was a dried-up branch in the family tree that would no longer sprout new blossoms. Jews are raised to accept it if God takes away a child and that they should bow to the Supreme One, but they are not prepared to see a child's life erased in shame. Few, if any, were willing to gracefully accept such events in their families. And though we strayed in many customs and were sometimes estranged from traditional Jewish observance, our reaction to intermarriage was just as visceral as our more traditional brethren. We mourned that the lifestyle steeped in Jewish philosophy, ethics and faith would come to an end.

In the case of our Milada, all these arguments were valid, aggravated by additional complexities specific to her boyfriend's family. Tom, her handsome and charming beau, was born into an old and well-established Prague family that had played a prominent role in Czech life for many generations. They proudly traced their family tree back to Jan Hus, the leading member of the Czech religious reformation of the fifteenth century. They considered themselves a part of the national elite and, while they did not profess and expound noisy and crude anti–Semitism, they were no friends of the "Chosen People." Certainly none of their invited guests at their elaborate dinner parties were Jews nor did they have personal friendships with them. They were not rabid Jew haters but their prejudices and biases were much ingrained in their circles. They were also very well off, owning car parts manufacturing plants and having many other business interests and other lucrative ventures. For good measure they owned hotels and invested successfully in the stock market. Politically they were members of the conservative Czech right wing, which was nationalistic, chauvinistic and reactionary. Tom, the pride and joy of his parents, was expected to follow the family's traditions and it goes without saying that he would marry a girl of similar background who would be compatible with his family's standards and expectations. That he would fall in love with a fellow student, a gorgeous Jewess, was bad enough, but that he would contemplate marriage was totally unthinkable. Tom's parents made it clear that if he were to proceed with his romantic notions, they would not only disinherit him but also use their considerable clout to undermine his and his future wife's plans.

While they considered themselves to be a form of aristocracy, they would not tolerate their son making a "morganatic" marriage (i.e., marrying someone of lower status). It was evident that Tom would be shunned and that the wrath of his parents would cause not only emotional turmoil but also extend into his professional future. The tentacles of the few powerful and wealthy families were long and mighty. Nevertheless, the two sweethearts were deeply and confidently in love and would not take such threats seriously.

My father was concerned for Milada's future. He was absolutely certain that Tom's family would never accept her and with time their contempt would corrode the quality of the couple's relationship. While our dad was well aware of the complexities of intermarriage, he still felt bad that Tom's family did not consider Milada good enough. There were few women who had the sterling intellectual, physical and personal qualities of Milada.

The impasse continued for months on end. Milada became an infrequent guest in our house and when she came she often spent a long time in my father's study, where they carried on lengthy debates. She no longer had time for Eva and me, only caressing our hair in passing or blowing a kiss from the door while coming or going.

On occasion she would come accompanied by Tom. They looked exquisite together. Both were tall, slim and handsome. And there was the aura of love around them. They looked at each other with great affection and adoring glances. Still, Tom lacked a hardened, virile expression; he could not deny the soft life and lack of hardships in his past. He had no exposure or chance to pass the litmus test of hard times. That is not to say that he looked effeminate, but anyone could see that he had grown up in the lap of luxury.

These two lovers were not destiny's favorites. The times were squarely set against them. During the mid-1930s the winds of anti-Semitism blew from neighboring Germany, where the Nazis came to power and quickly passed anti-Jewish laws affecting every walk of life. Impoverished of all material goods and reduced to social pariahs, the Jews were singled out for persecution. Although historically the Czechs had never been fond of the Teutons, such an enormous outburst of hatred and state-condoned robbery of all human rights of one small minority had to evoke some emotion from bystanders.

One of the first, and ferociously enforced, sets of decrees by Nazi Germany was the Nuremberg racial laws, which prohibited any sexual

Four. Portrait of Milada

contact between Jews and Gentiles. Both offenders would be liable to penalties. Even the offspring from already existing intermarriages were affected, as these "half-breeds" were subject to lesser deprivations but were still nevertheless persecuted.

All this did not bode well for my cousin. The couple completed the last year of their university courses with flying colors, both earning degrees in business administration. While Tom was offered a junior position in a branch of a multinational company, Milada was hired at the head office of a mining company stationed in Prague. The subtle discrimination became more palpable during these times, with few Jews finding work at any level. Tom's family could have pulled a few strings but they would not consider extending themselves for Tom's Jewish girlfriend. While they never considered her his fiancée, they waited for the couple to hit turbulence related to her racial and religious background. Events were moving quickly.

My father thought the time had arrived to test the quality of Tom's character and gauge his feelings for Milada. He reasoned—and justifiably so—that rough times were ahead and if Tom really and truly loved Milada he could shelter her from much vexation.

On one Sunday afternoon in 1937, Milada and Tom were invited for an afternoon coffee at our home. They arrived laughing and joking, happy and confident that they would weather the stormy days ahead and come out unscathed. I think my parents prepared the little scheme beforehand. My mother asked Milada to join her for a moment in the adjacent room and when they returned, my father and Tom had retired to Dad's study.

Later Dad told us that he invited Tom for a cigarette and a man-to-man talk. He told him frankly about his concerns for Milada's safety as a Jewess in the dark days ahead and he stressed that if Tom truly cared for her, he should marry her now before the Nazis' axe fell on Czechoslovakia.

When Dad fell silent, Tom did not answer immediately. Obviously ill at ease, he began to shift uncomfortably in his chair, hedging, explaining to my father that he was just starting out and was not at all certain if he would make his mark at his present position. Also, he could not afford to antagonize his powerful parents, and his income did not allow him to support a wife yet. He listed scores of plausible reasons to delay this marriage from his point of view.

My kind Dad wanted to make absolutely sure that he did not misjudge Tom, so he attempted one more time to explain that while Tom's reasons were perfectly valid, Milada's situation might become life threatening and that their marriage could ward off troubles. Dad went so far as to suggest that their timely marriage might save her life. This time Dad's point was crystal clear. Would Tom stand by Milada through bad times?

But still the young man would not commit himself. He assured Dad that he would do his utmost for the woman he loved but that it was his sincere conviction that my father saw events too pessimistically, his prism darkened by the panic-mongering regarding events in Germany. After all, they were young, they had just graduated and now was their time to lay a foundation for a solid future career. His parents had the necessary connections and once he was well on his way up, he would enjoy much greater freedom. He would marry Milada but not at this moment, when his parents could ruin his aspirations.

My father heard enough. He got up, signaling an end to the conversation. Now they would join the rest of the group in the living room. He knew right then and there that Tom was the worst kind of opportunist who would never make any sacrifice for Milada—or anyone else, for that matter. He enjoyed their affair and he might have even loved her in his own way but not enough to save her life and ruin his chances of being a young CEO.

The next days were quiet and sad. My father did not say much, but the next day, he sat with Milada in his study and they remained secluded for several hours. When they came out Milada had red-rimmed eyes and the appearance that her world was smashed to pieces. Had Tom died physically she might have taken it somewhat better. The man she loved was not the one she believed him to be. The death of her dreams was harder to accept in some ways; her romance was all a sham, Tom would not stand by her.

Much later, before our impending deportation, she spoke to Eva and me about Tom and her great love for him. She said only that had it been the other way around, she would have married him without blinking an eye, just to be sure to ease any undeserved burden. She told us that she confronted him with his reply to my father, and that he tried to hush her up. In his verbosity he tried to explain to her but he never said the right words. Then on the night she took her leave from him, with broken heart and indescribable pain, Tom tried to convince her to meet him and continue their affair. He claimed the future was not predetermined and perhaps the Nazis would not even bother with Czechoslovakia. But Milada knew better than to listen. Though her breaking heart wanted to agree with him, she knew that she had to act upon his cowardly, unprincipled lack of resolve. She could not afford the luxury of going into the twilight

Four. Portrait of Milada

with someone who would drop her at the first sign of danger. She had a mother and a grandmother she wanted to help, and this was a tall order, for the times we lived in did not allow for indulgences—no one could afford to coddle oneself or live in denial. Nevertheless, a part of her died on that night when she sent him away, parting with a last kiss, the sweetness of which was sprinkled with the salt of her tears. In the days to come she had to draw on all her strength not to answer his calls or talk to him when he waited for her as she returned from work. He certainly did not make it easy for her to break things off. Perhaps his heart ached too. Who knows what he felt when he betrayed the love of his life?

But events took a quick turn and all Jews were in a tailspin, heading straight to a man-made hell. Czechoslovakia was mutilated and torn; one part was annexed by the Germans and six months down the road, despite promises made, the remnant was taken. The country was split into two units: Bohemia and Moravia became the German Protectorate and Slovakia was proclaimed an independent state, headed by the fascist priest Father Tiso.

We, the trapped Jews of Prague, and the entire Protectorate became sitting ducks. The hunt began. We evaded as best we could but all to no avail. In the end we lost as we suspected we would. How could a tiny, unarmed civilian minority cope with the powerful Nazi military machine, unscrupulous, brutal and felonious? Our day-to-day life quickly deteriorated. We had no work. Our assets and bank accounts were inaccessible to us, and we soon hit the bottom of our cash reserves. Now were the days when we had little to eat and our clothes became threadbare. Luckily Milada knew how to sew and mend clothes. It was in this way that she was able to add to the marginal budget of the family. Times were tough and worse were to come.

At times I would ask her if she ever ran into Tom. She would answer in the affirmative: yes. He still tried to meet her but she knew that this fairy tale was over.

As our misery became more acute, we all looked for ways and means to help. At times I would be so hungry that I would steal a roll or a small loaf of bread at the bakers, forever trembling with fear that I would be caught and my parents would be held responsible for my actions. But hunger is a powerful force. But then, sometime in the year 1940, Milada found a way out of the predicament, at least for the time being. She met another man and quickly started a romance which was of paramount importance for all of us.

Milada, who lost her job as soon as the Nazis occupied the "Protectorate," picked up some administrative work in the offices of the Jewish community of Prague. On one occasion she met a young man with an unusual personality. He was in a liaison position between the much-dreaded offices of the Gestapo (*Geheime Staatspolizei*) and the Jewish community. He would communicate the orders of the Germans to the Jewish officials and he would carry material back and forth. He had the exceptional privilege of having a small motorbike at his disposal and he would zoom through the cobblestone streets of Prague, an unlikely sight: a Jew on a motorcycle. Sigi was also a speed freak, for he would drive through the streets of Prague at a prohibited velocity, moving unencumbered between the Nazi headquarters and the offices of the Jewish community. At this time Jews were not allowed to use public transportation except for two hours in the late afternoon, but Sigi roamed through Prague with few restrictions. Whispered hearsay had it that he was a very discreet operator and that he performed other services and errands for the Nazis, whose ear and confidence he enjoyed. Clearly Prague's police had been ordered to grant special concessions to this mysterious man who drove in such a dangerous fashion.

One has to bear in mind that in the early forties, in the wake of the deportation of Jews from Prague to concentration camps, the unfortunate people who stood on the verge of expulsion tried to unload valuables they could not take with them. They bartered them for precious stones, small nuggets of gold or other hard currency, all of which was easier to smuggle into a camp than precious oil paintings, carpets, or stamp and coin collections. The Nazis were hungry to put their paws on anything precious they could claim as spoils of war. The trapped Jews were glad to exchange priceless works of art at well below their true value for items they could hide on themselves and smuggle into the camps. But neither group could deal directly with the other. A German would risk his head, or at the very least his relocation to the Russian front, if he even talked to a Jew in an unofficial capacity—and no Jew could contact a German. Obviously a middleman would be of value to both sides as well as being a very special and rare commodity. He had to have the confidence of the Nazis who put their lives into his hands. As for the Jews, they only hoped that he would deliver the goods he bargained for them. Had he ever been caught or even suspected of such activity, he would have been killed. But the Germans involved would also suffer grave consequences. But nobody should underestimate the power of avarice and the grasp of covetous individuals when such a singular opportunity happened to pass their way.

Four. Portrait of Milada

Rumor had it that Sigi was not only a liaison between the two solitudes, but he also brokered some very hazardous, underhanded deals. He was one Jew the Nazis trusted to coat their pockets with gold. I never knew with certainty but it was likely true that Sigi enjoyed privileges and freedoms no other Jew in Prague could claim. While we all had to abide by the 8:00 p.m. curfew, Sigi roared on his motorbike through the darkened streets of Prague at will protected by powerful men who exempted him from the fate of the run of the mill Jews of Prague. Surely the Germans did not need a pet Jew: they exploited his agile, razor-sharp intellect and his absolute discretion. The Germans allowed him free reign in Prague for as long as he was useful.

It was Sigi who fell instantaneously head over heels in love with my cousin. He met her on one occasion when he dropped by the offices of the Jewish community, and it did not take more than one look for Sigi to know that this was the woman he wanted for a girlfriend.

Sigi was not the type of man who wavered when he saw something he wanted and he desperately wanted Milada, who had impressed him so much. Milada, however, though no longer the glamorous "femme fatale," always took her time with men, never in a great hurry to take any single one of them seriously. Tom, who swept her off her feet, had been the only exception. Besides that, I think she was still smarting from the disappointment of Tom's opportunistic decampment at the worst possible time. She never really spoke about her pain, only every now and then she would stare into some nebulous distance and her eyes would glisten with the unreleased tears and we knew she was longing for Tom. But we pretended not to notice, as she did not want to be seen in her moments of weakness.

Sigi was certainly not the man to take no for an answer. He was as persistent as he was impressive. In bygone days, he had been an engineering student who had almost completed his university courses in civil engineering when the Germans closed all centers of higher learning in the Czech lands. From the fall of 1939 no Czech Gentile or Jewish students had access to university-level education, for the Germans had imposed punitive measures in response to demonstrations staged by Czech university students. Sigi had all but completed the requirements but could not obtain his degree. A degree, though, would do little good for a Jew sentenced to extermination.

Sigi grew up in Ruthenia, the son of a small merchant whose endless hours of work brought little material comfort to his large family. Sigi was the oldest son, a brilliant student who made up his mind early in life to escape the dire poverty of the province in the Eastern tip of Czechoslovakia. He was largely self-taught, spoke some seven languages with ease and seemed able to master any task, jump any hurdle in his life. He was tall, slim and blond. He lacked Tom's dark elegance, but his face was manly and determined. Unlike Tom, Sigi's face was chiseled by hardship and each conquered challenge had left its indelible mark. Sigi nursed few illusions about the future. He knew that time was running out and he wanted to make the best out of whatever remained. He knew that in his position he courted death every day, many times over. One wrong step in his wheeler-dealer machinations could bring an end to his earthly existence.

Sigi later told us that he was never in love and never wanted to succumb to what he perceived as weakness. That had been the case until he met Milada. Though he wished to resist any commitment and perceived feelings of love as the fabrication of poets, movie producers and fools, he could not help but fall for Milada.

Their relationship was an interesting one, comprising two people who fought tooth and nail against any emotional attachment. Milada was always cautious—the exception being Tom—and Sigi considered love just a fanciful offshoot of sex drive. He was seemingly the ultimate arbiter of rationality, and romantic love was not a part of his repertoire. Then unexpectedly he was hit by Cupid's arrow.

Sigi found love at the least convenient time: the twilight of the Jews' existence in Europe. As for Milada, she found in Sigi an exceptional man but perhaps not the passion of her life. In those trying days he was the pillar she could lean on. For the first time in her life she felt in need of a strong shoulder. She was baffled and boggled by the challenges thrust upon her and unsure of how to ease the plight of her family. In those bleak, drab and impoverished times, Sigi could scrape up almost anything that was needed. He could work his contacts and he managed to provide for Milada and the rest of us. He helped us overcome the shortage of many essentials in our households. We never knew the details of his bartering operations nor did he himself ever touch upon them.

Milada and Sigi became inseparable. Slowly Sigi's presence and qualities helped Milada to see matters with a new clarity. Suddenly she saw Tom for what he really was: a boy rather than a man, pampered, malleable and spoilt, softened by good times. Milada never did become indifferent to Tom, but slowly her wounds began to heal. It was then that she found Sigi, the man who stood by her, who never wavered in his devotion and love for her.

Four. Portrait of Milada

I think he also stashed away some valuables in the unlikely case of Milada's survival. He did not want her to start a new life empty-handed. They helped each other in the most trying times and they became lovers as well. I know that Milada would often stay overnight in his bachelor pad. We all had to stay off the streets after 8:00 p.m. While Sigi could disregard any German ordinance, this did not apply to Milada, of course. I believe that theirs was the type of mature love of two people who understood each other and had mutual admiration and respect. While Sigi adored Milada and thought she was the embodiment of the ideal woman, Milada was perhaps not as infatuated as she was appreciative of this outstanding man.

Because Sigi had grown up in grinding poverty, Milada was unlike the women he was accustomed to. She was very different from the hardworking mothers who slaved from sunrise to sunset, cooking, cleaning, and bending over the washboards scrubbing the family's laundry. These were women who had to turn every penny twice before spending it to feed their large broods. Little wonder they aged before their time, losing their attractiveness, bent by the burdens of hard labor, the many pregnancies and, above all, the crushing privations required for survival during the early twentieth century. Their crisp, young faces wilted and wrinkled, their hair lost its luster, their eyes became encircled with deep, dark shadows, and their bodies became heavy and their legs distorted by varicose veins weaving their way up their calves like heavy bluish ropes. Sigi carried this picture close because it was the image of his beloved mother.

As a child he decided to flee this life, which was a never-ending succession of hard work with little compensation. Sigi recalled each Friday night's candles and festive dinner on a white tablecloth. He recalled the shimmering light of the candles, which softened the features of his mother, but to him it was not enough. He thought of the injustice of such poverty, especially for Jews who were tormented by rabid anti–Semitism. So when he began to read the writings of Karl Marx, he found the answer.

The answer to humanity's woes was to embrace Communism, which promised to give to all "according to their needs, while all will contribute according to their abilities." Sigi disposed of his lukewarm Judaism and substituted it with Communism. Still, he never joined the Communist Party, because he was not a "joiner" by any means. But all the same, he remained a dedicated convert of the new Left. Under the Nazis the Communist Party was outlawed and the Nazis pursued its members with unrelenting violence and vigor. The fact that Sigi was not inclined to belong to parties or clubs became his blessing because obviously the Nazis would have never trusted or employed anyone suspected of being a Communist.

When Sigi first came to Prague to study he discovered a new type of woman: fashionable, stylish, well-groomed and elegant. Their high heels made a staccato sound, proclaiming a different type of girl than the ones he knew in impoverished Ruthenia. He couldn't help but notice how they gently swung their hips, some more suggestively than others; few resembled the weathered women he was familiar with.

In the beginning he only admired them from a distance but with time, he plucked up his courage and began to date. He had quite a few affairs, most of which remained on a rather pedestrian, physical level. He never found a girl who could keep up with him intellectually and who he also found desirable physically. There were some who seemed to have rescinded their femininity and wanted to be colleagues with men only. These women he found enjoyable to fence with mentally but they left him cold emotionally and sexually. Then there was the majority: the pretty, attractive girls, the secretaries or bank tellers or sales girls who excited his masculinity. But once the relationship was consummated he became quickly restless and bored. And so he drifted from one to another until the day he ran into Milada, who left him thunderstruck from their first moment. After that first encounter he pined only for her and little else mattered. Sigi proposed marriage to Milada early on but she remained noncommittal, thinking they should wait to see if they survived these threatening times. She pointed out that she carried the responsibility for her mother and grandmother and it would be hardly fair to saddle him with so much baggage.

Sigi had an excellent plan he hoped to set into motion with the help of an SS man who had reason to be appreciative of Sigi. Sigi devised a scheme to disappear into the Aryan world. He had falsified documents indicating him to be an Austrian drywall worker. Since he looked like an Aryan, with his fair coloring, he had a chance of submerging among the Austrian working class and surviving the war without being deported with the rest of the Jewish community. Sure, there would be some risk but far less than that of being a starving, ill-treated Jewish inmate in a Nazi concentration camp.

The SS officer, who had become immensely rich through his dealings with Sigi, suddenly got cold feet. One evening as he attended a rather rowdy party in the SS officer club, he overheard a conversation of senior officers who voiced concern about underhanded business operations of their underlings with Jewish wheeler-dealers. Though no names or other

Four. Portrait of Milada

specifics were mentioned, the SS officer panicked and wanted to stop all his illegal activities. He also wished for Sigi to disappear. He didn't want any Jew around who could incriminate him.

Sigi was too clever to go down without a fight. He hinted broadly that if he were sent to a concentration camp he would have no reason to be silent. However, if the SS officer were to provide him with false identification papers as a Gentile, he would vanish into the dead of night, never to be seen or heard of again. Sigi indicated that he had a fiancée who wished to vanish right along with him. Surprisingly the SS man was willing to go along with the plan. He badly needed Sigi gone, just to be certain that he could not be incriminated as a partner in underhanded Jewish deals.

Now Sigi wanted to persuade Milada to join him and leave the accursed continent of Europe. He had contacts and once they were out of Prague he could arrange for an illegal border crossing and they could ultimately make their way to the safety of Palestine. Sigi knew people who would take them over the Slovak-Hungarian border and from there they would slip into Romania. There, some clandestine groups were operating illegally, helping refugees board rickety, barely seaworthy vessels. This was their best hope of getting to Palestine. Both were young and could easily withstand the rigors of being at sea for a few weeks. It was but a small price to pay for a chance to escape the trap that Europe had become. They could become free people.

At first Milada was elated, realizing that this would be her best chance of fleeing the Nazi reign of terror. But then the inevitable sobering thought brought her back to reality. What was she to do with her mother, a woman in her forties who was not very strong physically or emotionally? Only a few months earlier, the family had decided to place our grandmother in the Jewish old folks home and for a princely sum we were promised her permanent residence. Though the funds paid were ruinous to our family's financial balance, we thought it worthwhile because we were given a pledge that the old folks home would not be subject to deportation. Taking Grandma to an institution was difficult and her absence left a big void in our lives. But it didn't solve the problem of Milada's mother.

Sigi and Milada had only a few hours to reach a decision. They deliberated at length, trying to reach an acceptable compromise. Sigi pointed out that Miriam would not be abandoned: after all, as the rest of the family was still in Prague and could try to arrange for deportation together. Milada felt that this was a comfortable ruse to get her to shirk her responsibility for her mother. She knew that the Germans ordered the leaders of the

Jewish community to gather people together into transports with certain specifications and it was dubious if Miriam, a widow, would qualify to join a family of four. And all by herself Miriam lacked the fortitude so badly needed in times such as these.

Sigi, in turn, knew that in seafaring matters when all was lost and the ship was about to go under, the captain declared that everybody was on their own, freeing even the crew to try to save their lives. And this Jewish ship was sinking rapidly. Was Milada not duty bound to try to save her life? Would it not be right to present the matter to Miriam, who might be relieved to know her daughter could escape from harm's ways? Surely she should be involved in such crucial decisions, which could make the difference between life and death, shouldn't she?

Milada in turn felt that she could not place the burden of such a weighty resolution on her mother's shoulders and so she decided to reach an equitable and acceptable decision all on her own. She and Sigi argued back and forth without reaching a consensus. This was their last night together. During the course of the next day Sigi would get his papers and board a train that would take him to the Slovak border. Later Milada told me that they argued, made love, and cried the bitter tears of two people who knew that this was their final embrace before Doomsday. They did not shut an eye all night and in the gray twilight of the new day, they made love for the last time, spent and heartbroken.

Sigi, who always projected the image of a tough guy, steeled by years of grinding poverty, driven by intense ambition, did not try to hide his tears. Milada vacillated until the last moment, experiencing the strange emotion of sorrow mixed with elation in the arms of the man she was about to let go. In the end, she followed what she perceived to be her duty, namely to stand by her mother, whom she considered weak and unable to cope with the challenges ahead.

In the early morning hours Sigi used his motorbike for the last time. He went to the offices of the Gestapo, where he collected his papers that gave him a new identity. The last thing he had to do was to seek out the expert who attached his photo to the identification card. All this cost a small fortune. Sigi was cautioned by the SS man to vanish that very night. If pressed the SS officer could denounce Sigi, who could then end up under deportation order—or worse, the officer would issue a warrant for Sigi's arrest, which would result in Sigi's death in jail. The SS man made no bones about it: he had to rid himself of the uncomfortable presence of his Jewish co-conspirator.

Four. Portrait of Milada

Sigi made Milada promise him she would think it over and in case she had a change of heart she could use some of the valuables he left her. She could then get in touch with a friend who would help her join the illegal escapees via Slovakia. It would cost a mint but her life was on the line and Sigi hoped she would reconsider and join him. This was the end of the second love story of her life.

Sigi succeeded in surmounting the great number of obstacles and dangers, ultimately reaching Palestine. He voluntarily enlisted in the Czech army, fought bravely in Africa and later returned to Europe. It was after the war that the two of us met and painstakingly put together the missing pieces of the days after we were all torn from each other to very different directions.

After Sigi left, the apocalyptic events in Europe rushed ahead. There would be no reprieve for the Jews or a stay of our mass execution. Milada and her mother moved in with us briefly before our family was first ordered to report for deportation. The gathering point was at the annex building used for annual fairs in Prague. Behind this large building lines of railway tracks congregated with waiting trains that soon would chug out of Prague to Theresienstadt in slow motion. The transit camp of Theresienstadt was the next stop for most Czech Jews and had been since it was adapted in the fall of 1941. To us the camp represented the best of the worst: it was in Bohemia, still in Czech territory and not in far, distant and hostile Poland. However, we were well aware that the camp was only a transit station, from whence we might be sent away to another, certainly more gruesome, locality in the east.

On May 12 we took our leave from Milada and Miriam, picked up our bundles and traipsed slowly towards the appointed gathering area, where we began our "via Dolorosa." Milada and Miriam did not join us on our walk to the annex building because it would have been too dangerous for them to be seen with other Jews designated for transport. Some eager beaver SS man could include them if they were spotted with us taking a tearful leave. It was a hallmark of the perverted Nazi sense of humor to unite those who were heartbroken about separation and send them along without any sort of preparation.

We left on our odyssey, leaving behind my aunt, cousin and our grandmother. This phase of our lives was particularly trying for us. We were being sent into an unknown place, stripped of all we owned, left with little except the clothes on our backs and tormented by nightmarish expectations. The notorious optimists sketched our future existence to be one as slaves in one of the many labor camps the Nazis established. In this Nazi archipelago the Jews were forced to deliver their last pound of flesh to keep the German war machine operational. Believe it or not, that seemed like the preferable option to some of the alternatives that loomed on our horizon. We were haunted by hearsay, rumors and doomsday prophets predicting that we would be all be murdered somewhere in no-man's-land, in the vast expanse of Eastern Europe, poisoned or shot.

None of this made any sense. Most doubted the feasibility of wholesale murder, if only for technical reasons. Few questioned the Nazis' willingness to stoop to such depravity but most remained incredulous of their ability to bring such a project into reality. Although we were a minority across Europe, our numbers were still counted in the millions and you cannot simply do away with such a large group of people. Little did we know what would happen when German ingenuity met twentieth-century technology. We all escaped into denial and reckoned that the rumor was a product of panic mongers or perhaps the Germans themselves, who in their sadistic hatred of Jews relished any opportunity to torment us.

As well as taking care of her mother, Milada was still keeping a wary eye on our granny. She couldn't take it for granted she would be allowed to stay in the old folk's home. Milada shouldered a considerable burden but she tried to do her level best. When we were whisked away, she lost the only remaining source of advice and help, as she already had been separated from the support, love and guidance of Sigi.

Meanwhile in Prague, the situation would worsen for the Jews. The Czech government in exile was being pressured by the Allies to step up their resistance efforts against the German occupiers. The Allies intimated to the president in exile that perhaps the Czechs were not all that keen on independent nationhood if they so willingly coexisted with their Nazi overlords. Much intimidated by this ominous warning, the Czech government in exile ordered a spectacular action that would dispel any hint of passivity and willing subordination to the Germans. Their plan was striking in its audacity but resulted in enormous bloodshed.

The Czech government plotted the assassination of the brutal and bloody Nazi brute, "the Protector" of the Czech lands, Reinhardt Heydrich. If a man ever deserved the title "Butcher of Prague" it was this handsome, young, tall Nazi official who seemed to have been born without conscience or human sentiments. The assassination attempt did not go as planned but ultimately Heydrich did expire from wounds inflicted by the Czech government's heroic hit men. All hell broke loose in Prague [see "Portrait

Four. Portrait of Milada

of Arthur" for his involvement]. The first repercussions targeted the Jews, but the civilian Czech population suffered a nightmare of their own in the wake of "*Aktion Reinhard*." The German fury raged unabated, thousands of Gentiles were taken into custody, many were shot, and the two villages of Lidice and Ležáky were laid waste. There was no end to German reprisals for having lost their favorite son.

Immediately after the assassination 5,000 Jews were dispatched to an unknown destination. This transport stopped only for a brief while in Theresienstadt, where some wagons were added and the entire train went without selection to death. All were executed in central Poland, shot point blank by Ukrainian auxiliary SS, closely supervised by the German SS forces.

When she heard news of the assassination, Milada understood that their stay in Prague would be only a matter of days. Miriam and Milada took a teary leave from our grandmother, who was quickly fading, unable to cope with such heartbreak. Miriam and Milada were to be transported on July 27, 1942. As always, they had only two days to put their affairs in order and present themselves at the annex station. They arrived in Theresienstadt the next day with a transport with the designation "AAU."

Immediately after their arrival they were notified that within two days they would continue on to another camp. Panicked, they all tried to contact someone in Theresienstadt who could help abrogate their transport order. Milada hoped that we were still there and perhaps we had a connection that might help extricate them from their predicament. Milada managed to abscond for a while from the quarantine barrack when she learned from some friendly young inmate that I was confined to the hospital's isolation ward with scarlet fever. Thank goodness Milada was a resourceful girl who did not give up easily. I was suddenly summoned from my bed and directed to appear at a small, barred window. I staggered, my high fever depriving me of balance. I looked through the window to see my cousin, still gorgeous but deadly serious and worried.

Suddenly all my lethargy and fatigue were gone. I switched to high alert, sensing the mortal danger of a family member whose very existence was in jeopardy. I knew we had precious little time to defer their deportation to the East. Suddenly my mind became razor sharp and I quickly began to consider our options. No matter how hard I tried, I could not come up with more than just two. One slim chance was that the man who kept us on his list of protected individuals in the camp would be able to include two additional people. The other option was to contact one of

Milada's ex-suitors I knew had a rather influential position in the camp. He was still a bachelor, so perhaps he could be persuaded to claim Milada as his fiancée. Milada blew me quick kiss and told me she would follow through with my suggestions. As I watched her depart quickly in her elegant long strides, I prayed and hoped for her success.

I could not find a peaceful moment over the next two days. I lived on tenterhooks. I did not see her or hear her. But as the hours passed, I knew that she did not succeed. I am sure that if she had arranged a revocation, she would have found a way to send me word.

I was confined to the isolation ward for several more weeks. All this time I was certain that they had gone but I still nursed a flicker of hope. Perhaps her work assignment or some trivial illness prevented her from contacting me. But upon my discharge I no longer could deceive myself, hiding behind some rosy figments of my imagination. Mind you, I wished I could have buried my head in the sand like the proverbial ostrich and pretend that all would be okay. I knew that Milada was not a run-of-the-mill girl and that she had multifarious talents to draw on. If there was any possible way, she would contact find me.

Upon my discharge, I embarked upon an exploratory journey to trace Milada's last moments in Theresienstadt. Immediately I sought out the man who sheltered me and my immediate family, Dr. R. Tarjan, and he reported that, yes, Milada had found him and asked him for help but he could not oblige because the Council of Elders allowed him to protect only a handful of people. Though he attempted to find someone else to help out, it proved to be an impossible task. I could hardly blame him, for I knew that he would have done everything in his power to try to save her.

My next stop was the one-time admirer of Milada who filled a relatively high position in the camp's hierarchy. I could tell immediately that he was embarrassed and uncomfortable. His voice was hoarse and he was abashed as he recounted his sudden encounter with my cousin.

He related that he was willing to place Milada on his registration card and arrange for an immediate camp wedding, but he refused to include Milada's mother in the bargain. He tried to convince Milada that if he tried to protect her mother he would be putting his own mother at risk. He had managed to shelter his mother from transport for the moment. It is the sad and bitter truth that people over forty were considered to be dead weight not only by the Germans but also by the Council of the Elders of the camp. Their work productivity and survival in the camp conditions

Four. Portrait of Milada

were considered to be minimal. But Milada insisted that she and her mother would stay together or both would leave together. And leave together they did. No words could convince her to let go of her mother even if it meant a chance at life for her. Sigi's emphatic warning that she needed to abandon the sinking ship before it went under never held any water with Milada. She refused to consider her admirer's offer and they parted on angry terms. Therefore, both Miriam and Milada left, vanishing into the vast bottomless killing fields of the Nazi camps. I learned about their last days only after the war from the one man who escaped the most notorious camp in Belarus.

The transport left Theresienstadt and travelled for days on end. Those inside the dark, sealed cars were without food, water or sanitation. All they had was one pail to relieve themselves which they could not empty anywhere during the journey. It goes without saying that the bucket overflowed within hours of leaving Theresienstadt, filling the sealed-off car with an unbearable stench. In the early stages of the journey many cried, others prayed. Those who had some strength left tried to crawl between the packed bodies to get closer to the tiny window, which let in some air and light. As the journey proceeded, many died, some went mad and others just listlessly awaited their end. After several days of such travel, few of the passengers resembled human beings. If there was ever a Gehenna [a place similar to "Hell"] incarnate it had to be these packed, dark, airless cattle cars, where starving and thirsty people lay smeared with their own excrement and begging the Invisible for a merciful death.

Their transport was amalgamated with another one from Prague and they arrived at Maly Trostenets, on August 4, 1942. This was a death camp near Minsk administered by the Gestapo, the day-by-day supervision of the inmates entrusted to the Lithuanian paramilitary units, organized and styled according to the guidelines of the SS elite troops.

The skeleton workforce maintaining the camp searched the latest arrivals for valuables and then loaded them onto large trucks that had the exhaust pipes turned inward. The trucks drove off in the direction of the nearby Blahovstina forest and by the time they reached their destination, all those jammed into the enclosed truck were dead, poisoned by carbon monoxide. The trucks were unloaded by Russian prisoners of war who had the gruesome task of placing the corpses in layers and setting them ablaze. The grisly work continued for hours on end and upon its completion the Lithuanian Gestapo shot the Russian prisoners of war, so eliminating all traces of potential witnesses to the Nazi atrocities.

But our Milada suffered a different fate. I do not know if it was more merciful or less, a worse end from the one endured by the majority of the Jewish inmates. She was chosen to be part of a ritual customarily performed with the arrival of every transport. A victim was chosen, usually someone of striking appearance. That person would be murdered in cold blood. Often it was a young, beautiful woman. The nightmarish execution was staged as a deterrent. The newly arriving inmates had to be shocked into submission by a display of brutal murder, enacted as a warning in front of them. The rationale for this gruesome show was simple: the inmates were told that this was the fate of those who might attempt to smuggle valuables. The disorderly crowd just expelled from the packed freight cars were disoriented and did not even understand that they were being intimidated by such a ghastly murder.

Our Milada supposedly somehow had retained a semblance of her good looks. Her striking, tall and slim figure made her conspicuous and soon after she jumped out of the filthy car she was noticed by the SS man on duty. The SS man beckoned her to come closer. While she stood there filled with foreboding the SS man rattled down a customary warning: Anyone who was caught trying to smuggle valuables on their bodies into the camp or onto the trucks would be punished with severity. Then he concluded his invective with an order that one and all should drop all the valuables they hid on their bodies into the empty luggage next to the table where he stood. Those who failed to do so would meet a similar fate to this beautiful woman who was caught with a precious ring on her finger. In the middle of his diatribe he cocked his gun, pressed it to Milada's temple and pulled the trigger. Without a sound she collapsed, her body strangely contorted on the dirty ground. A fine trickle of blood slowly dripped from the small round opening in her temple. She was left lying there as a warning to those who intended to defy the Nazis.

The man who witnessed this scene also recalled that an elderly woman screamed and fainted as Milada slumped down. In order not to upset the already furious SS man, the guards picked up the woman and threw her on the truck, which soon became packed with the many others, all of whom passed by Milada's lifeless body. Horrified by the sight of the murdered girl, they poured what was left in their pockets into the empty luggage.

The mud of a farm in Belarus was the final resting place of my beautiful, brilliant cousin—the girl who carried so much promise. My aunt perished the same day in a large lorry filled with exhaust fumes. After the war, Sigi and I both mourned Milada's untimely death and the last tragic moments of her life.

How good that our grandmother never knew what happened to Milada, the pride and joy of her old age, and for that matter, all her granddaughters except myself, for all perished at the hands of the German killers. Our grandmother died while being transported to Theresienstadt on September 8, 1942, during another infamy, namely the deportation of the Jewish old folk's home of Prague, where she was supposed to remain until the end of her natural life. Instead she was enrolled into the BF transport, lost consciousness on the way and died on the floor of the Kavalirka stables in Theresienstadt. She never knew that I had discovered her among the dying senior citizens and sat next to her, patting her hand and kissing her matted hair. She was released from her earthly suffering, on the 10th of September 1942, barely a month after her granddaughter Milada was shot and her daughter Miriam was suffocated with poisonous gas.

I often wondered how many times a human heart can be broken and still continue to beat. In the words of Kurt Tucholsky, "And the best it sends is the knowledge that it ends, is the comfort of death!"

QUESTIONS AND ANSWERS

If Tom had said he would marry her, would this have been accepted given that it would improve her chances of survival?

It certainly would have been life saving for her if Tom would have married her and stayed with her, as her chances of survival would have been excellent. This was because Jews in existing mixed marriage unions were deported only in January 1945 to Theresienstadt and most of them survived. Yes, Milada would have survived, but the fact that Tom got cold feet and no longer wanted to endanger himself with a relationship to a Jew of course sealed her fate.

Was it common for a woman to want to move up the corporate ladder and was there acceptance of this by men?

It wasn't common in the first half of the 20th century for women to move up the corporate ladder. Few tried to break the glass ceiling. But Milada was one who had the ambition and the ability and the looks to go with it. But unfortunately she was not given the option to develop all her God-given talents. As you know from the story, she of course perished during the Nazi persecution. Still there were marginal expectancies by society. Not only men looked with skeptical eyes at ambitious women but also women themselves did not try to change their course. Many of them were happy to not embark on higher education, instead living their life as their mothers did with total compliance to the man in their life—with his wishes, with his desires, and with her taking care of the family.

Of course there's nothing wrong with that, but there were some women for whom marriage wasn't the ultimate answer for bliss and Milada was one of them. And she would have gone a long way because she had all the talents for that, but she wasn't given a chance.

Why did women have to choose between marriage and improving their professional life?

In those days there were very few chances for a woman who was married and had family to take care of to also pursue a professional life. There were few child care services or nurseries available and although large families often lived together it was still very difficult for a woman who took care of the household to pursue a career. Some women opted to have a family; some of them went into professional life. But usually they were content to be on a level where they were not necessarily competing for the highest position in the corporate world but rather remained in the middle level of secretaries and consulting. This eventually began to change but in Milada's lifespan it was exceptional for a woman to reach for the top, break the ceiling and become an executive.

Would Sigi be considered a good person for being a liaison between those Jews selling and those Germans buying?

I don't think he would be considered anything to do with being good and bad. It has a lot to do with survival. A lot of things were inaccessible to Jews under the Nazis. Jobs were unavailable; Jews were not allowed to work; and all they owned was confiscated. This was a mode of survival. If you stand at the end of your tether you do what is needed to organize some means to survive. So I don't think it has much to do with good or bad. I guess it's got a lot to do with those who marginalized us—those who did not give us a chance to work, who impoverished us, isolated us, and then expected us somehow to exist. So this is on their shoulders. On them rests the total crime and responsibility for the people who tried whatever means left to them to live another day.

Did the poverty and types of jobs (selling textiles, etc.) help when in the camps as opposed to academics, who might not have the skills to barter?

No academics—no matter how knowledgeable or well-schooled they would have been—had anything to offer in camp, where life was rather on a raw and basic level. No amount of knowledge helped the academics. They might have worked out their roots in their life philosophy or religion but certainly they would not have the skill to turn around somehow and exist in a camp where whatever you needed you would have had to barter for it. So certainly the skill to adapt and to accept new realities was a great advantage in order to live another day.

In Theresienstadt was there a hierarchy of individuals based on what they did before the war or while in the camp, e.g., what they could do to assist in the running of the camp or in the thwarting of the Nazis? Can you provide examples?

There was in every camp a hierarchy of individuals who would meet. Often they were chosen people who were active in Jewish communities before the deportation. For instance, Jakob Adlerstein was the first Jewish elder of Theresienstadt. He had been an active Zionist working for the Jewish community in Prague. In Berlin it was Rabbi Dr. Leo Beck, who had been working in the Jewish communities as a leader and who was eventually brought to Theresienstadt. Those are just two examples and there are many who others who were eventually assigned work in concentration camps by the Nazis because they had organizational skills with which the Germans were familiar. There were of course very few attempts to thwart anything, any Nazi attempts, because the Jew never had a clout of power to do any such thing. But people who were active in Jewish life before the war were often those who were transplanted to the camps to be in a position of leadership. But any such position was always short-lived. Germans never allowed people in office for any length of time because to their understanding these people knew way too much about the infamous murders they had committed so these people had to be periodically changed and they were unceremoniously deported to their deaths.

Many people were caught with having family members who needed their assistance, or so it seemed. Does a child have a moral responsibility to the parents (such as Milada not wanting to leave because of her mother)?

It depends on the philosophy of the society. In those days Jewish society, a minority in Europe, was a close-knit type of family-oriented group who were standing by one another for better or for worse. And of course when the worse came by the Nazi occupation it brought people even closer together. And then of course if you stand at the crossroads and you know that you are the only child or family member who can make a difference to the one who is weaker or older or perhaps not capable of resisting, you have the dilemma to decide: Do I save my life or do I stand by my weak family member? Few knew that standing by would not help. Few knew that people like Milada would have died in vain. She could have saved her life and she couldn't help her mother. But she had hoped when she made her decision that it was morally right and that she owed it to her mother to stand by her in the worst possible hour. She hoped, but of course she couldn't have known what was in store for her. She hoped that she might make a difference in the life of her mother.

Was this list of protected people that Dr. Tarjan possessed fair? And on what grounds were people put on it or taken off?

The leadership of any camp had a possibility to protect few individuals. In Theresienstadt it was a list upon which people placed these few members of the Judenrat, the Council of the Elders, and the ten or fifteen names permitted to them to protect from deportation; usually it was family members. Those who did not have family, like Dr. Tarjan, put their close friends or somebody they had an emotional or intellectual tie to. But mostly it was family members. Eventually, when the man fell out of grace with the Germans—and recall I said before that this was frequent—those people who were protected by him also lost their protection automatically and they were either deported or left without protection from deportation in the future.

Milada was murdered because she was beautiful. This is a twist of the usual situation—where beauty often helps a woman—and suggests that fate or luck played more of a role than any ability of the person. This would seem to make life chaotic—suggesting that one can't plan on using one's assets tomorrow in the same way one used them the day before. Are there examples when one's assets backfired or when one's weaknesses actually helped?

Milada died because she was beautiful and when she arrived in Maly Trostenets they wanted to set a warning, an example of what they do to people they believed were trying to smuggle in a ring or some kind of valuable. It was to intimidate people before they died, that they should bring the valuables out and give it to the Nazis. On occasions there were cases where beauty worked in the reverse. Beautiful women were chosen as mistresses to men in power and for a while they were protected. It cannot really be said that there were weaknesses that would have been assets in the structure of the Nazi hell we were forced into. But I think there were some women who capitalized on their beauty and had a relationship. There is the story of Rita, which you might have read about in my book *Hitler's Inferno*, who was a mistress to Von Bebouf, who was one of the leading German figures. In Milada's case her beauty really backfired on her but that was coincidental. She stuck out as good looking, so the Germans decided to make out of her a warning for the rest of the newly arrived. But I think people couldn't have planned for anything on a lasting basis in the Nazis' world. You have to live day by day and be flexible enough to restructure and watch closely to determine what is better for you or whether you can escape or perhaps not escape but at least delay it.

Many of the acts of brutality (e.g., murdering Milada so others wouldn't smuggle valuables) seemed not to be about the person being punished but about sending a message. This seems to fit with the objectification, or dehumanization, tactics of the Nazis. Was this your experience?

A lot of things were done by the Nazis to send a message to the masses, such as not to do what they didn't want, e.g., hide assets or try to conflict with the rules of the Germans. These messages were useful to the Nazis. And it was understood by the inmates that it was a message that should facilitate the German rule over us. And of course the Germans from the very outset of their persecution planned to dehumanize us profoundly as quickly as they could. It was not only the subhuman lifestyle that they imposed upon us. There was also the inability to maintain basic hygiene and basic human needs that were denied to us. But this of course was the way they hoped many would succumb. And the more people who died due to the terrible lifestyle then the fewer they would have to gas. That was the philosophy of the Nazis in those days. So I think the best situation was a very much integral part to the Jews in the world. "Do not try to violate our rules." "Do not try to develop any tactics to escape because you are lost and you will be paying a high price should you make any attempts of that sort."

Five

Portrait of Arthur

He was certainly a most exceptional man! He lived in the most unusual times of history, the first half of 20th century and during the Holocaust.

Arthur, known to his friends by his nickname, Turek, was born in the mining town of Moravska Ostrava, the capital of Moravia and a city that boasted a dynamic, vibrant Jewish community. His family followed the orthodox tradition of Judaism by observing Kashrut (dietary laws) and marking all the highlights of the Jewish calendar.

During Arthur's childhood, immediately after World War I, it became fashionable and also expedient to explore options of assimilation into mainstream Czech society. Although Arthur's family withstood the temptations that at times were tantamount to pressure, the gifted youngster was more than happy to explore life on the more secular side of the tracks. He had many non–Jewish friends, at first many boys and later, in his teens, even more girls. For Arthur was an easygoing chap, handsome, affable and able to fit into almost any group, like the joker in a deck of cards. But beneath his affable exterior was a granite-like firm character, unwilling to bend or follow anyone's path but his own. Arthur was exceptionally gifted in many fields, including the sciences, technology, athletics, music and much more. Though welcomed with open arms everywhere, Arthur remained in his heart of hearts a devoted Jew, an ardent follower of the Zionist movement and a shining star of the local Maccabee sports club. Truth be told, he also tried out for the Czechoslovakian sports club called Sokol, but in spite of his stellar athletic achievements he was rejected, for in those days Sokol did not welcome Jews.

Arthur's father was a local textile merchant and his greatly indulgent mom was a stay-at-home housewife. He had a younger sister, with whom he had a rather rough and tumble relationship. Conversely he was greatly protective of his much younger brother, for whom he represented a strong father figure. After completing his high school studies in his hometown Arthur moved to Prague, where he hoped to study medicine after graduating from the school of pharmacy.

Unfortunately, his plans were thwarted by the political upheavals of the Nazi era. The political and military situation, exacerbated by threats from the rising power of totalitarian Germany, prompted the Czechoslovakian government to cancel academic deferments to most university students. And so Arthur found himself drafted for two years of army service immediately after finishing up his pharmaceutical studies. His plans to proceed straight to medical school had to be postponed. Unbeknownst to him, his plans were shelved permanently. At that time such changes were a common experience and Jewish existence was complicated by arbitrary restrictions in all walks of life. Gone were the days of athletic activities with many victories; even Arthur's studies of music came to an end. Though his mastery of the violin showed great promise, further study was deferred to better times, which unfortunately never came. Not only did individuals have to adapt to the new realities, but even the incumbent government also had to face a rapidly evolving crisis. Every effort was invested in upgrading the military preparedness by purchasing state-of-the-art hardware and training of personnel. The warlike threat emanating from Nazi Germany loomed and the vulnerability of a small state squeezed in a neighborhood of aggressive bordering states mandated this necessity.

Arthur, being a university graduate, qualified as an officer in the Czechoslovakian army right after completing basic training. Here too he stood out and was awarded a special distinction for his sharpshooting abilities and commitment to excellence. Most of the young officers were determined to defend their threatened country at all costs, but that opportunity was to be denied them.

The leading European politicians decided that Czechoslovakia was expendable and, hoping to appease the fury of the Nazi leader they perceived to be all-powerful and invincible, Czechoslovakia was forced to cede the regions Hitler wanted—the mountainous and well-fortified Sudetenland, where the Czechoslovakian citizens of German descent resided—and to disband the army. In short order the inevitable happened: what remained of the amputated nation, the remaining indefensible rump, acquiesced to the well-armed German military. In 1939 Hitler's armies overran the democratic country without firing a shot.

Several highly visible political leaders, men known for their firm opposition to the Nazis and fascism, fled in the nick of time, mostly to England in the west or Russia to the east, where they hoped to carry on the fight against the darkness. One of these men was General Prchala, who planned to organize a nucleus for a Czech fighting unit in the East. Eventually he hoped to build this force into a regular army. This Czech battle group joined with the Red Army in the struggle to liberate their subjugated homeland and in the year 1945 was the unit that entered their homeland from the East as a Czechoslovakian army.

General Prchala selected handpicked officers to join him in Russia but he could bring only a limited number. So he chose trusted men who were recognized for their outstanding abilities, talents, courage and reliability. Among the few, he turned to Arthur, asking him to enlist for this important patriotic mission. It was a great honor to be chosen, for General Prchala wanted only the best of the best for the difficult war ahead. Arthur's first reaction was one of enthusiastic consent. Yes! Of course, he would go and become a member of the Czech army-in-exile. He would flee the victimized land and fight as a free man, with arms in hand, against the dark Nazi evil and he would return bringing back freedom!

Only a few hours later Arthur's mind began to fill with sobering thoughts. His father had an untimely passing due to a heart attack, so what about his now-widowed mother and younger sister? Could he leave them behind, without the protection of a strong male or head of the family?

Such were the close ties of Jewish families then that this consideration alone began to cast deep doubts on his determined resolve. Arthur agonized over this dilemma for a few days while General Prchala impatiently waited. The general was a wise man but with little time left. Ultimately Arthur's sense of responsibility to his immediate family, who would be left alone, exposed to Nazi persecution, convinced him that he must stand by his womenfolk, that this in fact was his primary duty. And so he, brokenhearted, informed General Prchala of his decision. Both men were unhappy about this impasse but the general understood Arthur's dual responsibilities and wished him success in his resistance work. For Arthur was now about to embark upon sabotaging the Nazi rule from within rather than from without. From that day on he battled the Nazis from within the belly of the beast. Incidentally, it was but for the grace of God that this loyalty and protective attitude to his family didn't cost Arthur his life. And it came just within a hair-width of doing so.

So Arthur joined the other well-trained, freedom-loving officers of

Five. Portrait of Arthur

the Czechoslovakian army who were humiliated, frustrated and of one mind. If they could not defend freedom and their country in open warfare, they would do so by going underground. Thus, early on the seeds of organized resistance were planted. All preparations were made in utter secrecy, during clandestine meetings by men and women sworn to fight the brutal occupation by the Nazis. Furious, gnashing their teeth in impotent anger, they began to form small underground cells with the solitary focus of fighting the Nazis to the bitter end. Arthur was one of the first to join and from that day on he began to lead a double life. Officially he worked for a while in a pharmacy that still hired Jews, but, more important, he was an active member of the secretive squad that worked assiduously in planning to sabotage the Nazi occupation that had materialized within months of the betrayal of Czechoslovakia by her allies.

These resistance cells were organized in a manner to minimize the risk of capture by immunizing them from detection, yet allowing them to be effective in spite of the brutal rule of terror the Nazis perfected and deployed. To that end the members knew next to nothing about members of the group and were familiar only with the conspirator conveying instructions, and possibly another needed to complete the mission.

One of the vital and urgent needs that surfaced early in the days of the Nazi occupation of Czechoslovakia was to spirit individuals who were blacklisted by the Nazis out of harm's way. They had to disappear lest they be incarcerated, tortured and more than likely put to death. The list was a mile long and included members of the Communist Party, politically active representatives of the Jewish community, and members of the assorted antifascist organizations from academia to the political and cultural arenas.

Every member of the newly formed underground had to adopt a nom de guerre, and Arthur's was "Len." Soon "Len" became the key person in forging counterfeit identity cards. Under his guidance it became a successful lifesaving operation for many. The responsibility and programming of the identity cards project was left up to "Len." He began to work on it and soon emerged with a solid plan. A casual friend who was employed as a minor official in the ministry of interior became a key person to the project. The girl was uniquely suited for the role, as she seemed insignificant, an almost homely girl, surely not an eyeful and not one to arouse suspicion; but what was more important, she was an insider in the office of the ministry of interior. Ultimately she turned out to be of great value.

The underground needed access to the blank red booklets used for identity cards. Once filled properly with convincingly official-appearing but falsified data these became lifesaving documents. Even before the occupation every citizen owned such an identity booklet, which was furnished with a photo and personal information. One and all used to have these identification cards on their persons, for these were times preceding driver's licenses or any other pictorial ID.

Arthur was assigned the responsibility of producing these counterfeit identifies. He worked out an elaborate scheme. First of all he had to remove the blank identity booklets from the safe of the ministry. This task fell on the shoulders of the above-mentioned junior clerk, whose plain appearance helped her blend with the walls; she also had no enemies or rivals looking over her shoulder. She was thought of as the office gofer, smiling obligingly, bringing coffee and croissants to the bigwigs and then fading back into her cubicle to file. Arthur managed to befriend her and realized that she was smart and for her age quite astute but that she much preferred to stay out of the limelight. He also sensed that she was a true patriot willing to help the cause. Now it had to be seen if she could be convinced to shoulder the risk of dangerous work against the occupiers.

It would be up to Arthur alias "Len" to see if she would be able and, if so, willing to pick up some of the precious blank identity cards. It helped in no small measure that he was a good recruiter, for he was handsome, charming and usually had his way with the fairer sex.

It took only one meeting in a corner coffee house to form a solid alliance with the soft-spoken, gentle Lilly. Even Arthur, who suspected that there was much more to Lilly than met the eye, was surprised how much artfulness and caginess hid behind her naïve exterior. Lilly was anything but the office simpleton. Arthur would have loved to learn more about this girl, whose bland, noncommittal front was clearly a well-chosen decoy for a more complex personality. But the rules of the resistance forbade any personal attachment, allowing only the most minimal contact and information transfer and thus minimizing the danger of potential disclosure by betrayal or under duress of brutal interrogations. Lilly understood and agreed to work out a scheme for lifting blank identity cards, one at a time, in an inconspicuous and careful manner. The last necessity was to establish a drop system signaling the possession of the cards and a safe location for Arthur to pick them up far from their offices or their homes. This system provided the foundation for an elaborate scheme that would save many endangered lives.

Next Arthur had to identify credible identities to replace the true

Five. Portrait of Arthur

names of those needing to vanish. He would stroll inconspicuously after work to the local cemetery and respectfully stop at some graves, memorizing names and dates of those he perceived useful for the rescue operation.

Arthur was extremely dexterous and attentive to detail. The Nazis were known as perfectionists but he managed always to be a step ahead of them. Into the falsified identity card a photo of the new recipient had to be glued and lastly Arthur had to produce an official stamp to make the document credible. He worked for long hours in the secrecy of his room until he had a perfect facsimile of a stamp. Then he inscribed the information in his elegant handwriting and glued the photo and pressed the stamp over it. The result was a perfectly forged new identification card.

Coincidentally, I saw one such document after the war that had been issued to engineer Bella Kraus that not only saved his life but also allowed him to work as laborer right under the noses of the Nazis although he was wanted for acts of sabotage. There were many like him who owed their survival of the Nazi rule of terror to the ingenuity, dexterity and perfectionism of this skillful forger. Tremendous courage and exceptional talents, with the knack to act calmly while also maneuvering at the very edge of real and grave danger every minute of the day, were required to carry the work out. In those days the walls had ears and eyes and many chose to ingratiate themselves to the Nazi occupiers by informing on members of the underground.

In 1941 Arthur was handpicked and entrusted with yet another incredibly dangerous, in fact, almost reckless, mission. The assignment, though hair-raising, was another must, needed to save even more endangered lives. This time it was Jews whose lives were at risk. Starting in the fall of 1941 thousands of Jews were being deported from their homes to the transit camp called Terezín, which was the Czech name, or Theresienstadt, which was the original German name in the Protectorate, as the Czech Republic was called during the occupation. The leaders of the Jewish community were well aware that in the camp subhuman conditions reigned and that the erratic supply of life-sustaining necessities included medications. A decision was made to find a man who was intrepid enough to alter that situation.

After a family boarded a transport, their flat was sealed and all the contents confiscated, sorted, and transferred to specific warehouses pending disposition by the Nazis. These warehouses had once been synagogues.

Most useful material was sent to Germany to support the war effort or given to German citizens. Arthur was appointed to manage the synagogue that stored drugs and medical supplies. That post would have been arduous enough by itself, but that was only the minor and safe part of Arthur's duties and served as cover for his real assignment. For Arthur accepted the onerous and risky duty of developing a secret plan to divert some of the Nazi loot of medical supplies to the concentration camp, where the rightful owners were dying.

As mentioned, our protagonist was a man of many talents, creativity, courage and imagination being a just a few. And he was well aware that the Nazis were paranoid enough to fear a dark retaliation by the Jews. As much as they hated and loathed Jews they were also superstitious of alleged Jewish powers and secret skills. Arthur used their anxiety to present them with a plan they would readily accept and would appeal to their avarice and simultaneously serve as a cover for Arthur's elaborate strategy of redirecting medicines to the camp.

Armed Nazi officers constantly patrolled the synagogue, now a drug storage warehouse, looking out for acts of sabotage or slothfulness. The Nazis were mostly concerned with tampering, altering or even poisoning with medicines being sent to the Fatherland or their soldiers or even the good citizens of the Czech protectorate. It goes without saying that if someone was suspected of lack of compliance that person, male or female, would be shot immediately with no questions asked. The SS officers did not have to answer to anyone or justify their actions for the killing of a Jew. Few can imagine the tension and pressure while working under such circumstances. At times the patrolling SS man would bark some orders and these had to be responded to instantaneously and in a smart and deferential manner. On one such occasion Arthur plucked up his courage and while showing a paper trail to the inspecting SS man, he politely asked if he could offer a suggestion. The warehouse was overflowing with medical supplies and in dire need of reorganization. Arthur had an idea. The medications that were intact, never opened and still in their original packaging, could be used by the general public; whereas those that were already in use and opened should be discarded, for how could one guarantee their safety? In this way the synagogue/warehouse would be less congested, become compliant with the request for safety and still remain functional, serving their intended purpose.

The ever-ready Arthur offered the plan in written form, aware that the patrolling SS officer was in no position to accept the proposal on his

Five. Portrait of Arthur

own. The Nazis had an exact hierarchy of authority and this suggestion would have to make its way up the ladder. Still the SS man gladly took the document outlining the program, as he decided to advance it as his own idea, which might work to his advantage—a feather in his cap, so to speak. If it was accepted he could bank on a promotion and who wouldn't want that?

The document was precise and accurate, easily understood and written in flawless German. Arthur knew that it would be appealing to the Nazis, for they were thrifty—one can say even say miserly—and to save some cash by utilizing drugs still in their original, untouched condition was not only safe but resonated with their rapacity.

A few days later Arthur was summoned by the SS officer in charge and informed that Nazi headquarters in the Prague neighborhood of Stresovice had decided to implement a new program for disposition of stored medications in the synagogue assigned for this purpose. Arthur politely accepted the innovation, smiling under his breath, as it was the exactly same plan he had offered to the supervising SS man only few days earlier. Arthur's plan had several layers of complexity unknown to the Nazis. Yes, he had suggested the transfer of unopened packaged drugs to German use but he omitted to mention that those medical items that had already been handled would now be discarded and their disposal was unsupervised. It was those drugs that Arthur kept and then worked out a system of delivering them to the concentration camp, where there was a crying need for them. There was more to Arthur's blueprint of how to help the drug-starved camp. He took it upon himself to participate in sorting the many bottles and containers and while doing so he inconspicuously tampered with the original seals of those that had not been opened already, thus rendering them unusable on the premise that only unsealed meds in their original packaging could be handed over to the Nazi authorities.

Although he had a few assistants, as the volume of work was huge Arthur did not share this scheme with anyone. Every single family had owned a first aid cabinet and the many Jewish doctors' offices that the Nazis shuttered had injectables and oral pharmaceutical products. Although Arthur was well aware that he could divert larger amounts of drugs with an accomplice he feared that the constantly patrolled premises were not conducive to this. One careless moment while tampering with perceived Nazi property would spell disaster. And so he worked long hours on this humanitarian operation, always remaining on high alert, always aware that a second of slack concentration could be his last. A bullet to his nape would be the immediate and guaranteed response for being suspected, let alone being caught red-handed doing something like this. It is hard to fathom the level of tension trying to sense and being aware of the ever-patrolling SS men marching behind your back, cocked guns at the ready, as you sabotage their goods. Nevertheless, as he pretended to be casually working away he would surreptitiously break many of the seals on countless bottles and packages, now rendered useless to the Nazis but of paramount importance to the inmates. His was a solitary labor of love driven by concern for his suffering coreligionists in Theresienstadt, who were sick and dying by the thousands from the abysmal conditions of deprivation.

Now he had to solve another major obstacle: how to deliver the salvaged medications secretly into the camp. Ultimately, Arthur knew that he did finally need an accomplice, someone involved in organizing transports from Prague to Theresienstadt. He found such a man in the person of Salo Kraemer, who was involved with the collection of Jewish assets. Salo K. often accompanied the transports to the loading site, right to the cattle cars and the final phase of embarkation. He was able to load a shabby suitcase filled with precious medications onto the train through a confidant in charge of accompanying the deportees who passed the case to a member of the Judenrat who was officially taking the census of the newly arrived. Though it was only a trickle, a veritable drop in a bucket, the regularly conveyed suitcase made a world of difference to many. Arthur persevered in his secret mission till the day of his own deportation, which arrived rather late, in June 1943. But before that occurred he did more work for the underground, all aimed at subverting the success of the Nazis.

Arthur, as a member of a resistance cell of ex-officers of the Czechoslovakian army, was ordered to provide his bicycle for a mission in early 1942. He was instructed to remove all markings of his ownership by stripping all numbers, registrations or possible identifications. It was to be rendered in pristine condition, untraceable to its owner, even by the store where it was purchased and the factory where it was manufactured. The highest level of secrecy was mandatory. Arthur knew that the mission was highly classified and very dangerous. He set about to inspect his bike with a thoroughness second to none. He examined the bike inch by inch with a fine-tooth comb. He scraped it with chemicals that removed the outer layer and thus erased any inscriptions or markings of the manufacturer or of prior owners. He used strong acids and right after he erased serial numbers he applied a coat of new paint on the handles, changed the light

Five. Portrait of Arthur

bulb and much more. He went so far as to exchange the pedals for well-worn ones manufactured by another plant. Deliberately, the bicycle was now a hybrid of unrelated bits and pieces, so no matter how thorough an investigation of it was, it would be virtually impossible to trace its original owner.

In June, right after the assassination attempt on the "Protector," Reinhardt Heydrich, Arthur received word to stay away from his residence. He quickly put two and two together, for the headlines informed the public that the bicycle belonging to one of the assassins was found and would surely lead to the apprehension of the assassins. Though Arthur was confident that the bike could not be traced back to him or provide any clues, as with all disciplined underground fighters, he obeyed the orders to stay away from his flat. So he stayed at the homes of his many friends, moving every night, always to a different district of Prague. The dragnets of search parties proceeded with merciless persistence and precision street by street to every high-rise and shack no matter how dilapidated. The thoroughness of the Nazis was stoked by their fury. How could these lowly Czechs dare to murder their Nazi overlord and Hitler's potential heir? Never mind that he was a classic brute and cruel oppressor. The Czechs were going to learn how the Nazis punish those who take justice into their own hands and commit rebellious acts against their occupiers. The Nazis set out to teach the impudent, disobedient Czechs a long-overdue lesson.

The searches went on and on. Arthur eventually ran out of places to stay, so he stealthily snuck right behind the search parties and once they had combed through his district he would return home for a short rest and a change of clothes. It was his good fortune that he was registered with the Nazis as the administrator of the drug warehouse and as such not subject to the curfew all Jews had to observe.

Meanwhile, the underground lay low, hoping the Nazis would run out of steam and give up. Sadly, that was not to happen. The two assassins and many of the underground workers were betrayed by one of their own who double-crossed them, motivated by greed, of course. There was a huge monetary reward offered to the one who would lead the Nazis to the capture of those who killed Heydrich.

The Czechoslovakian soldiers who had come to avenge the victims of Heydrich's bloody rule were holed up in the basement of a church in the heart of Prague. The Nazis caught up with them and, unable to force the soldiers out, they at first staged a shootout. When this fiery exchange failed to force the men out the Nazis flooded the basement with water, hoping to drown them. The two conspirators did not oblige the Nazis. They left one last bullet for each of them and as the water level was rising to their lips they embraced and shot one another.

The Germans were beside themselves with unabated fury. The hunt went on and on to find who else might be involved. Luckily, however, the corpus delicti, the bike used by one of the assassins, was never traced back to anyone. Yet, in one of the many horrors that the Nazis committed during the war, Hitler took his revenge on the villages of Lidice and Ležáky, which were falsely believed to be connected to the affair. There, thousands were murdered or deported to camps.

When the dust settled following the Heydrich affair, Arthur returned to his conspiratorial activities in the synagogue/warehouse. The daily stress took its physical toll on Arthur's health. He began to suffer from severe stomach pains, and the diagnosis of duodenal ulcer disease did not come as a surprise. The lesion bled and he was advised to undergo major surgery, a stomach resection. The awareness that sooner rather than later he would be deported to a concentration camp seemed to make the operation that much more imperative. Throughout his surgical recovery Arthur never slackened in his project of keeping the pipeline flowing that allowed a trickle of drugs to the sick of Theresienstadt. Yet in June of 1943 Arthur was ordered to join the ranks of deportees to Theresienstadt. As the number of Jews in Prague dwindled, with their disappearance there was no more loot to sort and his usefulness in Prague had come to an end.

The nucleus of the resistance in Theresienstadt was aware of his arrival. On the face of it even he had to join the *Hundertschaft Kommando*, where all arrivals had to work at hard manual labor the first 100 days with the exception of children and some famous people. After that he was assigned to work in the Magdeburg barrack, which was the block housing the offices of the Judenrat. Without delay Arthur set about creating a network to smuggle radio parts into the camp, which was isolated and completely out of reach of the outside world. Since Theresienstadt was a transit camp it was unimaginably difficult to plan any activity because thousands arrived at a time, spent a brief period in this makeshift place, and then continued their journey to the East. To organize anything by stealth was not only very risky but also very complicated. Accordingly, Arthur had to establish a trusting relationship with the Czech gendarmes who assisted the SS men in guarding the camp. While it was lucrative for the SS and the gendarmes to engage in wheeling and dealing with the Jews it was also so perilous that many of the Germans, though tempted, refused to

Five. Portrait of Arthur

get engaged. Arthur encountered huge hurdles, some seeming insurmountable. And as if the continuous state of flux, the transitional nature of the camp, and the reluctance of the fearful members of the guards were not bad enough, he still had to deal with the unwillingness of the Judenrat to support his endeavors.

Arthur arrived at the camp in June 1943 and it was unfortunate that in January 1943 the Judenrat had been replaced and was now headed by Professor P. Eppstein, who replaced the hitherto Judenaelteste (Elder of the Jews) named J. Edelstein, who was a man of considerable spunk, great courage and fighting spirit. The new head of the council was greatly influenced by the previous chief rabbi of Berlin, Rabbi Leo Baeck, who lived by his conviction that the best approach in this predicament was for the Jews to lay low and hope that way that some—even if only a few, precious few—individuals would thus survive the mass slaughter. To risk rebellion or attempt to sabotage the Nazi decrees was not supported since such things could result in the massacre of inmates and the obliteration of the entire camp. This in fact was the common pattern of collective punishment that the Nazis dished out to those who dared challenge their rule.

There were only few members from the original officers' resistance cell still present in the camp, as most had been previously deported to the East. Still, in the spring of 1944, Arthur met with Slavek Lederer, who escaped from Auschwitz, returned to Theresienstadt and hid in the underground passages (see "Portrait of Lederer"). He too was trying to help establish a connection with the outside world via radio; he was also bringing in some firearms. Yet, in keeping with the philosophy of lying low, the Judenrat also vetoed these efforts and Lederer was asked to leave, as in their eyes he constituted the gravest possible danger to the inmates of Theresienstadt.

In the fall of 1944 the camp was almost completely drained of able-bodied inmates and that put an end to further attempts to develop some form of meaningful resistance. In October of that year Arthur received a summons for deportation to Auschwitz-Birkenau. Since even the most able-bodied people, along with the Judenrat, were being sent, it didn't come as a surprise to anyone, least of all to Arthur. What followed, though, was an unexpected miracle. Even today I have no other explanation of what happened.

Arthur reported to the deportation site, the Hamburg barrack, in due time. Though it was off limits to all but the deportees, I sneaked in hoping to see him one more time. When I saw him I was worried. His appearance was changed. Arthur appeared ill, pale, drawn. I was not at all sure what was afoot but right then came the call for medical inspection deemed absolutely mandatory. Fear of contagion and major epidemics caused by infected inmates traversing the Fatherland on their way to the gas chambers worried the Nazis, resulting in travel prohibition until their health improved. The physician's inspection was usually cursory, followed by orders to board the cattle cars. As it was more a formality, all went quickly, with the aim of expediting the departure. This time, however, the inspecting physician stopped as he passed near Arthur and ordered him to go near the smudged windows. There, after examining him, he exclaimed, "Man, you are sick. You have exanthema [a skin rash] and a full-blown case of scarlet fever! You are going to be removed to the department of infectious diseases and right now." Arthur remonstrated, insisting that he was fine, only a little tired, and he was all ready to leave because included in this particular transport were most of his friends. The physician waved off all of this as irrelevant and motioned to the orderlies to place Arthur on a stretcher and carry him to the isolation department for the six-week mandatory confinement. And there the mighty microscopic streptococcus saved Arthur's life, for had he been deported in that pathetic condition he never would have passed selection by Dr. Mengele on the Jewish ramp. Was it a miracle, God's will or serendipitous fate? Many thought Arthur, known for his ingenuity, somehow managed to bring about this acute phase of scarlet fever by one of his ingenious tricks. I believe that this one time Arthur was not interfering with the summons of fate; he didn't try to "*corriger la fortune.*"

It was obvious that the Nazis deemed the further existence of Theresienstadt redundant and the camp faced impeding dissolution. The plans of the Nazis were thwarted only by the military situation. Though we, the inmates, had no clear idea of how the fortunes of war were progressing, the Nazis began to realize that their retreats in Russia and the situation on the Western front did not favor them. As a matter of fact, barring secret weaponry, the military situation was essentially irreversible. Their reaction to the new realities differed. Some realized and accepted that their Third Reich was in free fall, collapsing in front of their very eyes. Others, the most rabid and fanatical ones, wished to follow Hitler's scorched earth policy: kill, burn and destroy as much as possible and then when defeated retreat to the netherworld in Valhalla. The more sober-headed conceived their escapes by searching for new covers for their identities and modes by which to hang onto the stolen assets. These somewhat less destructive

Five. Portrait of Arthur

Nazis did not want to go down with the aborted Third Reich. Rather, they contemplated contacting the Vatican, where a highly positioned cleric and Nazi sympathizer, Monsignor Hudal, began to build the Ratline, a scheme to spirit Nazi officials out of Europe to South America or elsewhere so they would escape justice and find safe haven.

As always, Theresienstadt was filled with conflicting rumors. Most inmates were convinced that the Nazis would murder every one of us, for the last thing they wished for was to leave behind eyewitnesses. The mood was one of SOS, each person on his own, trying to figure a way to escape the final verdict. Arthur, who was my boyfriend by then, was feverishly at work creating a shelter or a lifeboat for the two of us. No longer could anyone hope that rescue would arrive in time; our ship was sinking and it was Mayday time for us. It was also common knowledge that the gas chambers built by the Nazis in the catacombs of Theresienstadt were all but complete and that the key to the storage room of the insecticide Zyklon B was controlled by the camp commandant, Karl Rahm.

Arthur developed a three-pronged plan for us to try to avoid death. By that time he was in charge of the hospital's sterilization room used to disinfect our very limited operating room instruments and hospital supplies. Arthur chose to dig a deep pit close to the huge sterilizer that was large enough for the two of us and a few basic items. That shelter would protect us from an air raid that, according to some people, would turn Theresienstadt from a fortress city to a pile of rubble. Should the Nazis choose a different approach, perhaps gassing us, then the pit would keep us protected at least for a while from the mass murder in the catacombs. Another hypothesis postulated that the Nazis would drown us in the large pond near the fortress and that, too, we could dodge by hiding. In case of a direct attack, Arthur believed that the huge sterilizer would for a brief time protect us. Obviously Arthur had covered all the possibilities and did not leave a thing to chance. He planned all meticulously but at the end we did not need any of it. The Nazi bigwigs fled the camp, panicked by the rapid advance of the Russian troops.

On the day of liberation Arthur was ill. As soon as he picked up some strength he worked indefatigably, helping the many dying, for the camp was ravaged by sweeping epidemics of typhus, typhoid, cholera and much more. It took quarantines and time to bring the perilous situation under control. Arthur remained for some time in Theresienstadt and only when the Red Cross arrived and stabilized the conditions did he leave. Midway through the year 1945 he returned to Prague, to a very changed world following the Nazi era. Subsequently Arthur faced new challenges, and, though they were complex, none were comparable to those of the Holocaust years. Arthur rarely spoke about his resistance work, for he was a low-key man who felt that even a simple narration of his work was boasting. He believed it to be the self-understood duty of every decent man to fight oppression and criminal regimes.

After liberation, Europe was initially euphoric, filled with hope for a better tomorrow. It was a short-lived dream, however, for Czechoslovakia. After a brief period of democracy, another period of darkness descended on the unfortunate land. In February 1948 a communist coup d' état toppled the fragile republic and enthroned the Communist Party, which was totally subordinate to the master manipulators from the Soviet Union. Right along with the better part of eastern and central Europe Czechoslovakia became a vassal state, victim of the expanding hegemony of the Soviet Union.

Again cut off from the rest of the free world, filled with anxiety and dark foreboding, Europe's hopes were dashed and a time of isolation and moral decay returned. By then, however, Arthur and I were far away, having left the crumbling continent forever behind us.

QUESTIONS AND ANSWERS

Why have we not heard more about these examples of resistance and the underground as you reveal them here?

There had been quite a lot of resistance and underground activity but all of it was of course very secretly kept because every attempt was punished with brutalities second to none. It would not only include members of the resistance but also, of course, families, relatives, and sometimes even friends. In several cases their neighborhood and maybe even an entire city were laid to waste. So every resistance had been kept secret. And after the war I think there was not a great attempt to investigate all these individual cases. This is perhaps one of the reasons why not enough had been heard about it.

Also, a lot of the resistance members did not survive to the end of the war because we were dealing with a time that did not have normal values or normal structure like society has now. For the Jews under the Nazis, life was on a different planet of horror, with suffering, tears, and

Five. Portrait of Arthur

misery. So a lot of it wasn't recorded and most of these valiant efforts have not been known to the greater population.

Would there be different reasons why one might have wanted to become part of the resistance movement? Are some of these reasons ethically better than others?

Well, of course in every activity there may be motivations that would not be considered, perhaps, to be on the same level. People who were in favor of a resistance to bring to an end the rule of terror would have been motivated by ethics, and of course perhaps nationalism and hope that their nation could somehow survive the onslaught. If people were entering the resistance for personal reasons—for example, vindication or some kind of personal revenge—that would be lowly motivated and ethically much less validating. But I think that given life in the hell of Nazi rule in Europe, those who resisted were highly motivated, heroic individuals who realized that they stood at a historic threshold of change. And if they wanted the world to survive the way we had known it then they believed they should contribute their part to bringing the Nazis down to their heels.

If appeasement had stopped Hitler, would it have been justified? Would the Czechoslovakians have approved of it if they had been involved?

Anything would have been of high merit if it would have stopped Hitler. Only logic tells us that appeasement couldn't work because he had a goal. He was about to conquer Europe and his ambitions were exceeding European boundaries. This hope that the handing over of the Sudetenland would stop these ambitions was not realistic. It was almost naïve, cowardly, and childish.

And of course I think that Czechoslovakians would have approved if they had thought that by their giving up territory it would bring the world to peace and calm and harmony. I am sure they would have found it in their hearts to sacrifice it and come to terms with it. But everybody who had some understanding of what the Nazi movement was knew it was a delay and that it was a time-gaining, arms-gaining strategy, because they would get all the armaments from the country. It was not an appeasement that could work on any sort of lasting basis. But ethically I think the Czechs would have come to terms with the sacrifice if they had been convinced the world would, as a result, come to a peaceful relationship where we all could live and get along with one another.

Smuggling medicines was extremely dangerous but lifesaving. Are there other examples where the underground clearly changed things for the better that you are aware of in Theresienstadt?

Although the smuggling of the medicines to Theresienstadt was very dangerous it actually saved very few lives because the amounts smuggled, in comparison to the actual need, the enormous need of thousands of ill, starving people, was just a drop in the ocean. The amount was so small that really maybe for one individual person it would make a difference but not to the enormous disaster of the final annihilation of Czechoslovakian Jews. But every such attempt was heroic, ethically motivated, and altruistic, because the people who did it took their life in their hands. They knew they did so and yet they tried to help the others on the end of the line, those who were no longer able to help themselves and were dying in dire straits.

How was medicine given out? Was it based on age, illness, a person's role in the camp, a person's role or status prior to the war? If so, why, and, if not, why not?

The medication in Theresienstadt, as I said, was a drop in the ocean. Most of the attempts were somehow geared to support the lives of the children. We had some 15,000 children in Theresienstadt, from the age of those in diapers to the age of twelve when, according to the Nazi concept, they were no longer children but young adults. These "young adults" between ages 12 and 14 were not assigned backbreaking work but were given some kind of work they could cope with.

The Judenrat was administering anything that happened in the camp. So with reference to medication, anything that came in they first channeled it to the children. Of course, perhaps if people connected to those who were distributing were at the receiving line—I don't know if they were able to steal something. But I do know that when my sister was ailing and we needed medication for her that wasn't available, we still had sewn into our shoulder pads some valuables, which we exchanged with the gendarmes, who gave us a piece of bread or something she needed in her dying days. Giving out the medicine wasn't done in a formal way because there was not enough of it. What came in was given to the children. And then if there were some opiates like morphine available it could be given to those who were in pain, dying in pain, and nothing else could have been done for them.

Given the scarcity, was it better to give more medicine to one who had a better chance of survival or one who was very sick? Would it be better to divide

Five. Portrait of Arthur

the medicine up and give a little of what there was to more people or be selective and give as much as possible to one person?

I think the previous answer will relate to this question because the philosophy of the camp was this: "Let's try to save some lives, young lives of children, who may have a chance to live on in the liberation days and eventually start new families and bring the Jewish way of life back again, which is nearly extinguished." All of what was there—a little bit of food, a little bit of milk, or maybe a bun—the children got, a little bit more food than the older people because the hope was that one or a few would survive and start the procreation of Jewish life again in Europe or perhaps elsewhere.

There was a lot of discussion after the war about whether it was ethical to give more of what little food there was to the kids and take it away from the older ones who had worked their life honestly and who tried very hard to live a decent life. At the end, they were not considered to be eligible for larger rations and the food was channeled to the children with the hope they might live longer and thus reach an age of maturity and renew the Jewish life, which was obviously at the end of the line. So while the ethics of it are debatable today, we could say the lack of complete ethic was on the side of the Germans, who brought us to this situation and forced us to makes these "choiceless choices." The tragedy of these choiceless choices was that they had to be done and yet there was not one way better than the other; there was not one more correct than the other. The hope that the children would live, to perhaps let them live another day, justified denying it to the older ones.

Was it justified? You have to search your conscience to try to see if there is an answer in your heart of hearts. I think in my heart of hearts the Council of the Elders was on the right path, knowing that the old are beyond saving and that it was a matter of days. Even if the medication would prolong an older life for a few hours, it could not be a lasting one. The hope that the young life might last longer, maybe even to the day of Nazi defeat, was perhaps not realistic, but some people did believe there was a chance. Unfortunately, the children who were given this privileged supply of all of what the camp could provide did not live long enough to provide what was hoped for, but nobody could have known that then.

Had Arthur been put on the transport, not only would he have died but he may also have doomed others. Was putting people on transport to Auschwitz who might infect and sicken others avoided?

The people who were suffering from contagious diseases were not to be put on transports to Auschwitz or to other places. But the idea was not to save or protect the other deportees who were sentenced to die; rather the idea was based on the fact that trains were passing through the countryside and Theresienstadt was in heart of Bohemia. The Germans were always concerned that the contagious epidemics could spread outside the camps. The people who were infected by contagious diseases were not to be sent away until such time as they were not considered infectious anymore and were cleared by physicians. Again, the thought was not to protect other people in the train, in the packed and jammed wagons, as this was of no concern to the Germans. These were Jews. But it was a concern of theirs not to spread it to the surrounding civilian populations. It was a possibility the trains were passing each other and sometimes stopping for hours on end because they could not proceed, as the railroads were sometimes jammed with trains supplying the German army fighting in the Soviet Union. Excrement had to be poured out from the freight cars and all these circumstances could potentially spread the contagion.

In the orbit of the Planet Auschwitz—which was such a different world—there were these different rules extended to Theresienstadt and any other camps run by the Nazis. However, the concern for the well-being of the inmate was never there.

If fighting oppression is the "duty of every decent man," as stated in this chapter, why did not more people fight?

First of all, we do not know how many people fought on different levels against the oppressor and the invader. But it is also a man with not only integrity and who knows what is right but also a man who has tremendous courage to fight against an overwhelming power well known for its brutal response to any dissent or disobedience. So it would take an exceptional man to oppose or, within his limits, fight the people who were supporting oppression, brutality, and wrong philosophy. So more people didn't fight, some out of fear, some out of concern for their families, because the Nazis always punished not only the perpetrator in their eyes but also his family, sometimes his friends, or the entire group, even a city. It's known Nazis have laid waste cities, localities in the protectorate of Bohemia and Moravia, because of what they perceived as opposition. So it took a great deal to fight. Even if you were willing to risk your own safety and life, you had to have an eye for your family; you might have second thoughts when you look around and ask yourself if you have the

Five. Portrait of Arthur

right to take the lives of those around you, those dearest defenseless people around you.

So this may be the answer to why more people weren't uprising. But then of course there was the average person, perhaps, who perceived that if he complied with the Nazis then he could live his life and close his eyes to the injustice and brutality around him. We cannot think that everybody is a hero or people aware of their ethics. There are people who are opportunistic, who think it's not so bad really. For example, more food is available and there's no problem with inflation and there's no problem with unemployment. Those people may opportunistically look at the situation and say, "Well, you know, why should I get involved with something that allows me to live a very comfortable life?" So that might be the answer to the question.

Why do people who do ethically important things (such as helping others or playing a role in combatting Nazism on any level) sometimes not share this information afterwards? What could others learn from these tales?

If people do not share this information it is partially understandable. It was a difficult time, a time of pain, a time of a lot of problems, and people do not want to return to these days. I know from my own experience that for decades I tried to avoid mention, discussion, or anything about it because there was so much pain and one does not want to revisit it. But of course with the realization that this information is important, that we should learn from these tragic times, then we should really come back and share with the next generation and the generation that follows what has happened just in order to recognize the signs of impending danger and learn how to cope with it before it becomes a full-blown power and disaster in our lives. And that is what happened with the ascent of the Nazi Party in Germany. By the time it acquired power it was so well organized and so powerful that surely few could have coped with it, and those who could have coped with it were perhaps not willing because the Nazi Party consolidated power quickly, controlled inflation, expanded on military exploits, and controlled unemployment.

It is important that people should come and share their stories from those difficult times but you cannot force people who find it emotionally very difficult to do so. Most people who lived through the Second World War are gone by now, so there are few individuals who have an accurate recollection and the presence of mind to remember it as it was. It is very important, but I can understand people not wanting to go there unless they see a really imminent purpose in it.

Were persons who had different roles in life prior to the war in better positions than others in terms of having skills that would be more "useful"? For example, would a tailor be more "useful" than an intellectual? Or was it possible that everyone had a gift, a talent that was useful?

I believe that in normal life everybody has some talent he can contribute and bring to the table of societal well-being. But in those abnormal times intellectuals were really at a great disadvantage. For one, the Nazis forever loathed and hated Jewish intellectuals, even more so than the crafts people. They perceived the Jewish pursuit of education and the intellect as something specifically Jewish and morbid. Remember, the Jews were viewed as "less than" so clearly—such persons were of no use to the Nazis. Some practical skill such as that of a cobbler or a tailor might have been useful in camps but usually only for a short while.

Six

Portrait of Gonda

Egon Redlich was born in Olomouc, a city in Moravia, in the year 1916. We called him "Gonda." The Redlichs were of modest means. The father owned a sweet shop that was supposed to support the family of five, which it did—although barely.

When the Nazis overran Czechoslovakia in 1938, Egon was a serious young man, his bespectacled face invariably immersed in a book. He was diligent and persistent in his studies, aspiring to become a teacher. To that end he had a gift to inspire and galvanize youths and encourage them to reach for the stars, to never give up on their hopes and dreams. You can say that he was born to provide scholarship. Although his appearance was quite ordinary, after listening to his words for a short while one could easily discern that he was a truly exceptional human being. He was a man who loved to impart knowledge to children and was in turn followed and loved by them. He used all these talents in the bizarre place called Theresienstadt.

Gonda came to the camp with a few others who were handpicked to upgrade and organize the new "settlement" of Theresienstadt in anticipation of the arrival of tens of thousands of Jews. Most of these men were veteran members of the Zionist organization, working within the Jewish community offices in Prague, where they were all attempting to pick up the pieces of their lives and reorganize the Jewish community in Nazi-occupied Prague. It was not an easy task and by no means a safe one. Unbeknownst to them, many of these Jews would soon be on their way to the death camps.

The Gestapo—which is the abbreviated form of *Geheime Staatspolizei*, or Secret State Police—whose main task was to deal with the "Jewish Question," deceived the leaders of the Jewish community, leading them to believe that the new resettlement areas would be autonomous areas similar to the Hachscharot. The Hachscharot consisted of units of young people assigned to work on a farm where they were taught agricultural labor that the Zionists fostered in preparation for Jewish immigration to Palestine. The young Zionists trusted the assurances of the Gestapo and worked assiduously to make the best out of the conditions dictated by the Nazis. The Nazis hid their dark plans very well and most of the Czech Jews were naïve enough to believe that Jews were merely to be expelled from the towns and resettled to some obscure, inhospitable place in the eastern regions of Europe. But, of course, Theresienstadt was actually a transit point on the way towards the camps.

In Theresienstadt the Nazis hand selected Jakob Edelstein as the first Elder of the Jews. He would act as a quasi-mayor and was supposed to organize the infrastructure of the new community, which in reality was designed to imprison tens of thousands of Jews before they were to be sent to their final destination. Edelstein was familiar with the many members of the Zionist Organization in Prague. Though he was from Poland originally, he lived in Prague for many years and grew very fond of his countless friends there. Gonda was one of them.

Edelstein handpicked Gonda to supervise the care of the children of the camp. As transports streamed to Theresienstadt, thousands of children became inmates. The children could not have had a more devoted and caring mentor than a man who invested his heart and soul into creating a home-like and safe environment for them. Most came with their parents but some came from Jewish orphanages. Initially the Nazis ruled that the children should be housed with their mothers in the barracks but that was altered after the Gentile Czech population of the town was ordered to leave, for it was a town now only for the Jews. The children were now housed on their own with teachers watching them, sleeping in separate quarters from their mothers and fathers.

To make the best use of the small, often dilapidated houses that were surrendered after the locals moved out, the council decided to establish homes for the children and those in their early teens. With time, the majority of the youths were moved to these *heims* (homes), which were independently administered and provided for by the council. There was a home for infants and babies, followed by a heim for preschoolers and also separate ones for older school kids. Teenagers were separated by age and sex. On the average there were about 20 to 30 children in one home, the majority from Czech lands. Eventually the Nazis sent children from Germany and Austria to Theresienstadt and these were afforded heims of their own with German-speaking attendants.

Six. Portrait of Gonda

The Council of the Elders took special care of the young ones. Everything possible was done to shelter the youth from the hardships of life in Theresienstadt. They were the new hope. The children were given larger food rations than the average inmate, and on a rare occasions they would even have some milk.

Although the children had to cope with the material shortages in the camp, worse by far was their emotional trauma. They had been uprooted from their families, homes, pets, toys, books and everything else that makes the life of a child worthwhile and pleasurable. The council went a long way to prepare educational programs for these diverse groups of children. There was this naïve, but at that time seemingly very valid, hope that some of these children, the more resilient ones at least, could survive until normal life would return. The education in Theresienstadt was designed to facilitate that transition by minimizing major difficulties one has when growing up and learning.

We were not all totally blind but we were hopeful. We still did not fathom that Hitler planned to kill us all. After all, Germany was considered a civilized nation in spite of its loudly proclaimed anti–Semitism. So the adults of the camp carefully laid out plans how best to educate and raise the unfortunate young prisoners. Teaching, while so important, was dangerous.

Each heim had its own teachers and caregivers. These men and women were charged with the planning of daily activities, which was extremely dangerous as it was contrary to Nazi orders forbidding education to school-age Jewish children. Teaching meant gaining knowledge. And gaining knowledge implied there being a future in which to apply it. Nevertheless, the educators endeavored to devise programs for discussion, recitals, theater performances and much more. According to the orders of the Nazi camp commandant, those over the age of 14 had to work. Their indefatigable attendants found special assignments that the teenagers could perform. Nothing was overlooked in the care of the children prisoners of Theresienstadt. The older children were taught and encouraged to write poems and essays and to keep diaries. They even published a magazine. Some of their creative work survived the war and is now on display in the Theresienstadt museum. Their poems and essays express their longing, pains, and fears but also some hope for a better future. Tragically, of the 15,000 children prisoners of Theresienstadt, only 132 lived to see freedom.

Jakob Edelstein selected a man he believed was the best choice to take charge of the children. For that vital task he handpicked Egon "Gonda" Redlich. Gonda was passionate about his work. He invested hours and hours to devising teaching strategies for an environment in which everything, even a scrap of paper, was hard to come by, where books were only a memory, and pencils and crayons were a camp luxury to be bargained for. Gonda begged, cajoled and bribed everyone he knew to bring these supplies to his young charges. Considering Theresienstadt's circumstances, he succeeded beyond anyone's wildest hopes.

Gonda was a complex man. In his diary, which was discovered hidden in an attic in Theresienstadt in 1967, he confesses his concerns about his work for the children. How would the future judge him? Did he do the right thing by the kids and the rest of the inmates? Obviously he was troubled by qualms about the fact that the youth received augmented rations at the expense of the elderly. He must have carried some guilt for allowing, or even fighting for, these larger food portions, thus causing even greater hunger to the elderly. These older Jews had worked their whole lives, were not guilty of any transgression, but were given the most meager of food rations. Did he, in his attempts to help some of the children survive, accelerate the deaths of the elderly, making their last days on this earth an even greater hell? Would G–d forgive him, understand his motives, or did he commit unforgivable sins? Tormented by these doubts, Gonda found comfort in the arms of his wife, Greta, who believed in him and supported him every step of the way. And then came the greatest dilemma to challenge their young lives: Greta became pregnant at the least auspicious time, while in Theresienstadt.

These matters were not all that straightforward as one may think. Usually female inmates stopped menstruating upon arrival in the camp or shortly thereafter. We never really knew why. Most of our scientists suggested that it was a result of chronic malnutrition, but during captivity we were convinced that the Germans, always delving into chemistry, eugenics and pseudo-scientific experiments, put an unknown substance into our food that prevented ovulation. Most women reasoned, wrongly so, that if they did not ovulate they also were unable to conceive. For some, it worked out that way but others were surprised to find that they were carrying a baby and that fact doomed them to certain death. The Nazis had firm rules in place: pregnant women were sent expeditiously to death camps. The Nazis were trying to exterminate existing Jewish lives and were determined to allow for no new ones at all.

When Greta found out about her condition, she was already in the

Six. Portrait of Gonda

last trimester and the couple had to confront this grave quandary. She could terminate her pregnancy, as camp doctors would perform abortions on inmates believing they might save the mother from certain death by gas. On the other hand, she could hope against hope that she might carry the baby to term and somehow survive with it until the end of the war.

In the winter of 1943, as a member of the camp's senior leadership, Gonda had access to some news percolating from the outside world. He would have known that the war had taken a turn. The hitherto victorious Germans suffered one military setback after another. Even among the rest of the inmates, there was hearsay that the Germans would soon suffer a massive defeat and that the end was at hand.

Nobody really knows exactly—but I can imagine—why the couple decided to take the risk that their little family would outlive the global fighting. This decision was a massive gamble with Greta's life. Perhaps the happiness of their young love and the baby filled them with so much optimism that they chanced such a grave risk. Although Gonda was an extremely intelligent man, he seems to have forgotten that even a dying beast can kill, and often in its last spasms it is the most perilously dangerous.

In March 1944 the couple welcomed a baby boy they named David. In Gonda's diary we read about his joy of having been blessed with the arrival of a son. Nevertheless, he was plagued by doubts and uncertainties. Did he realize then, already, that he might have overplayed his hand by gambling on an early end to the war?

In the fall of 1944 Gonda and Greta decided to get a pram for their little darling, David. That was by no means a simple task, but Gonda had connections and was an influential man. As matters stood in the camp, many a cook had a little child in one of the heims and was more than happy to help out the man who looked after his offspring so selflessly. Cooks were some of the most powerful people in the camps, as they dealt with food, which without a doubt was the most valuable currency in Theresienstadt. So with a lot of string pulling and maneuvering, Gonda accumulated an unheard-of bounty and, in camp terms, royal riches. He used this treasure to purchase a pram for his son. He paid a princely sum of 1 kg of sugar and 1 kg of margarine for a worn and battered baby carriage. At the time, I was not even able to imagine this amount of sugar or margarine being in any one inmate's possession. But, Gonda managed the unthinkable and little David enjoyed a pram all his own.

In October 1944 the Germans ordered thousands of inmates deported to Auschwitz. The Nazis were scrupulously eradicating the evidence of their genocidal actions during the war, sensing defeat was near. Those who knew too much were targeted. Members of the Council of the Elders and, tragically, Gonda, Greta and the baby were ordered onto transport designated "Er." The lives of all three ended in the gas chambers in Auschwitz on October 24, 1944.

The baby carriage remained on the deportation site at the train platform in Theresienstadt, in the very spot the young family boarded the cattle car. It stayed there orphaned and deserted, jostled by the wind of a rainy October night, the saddest baby carriage in the whole world. David, the tiny former occupant of this pram, was well on his way to Auschwitz-Birkenau, where his young life was snuffed out by the noxious gas Zyklon B. The raindrops fell on the empty pram, running down like tears, mourning the loss of the boy who was allowed to live for such a short while. The unleashed forces of hell swept David into the Netherworld, for this world was no place, and had no room, for a Jewish child. On this October night the skies wept openly for the lost hope, for the countless victims and the injustice of it all.

Gonda was really a man who was greatly involved looking after the children in Theresienstadt, together with Fredy Hirsh. They and other very special men and women were really and truly the educators who lovingly tried to diminish the pain and suffering of the innocent children inmates of Theresienstadt, children who were guilty of nothing else except being born to Jewish parents.

Questions and Answers

How does one act or live or hope knowing that one's fate is almost sealed?

It's very difficult to describe but it's comparable to people who are sentenced to death and are on death row waiting for their judgment or sentence to be executed. We did have, of course, one "advantage" over those people. Those people who are found by law criminally guilty of a crime or transgressions that mandates severe punishment such as the death penalty know they committed an offense against humanity. We, on the other hand, were innocent people. Because we were born to a nation, race, or religion that Hitler loathed we were sentenced to death. If you live in such a setting—one in which you know you will not have a chance to defend yourself or plead your case in front of an impartial and just court and you know that the sentence has been passed already—then you try to make best every day that is given to you. And it that respect we still nurtured the hope that, because there was a war in progress on both fronts and later in Europe, perhaps with some luck the Germans would be defeated. Although initially it did not look like that, as they were winning on all fronts, eventually the tide turned and the Germans were beginning to be defeated on the Russian front. Eventually, in 1944, there were the Normandy landings, which meant the entry of the Western powers into the active battlefield. So the hope that the war was in progress and perhaps it might bring an end that would be just and the criminal regime would be defeated fed into our day-by-day hope that maybe, maybe, the miracle would occur.

Fate later proved that, for a very few of us, the miracle did come to pass. You do your best to survive the day-by-day quality of life that you saw horrendously reduced. This was, of course, difficult, because in camps there were so many additional problems, not only that we had to work and live in horrible subhuman living conditions but also that people had hardly any time sit back, ponder, and think about such things. The bad thoughts would cross your mind while you were working, and when they did, you tried to dismiss them by saying perhaps the Allies will win and then we will hopefully assume as good a life as we will be able to.

Was having children in the camp seen as a good thing or bad?

For any normal human being a child is a wonderful thing. But in camp a child was a disaster for its parents because people knew they would be ordered for the deportation to the east, where the children were murdered en masse. Moreover, their parents forever feared that their malnourished children might fall sick and there would be no help for them. So it was a very grave concern.

But a child is always a future; and Jewish children were supposed to be the future life of Jews once that episode in our tragic history came to an end. But I think it took me a long time, many years after the war, to adjust my thinking so that I did not feel a child is an omen, that something terrible will happen to it. Because that was the fear for the innocent little creature who had fallen into the hatred of the Nazis. Nobody could have defended it and nobody could have done anything for it. So perhaps by and large we viewed the child with love and affection and it was a wonderful thing but simultaneously we feared its life would be very short and while it lasted, in spite of the valiant efforts of all those teachers who invested so much time and effort into the day-by-day existence of these children, their life would probably not be long.

Were there any animals and wildlife seen in Theresienstadt? One wonders if there were, whether it would be eaten. Or would it be cared for, in a way that might allow a person to have some sense of humanity or hope or compassion for an innocent creature?

There were animals in Theresienstadt, but they were infestations of vermin—rats, mice, fleas, bedbugs—which was due to the enormous jamming of people together and lack of hygiene. The vermin were infesting the place and spreading illness at the same time. We didn't have any pets, and actually even before the deportations began, since pets were forbidden to Jews. In my family we had a dog, and of course you know how we all love our pets. He was like another family member. Early after the occupation the order had been passed that Jews were not allowed to have pets. So at that point, when we were deported, all Jewish families had lost whatever they had, whether parakeets or canaries or fish, if they still had anything of that nature.

I never saw in camp any animal that would be anything but part of the infestation problem we had with rats and those type of life-threatening creatures. Another aspect of animals in camp was that the Germans had all of them; most of them had German shepherds and they would walk with them (but, of course, not when they were on horses); but these dogs were trained to rip apart inmates upon the order of its owner. Even historically, dogs were often trained to attack Jews in countries where anti-Semitism was prevalent. So there was the worry in the more religious Jewish communities concerning the presence of dogs. Even in camps we feared the dogs. The dogs belonged to the SS, who would come sometimes and allow the dog to take on an inmate and tear him apart for no other reason than simply because the German officer felt like it. So we really didn't have any animals, but also we wouldn't have the means to be compassionate, to feed and take care of an animal. So in short, the answer would be there were no pets because the situation did not lend itself to that.

In his diary did Gonda have any answers to his own questions?

Gonda was an optimist. He was a man who hoped the war would come to an end; that somebody would survive; that there would be a Jewish life after that disaster. It did not come to pass for him and of course not for the six million Jews who perished at the hands of the Nazis. But

Six. Portrait of Gonda

he was an optimist, because if he hadn't been an optimist how would he ever have sired a child in camp? But he hoped by the time gestation came to its end the war would come to a victorious conclusion for the Allies. A lot of people had different thoughts about the outcome of the war. Some were optimistic; most were not. The fact that Gonda wanted to have a child shows you that having progeny is a sign of optimism, and that was his case.

Did Gonda believe he was doing the right thing in trying to nourish the young? And did he do this knowing that so few would survive—not because of malnourishment but simply because they were to be selected due to their age?

From Gonda's point of view, anything that was done for the child in the camp—be it trying to get him a spoonful more of food of some kind or to teach him a song, to write a poem, to fill his day with some beauty, to lift it out of the bleakness of the cold barracks in which the child was sitting cold, sickly and hungry—was a good thing. He was working on the assumption that to improve the quality of life for those children might help them to survive and live another day and this would start a Jewish nation and bring a new life into the values he deeply believed in. The fact that he organized this teaching program and taught the kids to draw and write poetry (which today is published in many languages, as they were found after the war in the camp) was a helpful thing. And it is still helpful today, because I think it is inspirational to see what a man can do for the children if innocent creatures are being kept in inhuman conditions.

Gonda had done a great deal to lift the quality of life from the misery to a day in which the children were inspired to sing and write novels and write poems; and perhaps he inspired in them a belief that a better day was to come. So I think the educators of Theresienstadt were in the true sense educators. They invested all their energies, despite the dire predicament they found themselves in, into the improvement of the days of their young charges. Although in the end the children did not survive, I think the quality of their short lives was greatly improved. And I hope those educators took some comfort in what they had done for those children who all perished.

What was the Jewish faith view on abortion when it is done out of a need to try to save the woman's life (as would be in cases in the camp, not that the woman would die as a result of the pregnancy but because she and the child would be murdered).

The Jewish faith on abortion is to save the woman's life if it is in danger due to the pregnancy. This is in normal times. In times under the Nazis, any pregnancy in the camp was a disaster because every woman who was expecting a child was immediately sent to the nearest death camp, where she was put to death. The Germans hated Jews. They had a special strong feeling of hatred towards Jewish future; and Jewish children are the Jewish future. So if there are no children then there is no future.

So in Theresienstadt and in any other camp, any woman who found herself pregnant knew that her life would come to an end. But in many camps, and in Theresienstadt as well, there were a number of obstetricians who in normal times were trained to perform abortions. They would perform an abortion on any pregnant woman who was in the first half of the pregnancy, before the gestation came into the last trimester, and in that way they brought about the end of the life of the child.

Were there any discussions that revealed any changing views on matters of life and death within the camp?

I believe what changed about people's views concerning life and death preceded the deportation. Czechoslovakian Jews realized they stood on the brink of death and many of them judged that they didn't have what it takes to cope with such suffering and torment. So there was a wave of suicides in Prague. I remember before the deportation started after the Nazi occupation in 1939, 1940, a lot of people, especially middle-aged intellectuals who didn't think themselves to be strong enough physically to cope with such hardships, didn't see purpose in submitting themselves to such torment and ended their lives by means they had at their disposal to do it as mercifully or painlessly as they could.

Strangely enough, in camps there were very few suicides. I remember hardly ever any reported cases of people who took their own lives even when the summons came for the deportation to the east. I think many people were resigned that they had reached the end, but maybe they didn't even have means to do it in a painless way. So I think looking at life as being sacrosanct changed with the advent of the occupation of the Nazis in the Czechoslovakian republic when it was split to the protectorate of Bohemia and Moravia. That was when a lot of people resigned themselves to the belief that this was the end and the future would be only pain and suffering, and therefore they decided to release themselves from the situation.

Six. Portrait of Gonda

With the pram having no owners after the deportation from the camp, would someone else have taken it and used it? How does one block out the symbolism of objects in order to use them for survival or benefit?

I don't know. Probably somebody picked up the lonely, rain-drenched pram on the deportation site when the people were deported to Auschwitz. I am sure it would be left there for anyone to claim it. It would be collected with other leftovers and I don't know if anybody would have had a use for it in the camp. I have never had a chance to follow its path after the deportation. It is only such a symbol of tragedy, needless tragedies of an innocent family, which this abandoned empty pram represented in the drenching rain of this night in 1944. I don't think these things can be totally blocked out. And very often when I see a pram that doesn't have a baby in it the thought crosses my mind about the baby that was murdered in Auschwitz, whose parents so lovingly bought and purchased the pram in Theresienstadt, and it stood there abandoned when the family had left it on the last leg of their life's journey.

Of course, if somebody did claim it and it could be a benefit to someone I am sure it was without knowledge of who was really the original owner. Although, regarding whatever was left over at the deportation site, it was obvious to us all that at one time its owners were those who ended up in these cattle cars to be deported to their death, in this case, Auschwitz-Birkenau.

Was the decision made by the new parents to have the child seen as the right one? What concerns did Gonda express in his diary?

I think that very few people in Theresienstadt or any other camp decided knowingly to have a child. If it happened, if the woman was impregnated, it was not likely planned. Most of them, being realistic, decided for interruption, which was available with no difficulties in Theresienstadt and many other camps. Such matters were done with deference to the life of the woman, which was threatened the moment she became pregnant. There were people, perhaps idealistic optimists like Gonda, who believed the war was coming to a victorious end with the right cause and the Russians were breaking through. He, with his elevated position in camp, might have had information on the situation of the war that the average inmate did not have. By 1944, actually by 1943, the war was virtually lost. So maybe he knew something, maybe he knew about the advances of the Red Army into Europe and perhaps he drew optimism from it to hope to have a child and decided on this step. It proved to be a disaster not only for the child but also for both of the parents.

It needs to be mentioned that Gonda likely would have been killed in the last days of the war anyway because he was too high on the camp's totem pole in importance and he knew a lot about the Germans' infamies, with their intrigues and manipulations. But he would have had maybe spared his wife if she had not become pregnant. He would not have brought into life an innocent child who would be taken to the gas chamber, where it would die such a horrible death. So I think in retrospect it certainly wasn't a wise decision, but it was a decision of a man who firmly believed that if Nazi Germany was defeated there would be an end and a return to normal lives. He proved to be wrong in this case, but I guess I am sure they had some joy and hopeful thoughts and pleasure from the baby that unfortunately they could not translate into a lasting family after the war.

Was the education seen by the teachers as meaningful in ways other than merely occupying the time of the children?

The teachers didn't want to only occupy the children with an empty activity. They tried to prepare them hoping they would return to school. They hoped that these children would receive education so that once the war had come to an end they would become skilled people eventually. They were languishing in a camp where they had no meaning. They had no physical or intellectual stimulation whatsoever. And these educators in their initiative devised a plan on how to fill and stimulate those children, inspire them to aim higher and higher if they had an opportunity to do so in the future. So they were taught to draw pictures you can see today if you were to come to the Prague Jewish museum. You can see the sunflowers drawn on paper with dull pencils. You can see the children drew dogs or Friday dinners when the mother ladles the soup; you can see all these things. The teachers tried to show them the ethical life and how life was lived before the deportation. They were taught how to compose poems and write novels. There were some very gifted children there who had shown promise and they were all instructed. As well, even the physical aspect was never neglected. They were taught physical education and tried to keep in as good possible shape as the malnutrition and conditions in the camp allowed them.

Books were published after the war with the poems of the children of Theresienstadt in which you can see what the children were thinking. They were hoping to see their pets again and to see the sun and to be able to play. Yet there were some children who had the foresight of what was to come who talked about not living long enough to see a normal life after the war. But as you read these poems, as heartbreaking as doing so is, you can see what was lost to mankind because these children were not allowed to live.

There was so much talent, potential, and promise, and if only they could have lived to develop it society and mankind would have been richer for it. Unfortunately it did not happen. Still, I think that the educators presented a shining example of what it means to be an educator and not just a teacher who does it as kind of a routine job. They invented a play for them, *Fireflies* and the children's opera *Brundibár*. All of this was done as an investment to beautify their day. There was nothing in it for the teachers but effort and struggle and to develop the programs with no means to do so other than compassion, determination and dedication. So I think the educators were unsung heroes of the Second World War and the concentration camp Theresienstadt.

What did the children know about what was going on, why they were there, and what might happen to them or those around them?

The older children perhaps knew slightly more, but I think the educators tried to shelter them from full awareness of what was unfolding there. They really didn't know why they were there. They knew there was a war and they were fed the hope that better days would come and that they would return home to their nice warm beds and pets and toys and all that they were stripped of in Theresienstadt. Their teachers tried to feed them the hope and the will to study and to learn, which would open new vistas once they were free and lived in a normal society. I don't think the children were even remotely given a hint that there was a possibility they would be murdered. I think that would be absolutely prohibited for an educator to mention it. What they did know was that teaching was not allowed.

The teachers told the children that teaching Jewish children was forbidden by the Germans so they needed to avoid being caught. Furthermore, these teaching sessions, be they drawing or singing, writing or mathematics, were structured in such a way that one child was placed as a lookout, so to speak, and if the child saw a German or a gendarme approaching he would whistle and all this teaching would be suddenly converted into play. Play? There was no ban on that. So the children knew that teaching was something not allowed to them and perhaps it was more precious to them because it was not to be given to them. So this much they knew. But I don't think they knew or that there was ever a parent who would say to his child, "Listen, darling, when we are ordered out of here, we will all die." The sheer brutal truth fell on them only when they reached the death camp and there ended their young lives.

Seven

Portrait of Hanna P.

Hanna's story is one of a life guided by poor choices, sad complications and a tragic outcome. It is the story of life lost needlessly, for Hanna could have saved herself—she need not have died so young, thrown her life away. She could have eschewed her unfortunate end.

As it was, Hanna was the embodiment—a prototype, if you will—of a passionate woman who lived by her feelings, giving free reign to her emotions, including during times urgently demanding rational and cool judgment. It was on the rarest of occasions that Hanna would subordinate her feelings to sober clinical argument. It was this unreasonable bent of hers that ultimately led Hanna to the depths of an abyss that she could have, hands down, avoided. Of course it was Hanna's love for her man, which became her undoing.

But let us start at the beginning. Hanna was the younger daughter of an affluent Czech Jewish family deeply rooted in Czech culture, emotionally affiliated with the Czech people and rather detached from their Jewish roots. Already, long before the war, they considered themselves fully integrated and were accepted into the mainstream of Gentile society. A great number of Jews in the Czech lands nursed the naïve belief of complete assimilation, exceptional for one particular difference: their religious affiliation to Judaism, which though weakened and lessened with every successive generation was maintained. Most central European Jews lived in a make-believe world of their own creation, one deeply rooted in denial of existing anti–Semitism and often ignoring pointed facts, pretending not to notice that Jew-baiting was well and alive in the Czech lands.

Most did not dare to admit that it was wishful thinking on the part of the nationless Jews, who desperately wished to belong somewhere and set down roots within Czech society. Though the lack of enthusiasm for the rather sparse Jewish presence was undeniable in Czechoslovakia, still the Czechs could not be blamed for the wanton violence and frequent pogroms against the Jewish minorities in many neighboring countries. Still, the Jews of Czechoslovakia, no matter how many generations indigenous to the land, were well aware of the cool tolerance while they yearned for a warm embrace. Most hoped they might win over the majority if they engaged in hard work, hoping to gain recognition of their contribution to the society's prosperity. Hanna's parents enthusiastically embraced all those values. They were fully integrated and had indoctrinated both their daughters into this belief that their home—their rightful place and their future—was within the Czech community. Hanna's parents were in social contact with my parents and we visited each other's homes on frequent occasions. As a by-product, we girls developed a kind of friendship that was rather tangential but long in duration.

Hanna was not what you would call a serious youngster or a conscientious student. Many times she appeared flighty, impulsive and temperamental. She loved music, dance, shows and many sports. But all those took a backseat and became almost irrelevant once she discovered the opposite sex. From then on there was no stopping her. Boys became her main, almost exclusive, interest and her attention to them was reciprocated.

Hanna had little propensity for thoughtfulness or introspection; she would not question or challenge the wisdom of her parents and was rather a superficial, impetuous and emotional girl. She was never wanting of any material comforts, for her father was an excellent provider. He was a chartered accountant employed by a multinational corporation as one of the chief financial officers. Aside from his sizable income he grew his family's wealth by prudent investments, dispersed in diverse portfolios.

As was customary, Hanna's mother took care of the family hearth, helped by two domestics. They all were quite busy because one of the many duties of chief executives was to represent the company and entertain many business contacts and foreign visitors, which Hanna's parents accomplished frequently and in style.

Hanna inherited her good looks from her attractive and darkly handsome father. This, however, was only a part of his appeal, for if it suited his purpose he could be very witty, sociable and charming. Married or not, he was enormously popular with the fairer sex. His peccadilloes were legendary and he had the reputation of a philanderer who indulged in profligate affairs. He maintained liaisons with questionable paramours and was repeatedly involved in marital indiscretions. In those days, that was not particularly exceptional behavior: the double standard demanded absolute faithfulness of the wife, whereas the husband was hardly censured for licentious conduct. Hanna's father, however, was less discreet than most and was involved in some rather outrageous illicit relationships. It appeared that he was always surrounded by a cloud of fresh scandals, which he seemed to flaunt in the eyes of their hypocritical society, which took umbrage at his lack of pretense. Most successful men in those days kept a mistress and the wife usually pretended not to be aware of anything being awry. Most wives preferred to look the other way rather than blow up their otherwise comfortable station in life. Hanna's mother willingly complied with the time-tested mores, ignoring her roving husband's romantic exploits. If she was aware and called her roaming Casanova to task, it had to be in the privacy of their twosome, for none of the marital troubles were hashed out in front of children or servants.

Hanna, therefore, had no notion of any such trouble in her home. She adored her father, tolerated her mother and, like many kids born into an affluent middle class family, thought that all was well in her parental home. And up to a point it was, for most men engaged in extramarital affairs but were perhaps a shade more circumspect than Hanna's exuberant father. While most of the wives were less than enthusiastic about this state of affairs, they did not feel in the least threatened, for few, if any, marriages were dissolved because of men's infidelities. This was certainly not the case within the circles of the Jewish middle class, who were so self-conscious and concerned with appearances and proprieties that all was kept under wraps, hardly ever erupting into an open and messy divorce. All the involved actors played out their proper roles, places and duties. There was no ambiguity about it. The mistress was supported generously but never elevated to the status of an official companion. The wife enjoyed her legal status and was also provided for financially; but she hardly had the full passion of the man of her life. It's not that human passions were less important, only then it was a taboo to break up a family unit.

Hanna inherited her father's disposition, giving in to moods and emotional flare-ups of enthusiasm, allowing her ups and downs to be noticeable. Her peaks seemed higher and her valleys deeper than those of the rest of her family. She could not have been more dissimilar to her cool, self-possessed and controlled mother, and from her earliest days Hanna pursued whatever struck her fancy with fervor and hot passion. Hanna and her father were kindred spirits; they understood each other, yet that same disposition became a source of frequent anger and exasperation to her calm and composed mother. While her father adored, pampered and indulged Hanna, her mother was left to set the rules for the exuberant, often unruly girl resisting all controls.

School was a necessary evil for Hanna. She just barely passed her grades, biding her time in the classroom, waiting from recess to the school day's end. She was more enthusiastic about sports and she had a real talent and love for dance and ballet. She would wait patiently, her mind straying far from subjects being studied, for the bell to ring announcing the end of the school day and that would breathe life into her. While in the morning she was usually the last to enter the class, at day's end she ran out first at the speed of an Olympian.

Her parents noted all this but were not unduly perturbed. Hanna's sister, interestingly, was just the opposite: she studied with honors and was the pride of her teachers and everyone agreed that she would go a long way in the world of academia. As for Hanna, her obvious lack of talent and diligence convinced the parents and teachers alike that Hanna would not embark on a professional career. The parents hoped to find a field suiting her interests and disposition.

By all accounts, Hanna grew up in a generally happy and harmonious home and was provided a childhood and adolescence in a sheltered, safe and peaceful environment. Little prepared her for the rapidly approaching turbulence, which would shatter all that she took for granted to be her birthright.

Hanna discovered the opposite sex very early on and her eagerness and interest was certainly reciprocated. Hanna's mother, who behaved like a real lady, noticed the precocious attention her daughter paid to boys and while, at first, she was amused, before long she became nettled and ultimately was angered so much that she imposed a rigid curfew for Hanna. If and when Hanna attended a social event she would be accompanied by a chaperone who was entrusted with the task of never leaving Hanna alone.

Once in place, this rule allowed both girls to attend the many social functions to which they were invited. A female relative, usually an elderly spinster who had an abundance of time and few duties or functions within the family, routinely filled the role of a chaperone. In return, this unattached lady would receive support from the family. Hanna's chaperone was her aunt, her mother's single sister and a rather dour and miserable person who had little warmth or empathy for the two nieces.

When Hanna reached her 16th birthday and her sister, Meg, was 18, they were enrolled for an entire winter season in ballroom dancing lessons.

Seven. Portrait of Hanna P.

During those sessions the gifted, elegantly swirling, musically conscious Hanna became a focus of the young girls, few of whom could boast her looks or her polished, perfectly timed, supple bounce. There was not a young man in the class who did not long to invite Hanna for a round. One among them was a tall, blond young man, ruggedly handsome, whose manners and clothing pointed to his working-class roots. Hanna was immediately taken with the 19-year-old, who seemed to her more a man than a boy. That and his rather good looks and his self-assured, tough-guy image sufficed to fascinate Hanna. As we know, she was mercurial, impressionable and easily aroused, inclined to quick highs followed by crushing lows. Frank became her first passionate love. Hanna was convinced that he was the love of her life; the stormy emotions could not possibly be puppy love, no matter what adults believed about young people.

Characteristically for her disposition she suffered all the pains and delights of a girl in love. It was her first infatuation and she shivered with desire to meet him alone, fully aware that it was impossible because she just could never ever meet any boy alone. That is not to say that she did not see him often enough. She made sure to walk the same street he did on his way to school, but she could not stay or spend time with him alone, for her mother knew exactly the length of time needed for that walk. Hanna's mom did not leave space for leniency and soon Hanna began to hate her for her strictly enforced control. Such measures of heavy-handed supervision are mostly doomed to fail and they missed the mark with Hanna as well.

Her young-love woes induced Hanna's imagination and in no time she found ways to bypass and elude or shake off undesirable and imposed controls. The young man who became Hanna's heartthrob was not only handsome and, in his rather rough way, charming, he was also cunning and knew how to get what he wanted. He was three years older than Hanna and in one's teens, that is a marked difference. Moreover, he came from a working-class family where children matured more quickly and were less sheltered and pampered than in the more affluent circles. He knew of a few places where young lovers could find a modicum of privacy and seclusion, even if only for a short while. Hanna was awed by his seemingly worldly savvy and experience and slowly she came to trust him implicitly, compliant with every one of his suggestions.

They would meet at one of the hidden corners and find a spot behind an old, massive pillar in one of the many impressive entrances to the renaissance buildings of Prague. Covered and concealed from prying eyes they would steal a kiss and a passionate hug. Hanna discovered the magic of young love, spellbound and enchanted by his expert caresses and fondling.

Prague's old-city district boasts many patrician homes, built with impressive and imposing grandeur. They were erected in times when not every nook and cranny was placed for a function or practical purpose. These structures were built by affluent burghers of Prague and boasted richly decorated façades adorned with ornaments, pillars and statues, often carved in marble, a part of the aesthetic exterior. The richer the proud owner the more luxuriant the sculpted ornaments. These stately columns proved to be a windfall for young lovers who chose them as sites for their rendezvous. Hanna and Frank craved privacy, a rest from prying eyes, and, as many lovers before and after have done, they found their niches behind the many wide columns. There they hid from disapproving glances of the smug town-dwellers who looked them over with much disdain just for holding hands. At that time society tried to keep young lovers apart, to bring them to the altar and for fear of spreading promiscuity, venereal illnesses and illegitimacy. But, as it is now, it was a futile endeavor. People in love cannot be separated; perhaps wild horses could pry them apart.

Soon Hanna's life revolved around those palpable moments of her dates with Frank. As their kissing became more passionate, her ardor, desire and even lust intensified and with every kiss and embrace faded the innocence of their caressing. Frank, though much in love himself, was not as naïve as Hanna. He already had experienced several love affairs and was used to having his needs fulfilled. Though he understood that Hanna was not one of his run-of-the mill girls who bestowed their favors liberally, he began to take liberties, which initially startled Hanna, but then she acquiesced to enjoy their passions. She was too much in love to draw lines in their growing intimacy, but then she had only scant knowledge of physical love and the potential consequences of sexual intercourse. Though Hanna was well developed—and as a sixteen-year-old girl was physically a mature woman, at risk of conception if sexually active—her mother, faithful to the mores of her time, delayed enlightening her daughters till the age fitting a betrothal.

An active sex life before marriage seemed all but impossible to the middle-class matron, Hanna's mother. Yes, she heard of such conduct but not within her social stratum, for no self-respecting middle-class girl would engage in something as inappropriate as that. That was the way she

Seven. Portrait of Hanna P.

herself had been brought up and she always maintained her standards and principles. She knew that none of her friends would be entangled in such an egregious slip of morals and in spite of unsubstantiated malicious gossip about some young socialites, she was convinced that the right time to enlighten her daughters was still a few years away. Her girls were chaste and pure and would stay so till their wedding day.

Men—well, there's a different kettle of fish. In central Europe at that time they were, in general, notoriously polygamous and needed more than one partner for their sexual satisfaction. The clearly biased double standard was then the norm, hardly contested by any woman. While women met at their afternoon tea parties and confided their secrets, they mostly hinted and sidestepped their private concerns, for sex was not considered a topic discussed by a lady. To be sure, the subject of children born out of wedlock was sometimes discussed during those afternoon meetings, but the situation was dismissed as a calamity that befell only women of ill repute who came from different social spheres.

Hanna's mom had confidence in her girls, assuming as a matter of course that destiny would repeat itself and both her daughters would become, in due time, engaged and marry proper young men. They would enter their marriages as innocents, as she was when she met and wed her dark, handsome and gallivanting Romeo. Subsequently these carefully and correctly selected husbands would provide and care for their growing families. Hanna's mother hoped, and concluded, that history would repeat itself, only perhaps in a slightly improved version.

You probably wonder at how naïve and unwise Hanna's mother was. For starters, the times were changing and she should have been more observant, searching for signs of potential allurement of the flighty and frivolous Hanna. It was almost foolish to take so much for granted, to remain complacent while the danger signals flashed an uninterrupted warning red. Even a casual observer would notice that Hanna was at times reckless and foolhardy enough to risk all just for a moment of bliss. Somehow her mother missed all the signals of Hanna's elevated mood—glowing eyes, dancing steps, all the signs of being in love.

The lovers continued to secretly meet whilst their rapturous ecstasy slowly transformed into obsession. Hanna could not think of anything else but "HIM," and was consumed by overwhelming emotion that came to dominate her life. Almost imperceptibly their involvement became intimate. Frank prevailed upon Hanna, who only pretended to offer face-saving resistance.

The consummation of their relationship opened a new world to Hanna. She was overflowing with joy, happy beyond words, spellbound by the magic of the new adult world opened to her, even though she should have eschewed such exploits for yet a long time. Now a new phase began. Hanna's ardor and love for Frank grew by leaps and bounds, which soon began to irritate and bore him. He felt smothered and entrapped; her amorous prattle sickened him and sex with her soon lost the attraction of novelty. He had satisfied his desire and curiosity and now he wanted out, away from her. Youthful Hanna was not sophisticated or wily; she failed to notice the signs of the new spin of his sentiments. In her artless simplicity she believed that they had found each other and would live together happily ever after, like in the fairy tales she used to read in her younger years. She was in for a rude awakening.

Before long she discovered that he was not always waiting for her in their secret, concealed hallway, behind the heavy pillar. Actually he was coming on fewer and fewer occasions, leaving her waiting for him. He always had some handy excuse and if he did come he seemed in a hurry and barely bothered to mask his impatience with her sobbing queries about his absences and change in attitude. A slightly more sophisticated or smart woman would have realized that the romance was over and that he was tired of her and wanted to terminate what he considered a passing romance.

All his words fell on deaf ears. Hanna seemed obtuse, she lived in her own dream world, unwilling to accept the blatant evidence of his indifference, impatience and later near detestation of her. She lost all her pride, ran after him begging him to meet her. He rarely obliged, but she carried on like a woman possessed in her useless chase after a man who not only no longer cared but also showed quite openly his disgust with her shameless, brazen hunt for his affection.

Hanna sank into a gloomy, depressed mood. Her mind was preoccupied designing new schemes to rekindle Frank's faded passion, all of which met with abysmal failure. It was a devastating blow for a pampered teenager to be jilted by her first lover. Soon her anguish affected her physically; she began to feel unwell. Hanna was convinced that her fatigue and sickness were symptoms of her broken heart. She had just sustained the worst possible tragedy, the loss of the love of her life! Did she not read in the romance novels, secretly appropriated from the servant girls, that many a young heroine died of a broken heart? Hanna was certain that her death was imminent, for she could not carry on without him. Her sorrow was such that little else mattered. She barely paid attention to the fact that her

Seven. Portrait of Hanna P.

monthly periods failed to appear. Hanna was convinced her body was ailing, unable to cope with her emotional pain.

At no time did it occur to Hanna that the pleasure of her sexual relations could have consequences. She trusted implicitly in Frank's assurances that he knew how to handle himself and prevent any unwanted complications. Her faith in him was absolute; in her eyes he was the epitome of male sophistication and she never questioned his words. In fact, Hanna's confidence was misplaced. He was by far not as experienced as he claimed: he used these boasts only as a strategy to impress Hanna, who was young and gullible. In her eyes he was larger than life, but reality did not bear out his flaunting. He was a rather simple, if handsome, young man.

During the first part of the twentieth century, namely in the 1930s, sex education left much to be desired. In schools the topic remained an untouchable taboo and parental guidance varied greatly from home to home. In the more concerned homes the obligatory "heart to heart" talk was postponed till the age of marriage neared for the daughter and the male offspring would be enlightened sooner perhaps, but all depended on the wisdom of the *pater familiae* (the male head of the family).

The only timely, if not top-level, sex information was available from the household's servants, who were not as reticent to tackle one of their favorite topics. The youngsters would be the captivated audience, consumed with curiosity about the enigmatic secrets of physical love.

Therefore, most parental explanations came much too late and their sons' and daughters' instructions often came with the price tag of vulgar oversimplification, for those who recounted often had scant knowledge themselves but enjoyed being listened to and looked up to for a change. The "facts of life" were such an uncomfortable topic for most parents that many secretly hoped the servants would inform their charges for them. Some families with an adolescent son went so far as to hire as a domestic servant a comely yet simple country girl who was already sexually initiated with the tacit hope that their son would receive his first introduction into sexual life right under the parental roof.

Without any verbal acknowledgment the girl would receive extra monetary recompense, greatly enhancing her dowry, with which she would return to her village and attract a local suitor. The parents in turn were grateful that the boy was not tempted to search for an outlet for his physical needs among the streetwalkers of Prague. Like all large cities, Prague had an abundance of establishments catering to these needs—bordellos if you wish—but a young man could not enter, even with money, without being accompanied by an adult. And it seemed hardly befitting that a father and son should jointly use the services of the ladies of the oldest profession. Thus, a discreet arrangement was made and all sides were satisfied, sanctimoniously pleased with their hypocrisy.

Today it is hard to understand this silent, embarrassed attitude of those days. Why did people find it so awkward to engage in open, honest talk about sex, the primal and strongest instinct, a basic need of men and women alike? Why did they consider the major source of pleasure in adult life to be so unmentionable? To be sure, there were many passions, amours, paramours, no less promiscuity or dalliances in any social strata, right across the board. But protocol called for keeping all these human qualities tightly under wraps, unmentionable, only perhaps escaping in the form of titillating gossip.

Another topic considered unsuitable for polite conversation was the practice of birth control. The dearth of information for young adults was almost criminal, often resulting in tragedies of unwanted pregnancies. There was hardly any print devoted to sex education and many youths remained ignorant for too long a time. If and when sexual contact resulted in an unwanted pregnancy it was a major catastrophe in the making. By far, a very high majority were forced to marry. A shotgun wedding was the order of the day, and more often than not this resulted in ruined lives spent in incompatible marriages between immature partners coerced by their parents in an attempt to set right a moment of hot passion that everyone involved wished had never happened.

In the event of unwillingness or the impossibility of immediate matrimony the remaining solutions were equally foreboding. One of the unpalatable ways out was to offer the child for adoption or, worse yet, place it in an orphanage. Such places were cold, cloistered institutions, a loveless and pious atmosphere under the auspices of religious authorities and usually attached to a convent. There, the child might be subject to any number of abuses or neglect.

The most dreaded and tragic option available was abortion. This was the most horrid and dangerous option of them all. No respectable physician would perform an abortion, for he risked the loss of his medical license, charges of criminal conduct, and permanently besmirching his reputation within a society that prohibited the termination of pregnancy irrespective of circumstances. No amount of money could compensate and thus convince a qualified medical doctor to carry out such a procedure.

Seven. Portrait of Hanna P.

Some desperate women turned to remedies recommended by word of mouth, such as quinine and many others that rarely terminated a pregnancy. Equally ineffectual was bathing in scalding waters or jumping from heights, all of which resulted in some injuries but failed to produce the desired result.

The only way out for a desperate woman was a backstreet abortion performed by a criminal abortionist who knew little about the trade she plied and cared even less about safety or, indeed, the survival of the women who turned to her. Most abortionists had a lucrative business and extorted high fees, which often drove the girl into debt. Many a despondent woman tried to induce an abortion with the use of a coat hanger or infusion of a caustic emulsion, most of which resulted in ghastly consequences. Even those who scraped the money up and could afford the services of an abortionist risked much. Many died during these botched interventions, often performed on kitchen tables, without the benefit of anesthetics and under perilously unhygienic conditions. Usually, either immediately or a few hours after a botched abortion, disaster struck. It was not uncommon to have a severe hemorrhage caused by a perforated uterus, exsanguinating the woman before help could be summoned. In other equally tragic instances, massive infection set in, which in the time before antibiotics was nearly always fatal. Another danger, high on the list, was an embolism, which killed or maimed many.

Even when all went well and the woman survived she often remained unable to bear additional children; she was scarred for life both physically and emotionally by the horrific secret trauma of the criminal procedure. If she revealed or reported anything to the authorities she was culpable in the eyes of the law. She could then be charged and sentenced to lengthy incarceration. To avoid the criminal charge the victim would feign mental instability and in that case she was sent to an asylum for a confinement of undetermined length. In view of such dramatic consequences of abortions at that time, one can only wonder why the elder generation had such an implicit, blind trust in the chastity of their offspring. Admittedly, most middle-class youths refrained from sexual relations, but that was most and not everyone by any means.

Hanna was unhappy and moped about the cooled passion of her onetime boyfriend, whom she still adored. Daily, she grew thinner, looking drawn and haggard, her beautiful dark eyes underlined by dark circles. Her complexion seemed coated with an unhealthy sallow tinge. She hardly ate, showing all the signs of a person afflicted with a wasting disease. Her woeful sadness did not escape the attention of her doting parents, who began to worry, much disturbed by their daughter's strange malaise, and arranged for a medical check-up. The doctor was an old family friend and Hanna had no objections to a visit to "Uncle Doctor," as all in the family affectionately called him. She was certain that she suffered from a broken heart, which gradually drained and crushed her otherwise strong and robust body.

On the appointed day, Hanna, accompanied by her mother, went to see the doctor. While Hanna's mother sat patiently in the waiting room, Hanna submitted to a complete physical check-up. Hanna had to answer many questions pertaining to her physical and emotional well-being. From her early years on it had been impressed upon Hanna that all questions from a doctor had to be answered with painstaking honesty and truthfulness. During the examination, almost in passing, the doctor asked if her monthly periods were regular. Hanna paused, unwilling to lie or concede the truth. The doctor waited patiently and she finally admitted that recently the pattern had changed, but she rushed to add that all her woes were caused by her despondent frame of mind.

The old doctor looked at her with a kind, warm, but worried look. He began to probe deeper into Hanna's anguish and to direct his questions to her relationship with her boyfriend. Hanna was mortified by her own admission of intimacy but she rushed to assure the doctor that her lover used all needed precautions to prevent all complications. The old man nodded patiently as Hanna implored him not to tell her parents, who would be shocked by their daughter's promiscuity and loose moral standards. The kind doctor promised his silence under one condition: that Hanna allow him to check her over and satisfy himself that she bore no ill effects.

Back in the examination room, Hanna closed her eyes, gnashed her teeth and hoped that all would end soon. The doctor took a long time to check her over and then told Hanna to get dressed and join him in the office. Intuitively, Hanna sensed that his news was going to be bad, yet his warm expression remained fatherly although simultaneously anguished. Hanna began to panic silently and shuddered to hear.

She tossed her clothes on and soon sat across the desk in his office. He opened in a low-key voice, somewhat unsteady and upset: "Hanna, I have known you since you were born and I have been your physician ever since. Better yet, I am your fatherly friend and almost a member of your fine family. There is little I would not do to spare you pain, but there are

Seven. Portrait of Hanna P.

times when it becomes impossible to hide the truth. I cannot conceal from you the information that you are pregnant and at an advanced stage. You are already five months with a child. I would give anything to have better news for you and your family, but I don't. Would you prefer that I inform your parents or would you rather speak with them alone?"

Hanna begged that he tell her parents. As she anticipated, their fury was one of a kind. They thought highly of their girls and were so disappointed on realizing that Hanna behaved totally inappropriately. In their eyes there were no excuses for her weakness and promiscuous behavior. All the distress that followed the disclosure of her condition was kept from Hanna. The family physician insisted that in her condition she and the baby had to be protected from the explosive ire and tears of her parents. The only advice he could offer was acceptance of the unchangeable and make the best out of this difficult situation. They should support Hanna, who was so young and ill-prepared for her new responsibilities and role of a mother.

Nevertheless, Hanna's father flew off the handle. No sooner was he informed in the most considerate manner than he became enraged. How could something so outrageous happen to his daughter? Such happenings were common in the lowly, vulgar classes but no daughter of his could have possibly compromised her reputation by becoming intimate with such a good-for-nothing fellow! He was raving and ranting, shouting totally out of control, failing to notice the double standard as he repeated time and again that his daughters were supposed to remain chaste, marry in a virginal state, pure and untainted by premarital experiences. His anger notwithstanding, little could be changed.

He understood only too well that they had an emergency on their hands, but there were no palatable options for resolution. They knew that they had to come to terms with the facts as they were and do something. To begin with, Hanna's pregnancy was much too advanced to consider abortion; perhaps this would have been an option earlier in her pregnancy. Hanna's parents, in consultation with the physician, decided that Hanna's child would not be given up for adoption or placed in an orphanage as was the fate for most children born out of wedlock. What appeared acceptable, if only barely so, was the option of a shotgun wedding. Hanna had no objection. She was still very much taken in by Frank though he had jilted her so rudely and treated her with a total lack of consideration. His boorish, irresponsible stance only slightly tarnished her opinion of him. As soon as the family reached the only solution at hand, Hanna's father, faithful to his energetic and decisive character, did not waste time setting all into motion. He was a man of prodigious energies and now he set about to single-mindedly stave off this embarrassment of his family and salvage as much as possible by quickly doing damage control.

First he had to establish contact with the young man's family. Hanna's future in-laws were simple folk, a working-class family awed by a visit from a successful and rich businessman but who felt thoroughly uncomfortable in his presence. Neither did Hanna's dad feel much better about the deal. He tried to be polite and companionable but he could not help but see his future son-in-law's many generations of working-class ancestors as an affront to his own family's status. The humble flat in a working-class district, smelling of cabbage, onions and other stale kitchen vapors, offended his olfactory system. The simple if clean furnishings were cheap. The naked bulb suspended from the kitchen ceiling was a sure sign of poverty. To Hanna's dad they were living proof of unassuming working people who hardly tried to lift themselves by their bootstraps. But he had to put a positive spin on it as he tried to explain the situation to Frank's parents. Surprisingly they took it in stride, not at all shocked by their young son's reckless sexual exploits. They listened with civility as Hanna's father began to reveal the solution for the future of the two hapless lovers. They had a hard time following his refined language, presented at a fast clip. They were overwhelmed by his sartorial elegance, his matching tie, the pleasant scent of his after shave; all this made a deep impression on them.

It is debatable if they fully grasped his suggestions and, by implication, orders. They felt that such a polished, cultivated gentleman must be correct in his assumptions. They consented quickly to everything. The only one demonstrating little enthusiasm for this plan was the groom, but in those days young people were not asked for their input, especially when larger issues were at stake. Hanna's father outlined the future of the young couple in measured tones over several sentences. He would take financial responsibility not only for the wedding but he would also provide the young couple with a furnished apartment. He offered to underwrite all the financial expenses of the newlyweds with the hope that young Frank would be a caring and loving husband to his daughter and a devoted father to his grandchild. Soon it was considered a done deal. They drank a glass of cognac to the health of all involved. The first chapter of Hanna's tragedy, which later evolved into epic proportions, was signed, sealed and delivered.

Hanna's parents felt let down by what they considered to be a sordid affair but they could change little about the immutable facts. They both detested their new connection to the scarcely educated, working-class folk and, worse yet, observant Catholics, with whom they could hardly hope to share more than a nominal kinship. They feared for Hanna's acceptance within the fold of such a dissimilar group of people whose values, manners and preferences were alien to her background and upbringing.

There was yet another deep pain in Hanna's family. As much as they were assimilated into Czech society and believed themselves to be an integral part of the Czech nation, they realized they were still deeply rooted within the Jewish community. Never before had they felt the full emotional impact of such loss, for they never contemplated the possibility of intermarriage within their family. Like many others, they thought such things happen only to others and definitely not to them. Although most of the highly cultured and prosperous Jewish community of Prague practiced their faith only within marginal limits, they still were fiercely proud of their ancient heritage, unwilling to give up or renege on their identity as Jews.

Perhaps societal anti–Semitism, still deeply ingrained and imbued within the Czech people, decelerated the process of assimilation. At times this virulent racism would be expressed vociferously, at other times subsiding into a latent form, never to vanish completely.

Hanna's family faced the situation, which would change their lip service of belonging to the Jewish community into a real full-bodied kinship. And they found it so very difficult, humiliating and painful to have their daughter married in a secular wedding. But they knew their part: they had to bite the bullet, put brave, smiling faces up, and arrange for a rapid civil ceremony in the office of the justice of the peace. They went through the motions with grief in their hearts, trying to put on as good a show as possible. Family from both sides attended the brief ceremony but it was almost a somber affair. None of the participants appeared joyful; all felt, for different reasons, short-changed and alienated in the company of their new in-laws. It was only Hanna who did not have to act her part. Though pale and tired, she flashed several genuinely happy smiles, standing next to her morose bridegroom. She wore a smart off-white outfit that was loose enough to cover her growing belly.

Following the ceremony the small cluster of celebrants went to a nearby restaurant, where Hanna's parents hosted a festive lunch marking this special occasion. Though the meal ordered was scrumptious, it did not appeal to any palate. The palate of the groom's family was oriented to simpler fare and it was an insurmountable challenge coping with the assorted cutlery. They felt intimidated by the refined elegance of the restaurant. The hosts tried to enjoy the occasion but as they watched the questionable table manners of their brand-new relatives they felt repelled by their crudeness. Indeed, this lunch served as an ominous omen for Hanna's marital future.

The just-wedded twosome retired to the apartment rented and furnished by Hanna's parents. A honeymoon could not be considered in light of the special circumstances. The plan stipulated that Frank was to find work in construction or other gainful employment and persist for a full year, and only then would Hanna's family subsidize the continuation of his education. Nobody quite understood why this precondition was laid down but perhaps Hanna's dad wanted to teach him a lesson in the responsibilities of earning a living and supporting a family. What reasons led him to this resolution were not shared with Hanna or his son-in-law. As was befitting in those days, the senior head of the family, Hanna's father, assumed financial control and was the only one entitled to make decisions. He was never a man predisposed to leniency or review and consideration of other points of view.

In the beginning all seemed to go well. And what did go awry remained hidden to Hanna's parents, for she was too embarrassed to complain, already having inflicted more than her share of heartbreak on her family. Hanna now painfully noticed new personality features in her husband. Not only did he show little ardor or love for her, but also he often snapped rudely at her, at times using vulgar and outrageous language.

The weeks passed. Hanna's pregnancy entered the last trimester and more and more it affected her appearance. Gone was her exquisitely slim figure, and her pretty face was marked with ugly blotches. The bloated belly made her even unable to tie her own shoelaces. When she caught her husband's glances as he gazed at her up and down she noticed so much derision in his eyes that she almost shuddered. Often his expression was full of disgust. Clearly he could not stand the sight of her. Towards the final stages of the pregnancy he did not even try to hide his repulsion. More often than not he did not come home after work, returning late and hardly ever sober. Hanna always feigned deep sleep, as she grew afraid of Frank. His taunts and insults reduced her to tears. Hanna feared that he found her disgusting and unattractive and that he held a grudge blaming her for his loss of freedom and assumption of responsibilities he was unready to shoulder. When they first married he usually spent his evenings with his parents, but later he began visiting a nearby pub, indulging in drinking bouts with his buddies, who teased him about his upper-class connections and subservience to his Jewish father-in-law.

The young man felt humiliated being controlled by his domineering father-in-law. Even more, he loathed his friends' frequent intimations about his secondary status to a Jew, and a rich one to boot. All this teasing, even if at times benign, further corroded his union with Hanna. He returned home later and later, at times in the wee hours, almost at dawn, drunk and in a foul mood.

It was only on a rare occasion that Hanna would pluck up her courage and ask about his after-work whereabouts. He would ignore her question and if she was foolhardy enough to persist in her query he would rudely silence her. Initially he insulted her verbally but soon he became physically abusive. He would strike her with his fists or throw the nearest object at her.

Hanna entered a new phase of her life, a phase dominated by fear and panic. She was petrified of the man she had once loved so dearly. She tried her best to prevent the unleashing of his anger, all to no avail. It seemed he discovered a new pleasure, the pleasure of hurting Hanna and maintaining in her a state of permanent dread. The more she feared him the more brazen his aggression. Before long he began to beat her regularly, irrespective of what she did or did not do. He slapped her face but saved his most savage blows to her body, where the bruises were hidden by clothes. If she begged him to stop he would beat her harder, exhorting her to bear her punishment in silence. He singled out her bloated abdomen for some of his most vicious slaps, as if he could avenge his loss of freedom on her pregnant belly. Hanna spent her days in terror, her mind in constant panic, trying to come up with a scheme to placate Frank and avoid his brutal trashing. Many a time she was determined to talk to her parents or sister but when she finally was in their company she lost courage and remained mum. She hid her bruises, hoping that no one would notice her plight and the humiliation she suffered at the hands of her husband.

One evening ushered in an especially rough night for Hanna. Frank returned home totally inebriated and in a filthy mood. He cast one hostile look at Hanna and without as much as saying a word began hitting her with, even for Frank, unusual brutality. When she begged him to stop he began to scream obscenities and insults, his fury rising. He threatened to kill her but told her before that, she would endure his terrible ire. He called her his curse, an ugly fat Jewess and his nemesis. Perhaps he would have murdered her on that particular night—and Hanna certainly prayed for a quick deliverance from her torment—but before very long he was spent and fell fully dressed on the bed snoring. The death for which Hanna prayed so fervently that night did not come. Instead she felt the onset of labor. The contractions became more frequent and Hanna knew it was time to leave for the hospital. She would not wake up her husband, whose snoring droned loudly in his alcoholic stupor. She feared more blows and she was content not to have to deal with him and his unpredictable savagery.

She got up quietly, washed off some of the blood and surveyed the damage. Not only did she suffer tissue injuries, scratches and welts on her body, she had also absorbed a massive blow to her face. One of her eyes was nearly shut by massive swelling, the bruise discoloring and spreading on her pale, skinny face. Clearly this was one of the worst beatings and it had to happen on the night of her delivery! Or was the childbirth precipitated by the brutal attack? He also used his belt for the first time, thus leaving deep welts on her body that every midwife or doctor would question.

But Hanna had no time to reflect about the inopportune timing of this outrage. She washed and dressed in total silence, keeping one eye on her tormentor in his deep sleep. She was determined to leave alone for the hospital where she was registered for delivery. She picked up a bag containing a few toiletries she had prepared long ago for that very purpose. She slipped noiselessly out of their apartment, where once, a brief while ago, she had hoped to live happily ever after but where it turned out she endured more pain than she could imagine.

Hanna's body was sore all over, and her cramps were returning with stubbornly more frequent regularity, indicating that she was in labor. How could she hide her bruised face and body now, on admission to a hospital? Before, when Frank's abuse left visible marks on her body, she avoided contact with people and wore long-sleeved dresses, no matter how high the mercury climbed; she would never go out without stockings and even if the weather was overcast she wore dark sunglasses, professing a newly developed light sensitivity. Actually she became quite proficient at covering up and no one suspected anything sinister. Her family was slightly amused by Hanna's peculiarities, attributing her eccentricity to the changes of an expectant young mother. But this showmanship came to a sad end once Hanna was hospitalized.

In those days, especially among the poor of the working class, it was not unusual for a woman to be badly treated by her husband and in some

Seven. Portrait of Hanna P.

circles it was more the rule than the exception. Perhaps the staff would overlook or ignore the welts and the large discolored patches on her body. Some were more recent bluish-purple, while some were turning green to yellow. Hanna's body was like an array of colors on a palette indicating multiple episodes of physical abuse. But what about Hanna's family, who would certainly come and visit? Hanna thought it was such bad luck that he had to attack her so badly this very night, making her situation all but untenable. In fact, she was inordinately fortunate, for that beating on the birth of their child saved her life, as Frank was out of control. The harder he hit her the more he enjoyed it, and the most likely outcome was that he would either kill or maim her.

By then, already outside her apartment, she knew that there was no time to dally; her contractions signaled the need to reach the hospital soon. She boarded the tram, which meandered through the early morning gray of the streets of Prague in what seemed to take an absolute eternity. When finally she arrived, in the nick of time she was rushed to the delivery room, where she gave birth to a healthy baby girl.

An elderly midwife delivered the girl with the quiet efficiency of an experienced professional. With the baby safely sleeping, she approached Hanna, shook her head and said, "Listen, child, I have seen evidence of beating on many women during the many years I plied my trade. But the type of bruises and injuries you have often result in serious injuries just before delivery. Either you are married to a savage alcoholic or a brutal criminal, a lowly beast who abuses his pregnant wife to a black and blue mass of bruises." The midwife was a kind person and she would not be disabused by Hanna's rather feeble protests. She spoke patiently to Hanna, who sobbed softly and slowly stopped remonstrating against the midwife. The midwife explained to Hanna that it was common to find some evidence of abuse at the hands of primitive men who became disgusted with the altered appearance and diminished efficiency of their pregnant wives. They resented the lack of marital comfort and in their ire took it out on the poor woman. But the kind of injuries Hanna sustained were severe even for the rough and tumble neighborhood the hospital serviced. Hanna listened to the soft hum of her voice, barely making out the words, for her eyes were closing and suddenly the tension fell off her shoulders. It had been a long time since she felt safe; now she could relax and feel happy, holding her newly arrived baby daughter in her arms. She was lulled into a nap, feeling that no evil could befall her in the realm where this kind person was in charge.

But before she dropped off she asked a favor. Would the kind lady phone her parents and let them know of her whereabouts? Having received assurances, she relaxed in a moment of happiness. The hospital tried as a matter of policy to inform the husband, who so far had failed to show up. Perhaps he did not want to know if his child was born; perhaps he hoped that his wife, sickened by her ordeal and daunted by the prospect of continuous suffering at his hands, had finally left him for good. Certainly it seemed to be his plan to torment her for as long it took to have her leave of her own volition.

Hanna's parents came rushing in as soon as the good news reached them. They were delighted with the birth of their first grandchild, admired the bundle of joy in the nearby nursery, and began to deliberate for a suitable name. All were in high spirits, pleased with the new addition to the family, but Hanna's mom wondered why her daughter needed sunglasses in a shady hospital room. Both parents exchanged puzzled looks when the door opened rather abruptly and the affable midwife stepped in, making a beeline for Hanna's bed. The friendly woman skipped all preliminaries, even an introduction. Her white uniform and demeanor gave her credibility and standing. She bluntly informed the family that Hanna's body was one large collection of bruises, inflicted by savage beatings, not on one occasion but numerous times in the course of several months. Hanna had fresh injuries and also numerous old bruises in various stages of absorption. The caring midwife warned her parents that a man capable of such brutality might not only kill Hanna but also easily end the life of the baby, for he had to be a maniacal psychopath. Without soliciting Hanna's permission, she drew near the bed and pulled back the blanket, revealing Hanna's mass of bruises. Both parents suppressed cries of horror, and they gaped at the sight of their daughter, in front of their eyes, in utter and incredulous shock.

Next the midwife exposed Hanna's face, quickly removing her sunglasses, waving aside Hanna's protests, baring the massive swelling nearly shutting one of her eyes. The only sounds in the austere hospital room were sighs and whimpers of dismay. How could it happen that Hanna went through hell on earth without confiding in them? Had she shared with them her situation they would have intervened long ago, before she was nearly killed. They thought that they arranged for her the best of solutions under the circumstances and never contemplated contributing to such an ordeal. Both parents exchanged guilty glances, filled with pain and regrets. The first to regain composure was Hanna's father. He covered his daughter's battered body with the blanket and said in his firm, resonant voice, "Hanna, you will never return to the monster you married. You and the baby will come back to our home upon your discharge from the hospital. The fiend who beat you will never get near you or the baby. I will force him to give up his rights to the baby in exchange for exemption of his legal obligation to contribute financially towards his daughter's upbringing. I know that he will accept this deal and be delighted with it, and we in turn will rid ourselves of this outcast of a savage barbarian."

It happened exactly as he said it would. He confronted his son-in-law with charges of his atrocious brutality, threatened to report him to the authorities and offered him only one alternative. He placed in front of him a written contract stipulating his surrender of all rights to his daughter and in turn Hanna would wave her prerogative for financial support. He pressed, none too gently, a pen into his son-in-law's hand, ordered him to sign and told him he could never show up or come near their home again. The truth of the matter was that Frank was overjoyed to sign. He was happy to renounce his rights and obligations in regard to his daughter's upbringing. He loathed the idea of married life with Hanna and being responsible for a child; he was sickened by all marital commitments, which he felt had been forced on his young life.

Hanna returned to her parental home, her spirit crushed, unable to grasp what went wrong with her marriage to the man she loved so dearly. She blamed herself for having failed to please and satisfy him, but in the end she accepted reality and came to terms with her new life. She was aware that it was a stroke of luck that she did not suffer any lasting physical damage, though few claimed this about her emotional state. On occasion Hanna reminded herself how fortunate she was to have caring parents who took her in and provided a safe haven for her little Jean. Slowly the sounds of a turning key in the door stopped triggering panic attacks and she even began to sleep without fear that Frank would return and rain blows on her again.

The divorce proceedings were swiftly concluded. It was an uncontested separation case and the courts quickly dissolved what never should have been united. Hanna knew that she should be grateful and, moreover, count her blessings, for her baby daughter developed into an affectionate, bewitching toddler, with a ready toothless smile and charming the entire family. The presence of the little girl helped comfort the family in their painful disappointment with Hanna and her failed marriage. Little Jeannie also had relatively young grandparents who adored her and reminded them of their own early marriage, gone long ago. Lastly, her sweet grin erased the sting of the errors gnawing at their consciences, for they blamed themselves for Hanna's pain and smarted from it for a long time.

Meanwhile, the entire family settled into a welcomed lull, troubled only by the steadily deteriorating political situation in central Europe. And then, in Germany, the hatred exploded.

Hanna was never interested in politics, paying little attention to matters that seemed so very troubling to her parents. In fact, just the opposite was true. Following her physical and emotional recovery, she soon became restless and began to miss the carefree joys of other teenage girls. She was still one of them and she missed the fun, friends, company, parties and all the other activities that preoccupied girls her age. Was she not, in spite of all she had experienced, still a very pretty teenager?

On occasion Hanna would dream of finding a real boyfriend, a man who would love her and be kind to her, not such a rough clod as her first love proved to be. Her parents encouraged her to go out, try to make friends, and behave like other girls her age. They were willing to take care of Jeannie, taking that responsibility off Hanna's young shoulders. The parents were still reeling from the shock and guilt of their blunder of forcing Hanna to marry for propriety's sake and so nearly getting her killed at the hands of a punk whose background and character they hardly bothered to check. Now, to make up for it they bent over backwards, showering her with understanding, sympathy, generosity and leniency.

In just a little over a month Hanna met a young man who seemed seriously interested in her and whose affection, faithful to her impetuous disposition, she returned with hot passion. All too quickly she forgot that only a brief while ago she swore never to love another man or become dependent on one. All her good intentions dissolved and again she glowed with a white-hot, starry-eyed love for her new one and only.

Still, this time there was a marked difference. George, her new boyfriend, was not only a handsome, intelligent and serious young man but he also came from a background similar to Hanna's, all of which smoothed their relationship greatly. Hanna never did anything halfheartedly. She gave her all or gave nothing and for the second time in two years her passion flared up in an intense, unrestrained all-consuming blaze. Again, everything else became almost irrelevant, pushed into the background; the top priority was George and their blossoming relationship. Hanna lived for her new flame to the exclusion of all else. Little Jeannie was moved to the emotional sidelines and her doting grandmother cared for her.

Seven. Portrait of Hanna P.

Hanna's parents went along with her choice but they could not help but note with consternation her tendencies towards extremes. It seemed that she could love only with utmost passion; she could not find a middle way, with balance or a levelheaded attitude. It was all or nothing for Hanna. Still, the parents consoled themselves that this time good fortune was with them, for Hanna's boyfriend was a decent, reliable and well-educated chap who would neither misuse nor abuse her absolute devotion and affection. He obviously loved her, as well, even if he demonstrated it in his slightly more measured and reserved style.

But while all these positive developments were unfolding in Hanna's household, the external political situation deteriorated further. The Nazis occupied the truncated republic, forming a new, till then unheard-of entity, the "Protectorate of Bohemia and Moravia." In rapid succession they passed edicts restricting Jewish freedom and implementing the Nuremberg racial laws, converting Jews to a colony of social lepers. Gradually most professions, activities and rights excluded Jews and most commodities, including their own monies, were unavailable to them. Some leniency was extended to the "crossbreeds." The household included one such "crossbreed": little Jeannie qualified, for she was the offspring of a Gentile father and a Jewish mother. These special privileges accorded to the half–Jews allowed for some mobility and more generous food rations, not the starving allotments parceled out to the Jews. But most important, they were, at least in the early stages, exempt from deportation, which began to expel Jews from their homes to some obscure eastern camps or ghettos, a forced deportation against which there was no appeal.

Stripped of all possessions except for the 50 kg they could carry with them, the Jewish populations trudged to the unknown concentration camps, where they were stripped of all human and civil rights, defenseless prey of a bloodthirsty, hideous, felonious government. There was not a soul in the countries under Nazi domination that did not dread this. But there was no appeal or postponement of the sentence passed on the Jews, no glimmer of hope for the most abject, grievously harmed and demonized minority ever. The ejection of Jews proceeded at a fast clip, the Germans aiming at a universe cleansed of Jews. To the Nazis, the Jews represented emissaries of the devil incarnate, a parasitic infestation of the body proper requiring amputation. Silent despair blanketed the Jewish community, and all scrambled to find a postponement. But next to none found a loophole to slip the noose of the feared fate of deportation.

Hanna did need not to worry, at least not for the time being. She was considered the mother of a "half-breed" and thus was protected from early deportation. These persons were, till further notice, not subject to forcible removal from Prague. Their food rations were similar to that of the Gentiles and therefore they were not reduced to living on the brink of starvation.

All the same, misfortune befell Hanna. George was ordered to present himself for deportation in the fall of 1941. He, along with many others, vanished without a trace. The only sign of life was a postcard Hanna received a few weeks later. The message was brief, stating that he was well and working on construction in Theresienstadt, the newly established camp for Jews of the Protectorate.

Hanna sank into a deep depression. She was disconsolate, unable to find solace or hope. She could not accept what was perceived as a temporary loss of the man she cared deeply about. While she had only dabbled in her caregiver role for Jeannie before, now she distanced herself completely from the child. Instead of finding comfort in the presence of her child, she had no patience for her laughter and mischievousness. But then again, Hanna never responded to major upheavals of her life in the usual fashion. Being impetuous and guided mainly by emotions, her responses often made no sense. Now the despondent Hanna lived like a recluse; she would not leave the apartment even during hours permitted by curfew for Jews to run their errands. She neither read nor talked to her family; her depression robbed her of all common sense. She spent the better part of her days and nights bawling and moping for George and all she obsessed about was her hope of being reunited with him.

Hanna was the only one of the family aside from Jeannie who was temporarily deferred from deportation, and her family hoped that she would make use of it after their departure by sending them the "once a month food parcel" permitted by the Gestapo. It goes without saying that she was already doing this for George, as hearsay had it that the inmates were kept on starvation rations.

Though past experience should have taught Hanna that her judgment was often faulty when guided by feelings only, she did not learn from her painful lessons from a tattered past. She waived off all other considerations and decided to volunteer for deportation to Theresienstadt, where she hoped to reunite with George. In spite of the forceful objections of her family she pushed forward with her plan. To implement her idea, she had to take care of Jeannie first, for it was only a matter of weeks before her parents and sister would also be expelled, leaving little Jeannie homeless.

Hanna agreed with the rest of the family that the child should be spared this ordeal, if at all possible. She paid a visit to the offices of Prague's Jewish community, where the official, following German orders, promised everyone that deportation would allow for reunification with their loved ones. Hanna swallowed the bait, hook, line and sinker and decided to embark on the slippery road.

Again she delayed talking to her parents, leaving it for very last moment. But soon she had to cross that bridge and shared with them her irrevocable decision and all details of her scheme. Hanna's parents, as before, were shocked by their daughter's reckless abandon. They could not conceive of a reason that she should refuse to stay in Prague, benefitting from her special privilege and take care of Jeannie and trying to ride it out while in the eye of the storm. They attempted to plead with her, even if just for Jeannie's sake—but also for themselves and even George—for all would be better off if she continued supplying them from her particular vantage point. Tragically Hanna seemed beyond the reach of their words.

Hanna resolved to place her daughter in the care of the child's paternal grandparents, a couple she had not contacted since her messy divorce. Hanna's parents shook their heads in disbelief over her decision to forsake her clear parental duty towards her child for the unsure promise of joining her lover in the most perilous circumstances. But wizened by past experiences, they knew only too well that little could be done with Hanna when her feelings for a man predominated.

Little Jeannie was told that her mother was about to leave for quite some time and was to be followed by her grandparents. Gradually they won the child over to the idea of spending some time with her paternal grandparents. They in turn were persuaded, after their palms were greased with a lot of money, to take Jeannie. Though the family stipulated that those funds were destined for Jeannie's future education, all understood that schooling was not the top priority of Frank's parents. Hanna rationalized that this transfer was the best for the child, for life in the midst of a Gentile family would provide safety, unfettered by the restrictions and perils shadowing all Jewish existence in occupied Europe.

The separation from the little chubby darling was painful for the entire family, but Hanna persistently repeated a convincing view that Jeannie was the only winner and they must not be selfish and drag her into their misery. They all kissed and hugged the child and then Hanna quickly picked up the luggage with her clothes and the few toys she owned and they were off. Hanna did not stay for long. She felt extremely ill at ease with her former in-laws. She tried to reassure Jeannie, kissed her and whispered into her ear that she would be back to fetch her very soon and then they would never part again.

Absolute sadness reigned at home. The last vestige of happiness and joy, Jeannie, was gone and only last-minute preparations for relocation into the unknown were left. While everyone else dreaded the call, Hanna awaited her voluntary call-up with joy in her heart; and indeed she was included in a transport leaving a few days later. She took her leave from her parents and sister, all still incredulous that she chose to try to join a man whose exact whereabouts were unknown and give up the care of her little girl to, at best, people of questionable character. All Hanna had to go by was the one postcard, not followed by any additional sign of life. But Hanna had no doubts. She needed to join George and help him build what would perhaps be an impoverished existence somewhere far away, but at least they would do it together. In the final moments before parting from her parents she became sad, but she remained ignorant of the truth of the rather persistent rumors that older folks stood no chance of outliving the rigors of a German concentration camp. She embraced them all warmly and only on saying good-bye to her sister did she feel hope for a potential future meeting.

All choked up, she gathered her 50 kg of basics that were allowed to every deportee. She packed it all with great care but no item received more attention than the warm sweater she had just finished knitting for her beloved. She folded it neatly in the bottom of her luggage. Then she put in her own clothes and in between she hid some of George's favorite sweets. Hanna hunted for hours for these candies and paid a small fortune to the black marketers of Prague. As soon as she was out of her home her frame of mind improved. Unlike most deportees, who were wretched and miserable, Hanna stepped forward energetically in the direction of the building where all the castaways were gathered. She was neither fearful nor apprehensive about her future existence as a camp inmate.

The journey by train was relatively short, only about two hours. When they reached their destination, they heard orders shouted for all to get off the train, pick up their bundles and march some four kilometers towards Theresienstadt, where the gates shut tight behind them. Hanna marched cheerfully, vigorously, animated by the approaching reunification with George.

Once inside the gates, the newly arrived were subjected to thorough strip searches, supervised not only by Czech police but also by SS officers

Seven. Portrait of Hanna P.

who stood behind them, guns cocked. They checked closely the bundles and placed the contents in large bins, assigned for confiscation. It was not an inviting scenario but Hanna hardly cared. She kept herself busy imagining George's surprise when he would first see her. The only time she became apprehensive was when the man who rifled through her luggage paused and fingered the soft, woolen sweater, the one she knitted for her Man. He noticed her imploring look and quietly he placed the colorful garment back, smiling thinly at Hanna's beseeching glance.

Many men found Hanna's dark, elegant beauty fascinating and, now in her mid-twenties, she looked lovely, radiating the special glow of a woman in love. Her tall, slim figure was more like a mannequin's than that of the average young housewife. Many men tried for her favors but Hanna was steadfast in her devotion to George. Now the man who rifled through her bundle wanted her to notice that he saw her hidden sweets but overlooked them. Hanna gave him a grateful grin.

Soon all the screening procedures were completed; she lost some of her toiletries and part of her salami. The women were commanded to form a column of five and were ordered to march to nearby barracks. They were given some dirty straw and ordered to sit and wait. All of them were hungry and tired and most were outright miserable, again with the exception of our Hanna. They were given some watered-down soup and ordered to lie down and stay put for the night. The next day they received another bowl of watery soup and were ordered to pick up their belongings and march. They were led to another barrack, where they were assigned places in three-tier bunks and told that tomorrow they would be assigned to working commandos. The majority were enrolled in a unit working the fields.

Before long Hanna worked out the routine for her life in Theresienstadt and she was ready to proceed after her real objective: to find George. She found out which barracks housed male prisoners and made the acquaintance of some men who lived there. She questioned all of them about George's whereabouts but nobody seemed to remember the name at all. One of the men suggested that Hanna turn for help to the Magdeburg barrack, which housed the Council of the Elders, the men in charge of the camp. There they kept the archives containing records and statistics of all the camp's inmates, past and present.

The next day Hanna went straight to the Magdeburg barrack, where she found another young man who directed her to an official who could provide some answers. The result was the worst possible shock and disaster for Hanna. The man she loved so dearly and volunteered to be with in this God-forsaken place, had been deported only a few weeks ago to yet another camp. She was told frankly that conditions further east were indescribable, horrific and life-threatening.

Hanna's upbeat mood took a sharp dive. Once again she became lugubriously wretched. All her hopes came to naught and she failed to reunite with the only person she really cared about. Her misery was such that she failed to show up for work, and in any of the concentration camps this was the single most dangerous omission. She spent the better part of her time dissolved in tears; she felt numb, untouched by hunger or cold. She was informed that all the thousands of people dispatched to the East would not return and most inmates from Theresienstadt would eventually follow since Theresienstadt was a transit holding camp.

Hanna's barrack mates never really cared for her, as they considered her odd. Few admired her choice of opting for her lover rather than staying with her own child. Few, if any, of her bunkmates extended any sympathy to her; most held her in contempt, irritated by her fiery, impulsive emotions and undisciplined reactions. Even her copious tears had little impact on them. Theresienstadt, like most other camps of Nazi creation, did not abound with volunteer inmates and Hanna was viewed by most people around her with suspicion. Some believed that she was either an eccentric or, worse, a potential spy placed in their midst to report on them and their forages for food.

Poor Hanna. Not only was she heartbroken, she was also ostracized and abysmally lonely. For two full days, Hanna carried on like that. In the evening she sat on her bunk, her eyes flooded with tears, not noticing the hateful glances from her fellow inmates. Suddenly one of the women addressed her with considerable malice in her voice: "Listen Hanna, if you are so miserable here, why don't you volunteer for deportation east. Your woes here are getting you down. You might die if you won't do anything constructive. Here you do not have a chance to meet your man but he might be in another camp. Who knows? You might be lucky. Moreover, by volunteering for deportation you would fill one slot, exempting another person from forcible enrollment." Far from being hurt or suspicious, Hanna wondered why it had not occurred to her that this was her only chance to find the man she loved. Recklessly impetuous as ever, she decided within a few hours to voluntarily join the next transport out of Theresienstadt bound for some unknown eastern location.

Little could have been simpler to arrange in Theresienstadt. Though Hanna's decision raised a few eyebrows and prompted some astonished

Seven. Portrait of Hanna P.

looks, it mattered not to Hanna. She was never an approval seeker and from early on was accustomed to people finding her peculiar. Hanna gathered her few remaining belongings and with special care she put on George's sweater knitted back in Prague. Now a wizened inmate, Hanna knew not to risk its theft if she wished to deliver it safely. She carried her knapsack, on top of which she bound her blanket. She joined a large crowd waiting on the nearby tracks, which was quickly rammed into boxcars. The number of people jammed into the available space exceeded its potential by far, turning it into a mash of screaming individuals. Hanna forced herself to think about her upcoming reunion with George, trying to overlook the unfolding bedlam.

Hanna pushed her thoughts far from the squalor around her, far from those crying, yelling, praying, fainting, and eventually dying in close proximity. Few survived the prevailing conditions in a normal physical or mental state. For the entire duration of the nightmarish journey few knew the real stretch of time because hours merged into days in the darkness and airless stench of the boxcar, but Hanna held her own, sustained by her indomitable hope.

When the train came to a halt the doors were ripped open and all were ordered to jump out. To Hanna it seemed that all hell broke loose. They were jostled onto the platform amidst shouts, screams and beatings. Around them ran some strangely clad men in striped uniforms trying to establish some order in this mass confusion. They beat down aimlessly at the newly arrived with their whips, cudgels and truncheons. In the background, a heavily armed unit of the SS cordoned off the platform. The crowd were then pushed into a queue and ordered to proceed in the direction of an SS officer.

Hanna noticed that the smartly dressed officer was dividing the throng into two groups: one large, where most of the pathetic, dirtied, disheveled inmates were sent, and another one, much tinier in size, where the cluster of people consisted of stronger-looking inmates. One more time Hanna used her well-worn but effective trick. She concentrated her thoughts on the man she wished to meet up with, trying to dissociate herself from the wretchedness around her. Soon she felt impervious to the madness threatening to engulf her. Then she focused on the scurrying men in striped uniforms, for a moment thinking that they might know about George's whereabouts, but then she dismissed the thought. Nobody in this peculiar pack could be in the same league as George. They were most likely criminals serving time in forced labor camps.

Moments later Hanna found the thought of finding George among hardened criminals ridiculous. The thought was so absurd that for a second Hanna was forced to smile. Soon she reached the SS officer, who like an orchestra conductor moved his white-gloved hands gracefully in two different directions. The SS man was genuinely surprised to look into the eyes of a smiling and composed, pretty young woman. For a moment he stopped whistling his favorite aria, looking with some approval at Hanna. Then he quickly motioned her to join the tiny group on his right. Hanna was glad, at least for a moment, not to have to put up with the screams of the distraught children and the tears of the older folks, all of whom rattled her nerves.

From then on events moved at a fast clip. The small cluster around Hanna were marched to large shower halls and the big crowd on the left was shoved and thrown onto waiting trucks and driven away quickly. After showering, the hair of those assigned to forced labor was shaved off, a number was tattooed on their right forearm and they were ordered to run into the next barrack. During their gallop someone tossed pieces of clothing at them, all dirty and stinky. Though Hanna's teeth chattered, she hesitated to put on the skirt and top she caught. It seemed such a shame to place them on her washed body, for both pieces of clothing were smeared with blood and human excrement. But Hanna was freezing and, although almost overcome by nausea, she put the clothing on while dreading the thought of meeting George in such outlandish rags, her skull shaven and still dripping blood from the rough shave performed with a blunt razor. She need not have worried. Early the next day, following a restless night spent on the cold floor of the barrack thinly overlaid with filthy straw, she was included in a group of women destined for another camp: Bergen-Belsen.

Another short journey ensued. As if in a nightmare revisited, she was again in a boxcar, only this time the transport was composed solely of young, healthy women. The overall mood was better controlled, with next to no commotion or attacks of madness. No sooner had they arrived in Belsen than they received their work assignments, which called for them to join a commando in a nearby munitions factory. Each shift, and there were only two, toiled for 12 hours. The rations were deliberately so scant that the women were starving. The living quarters defied description. Most women began to lose weight, their bodies covered with sores and vermin. An epidemic of typhus spread by lice soon followed. Most succumbed after a brief stint there; little else could have been expected under such appalling conditions. Only Hanna lasted longer, sustained by her hopes of meeting George, if only she could persevere a little longer.

In Belsen, Hanna shared a bunk with a woman who miraculously survived the war. She later recounted to me her last days spent with Hanna, who defiantly never gave up her hope to find George. Hanna never missed an opportunity to ask every newly arriving inmate if they knew of or had seen him somewhere in this system of concentration camps. She kept her hopes and spirits up although she never met a single individual who had heard of him or knew him. Tenaciously clinging to her desire and trust, she hardly noticed the onset of her illness, the high fever; the first symptoms of typhus. It quickly took its course. She slipped into a semiconscious state and eventually into full unconsciousness, hoping till her last moment to meet George, her great love.

The tragic irony of fate was that Hanna contracted typhus in the first week of April 1945, the month Bergen-Belsen was liberated by the advancing British troops. For a few days Hanna slipped in and out of consciousness, too weak and run-down to put up a meaningful fight against the menacing typhus. She was still alive on April 15, the day the first British military units entered the camp. The first scenes there caused the soldiers to believe that Dante's inferno was a nice and cozy place when compared with Bergen-Belsen. Although the soldiers were toughened and brutalized by six years of horrible fighting, they recoiled with horror at the spectacle meeting their eyes.

Piles upon piles of emaciated corpses, amassed helter-skelter in heaps, all in different stages of decomposition, littered the camp's expanse. Among those shuffling aimlessly were the many "Musselmen," the thousands of infected, doomed skeletons, too far gone for any possible attempts at salvage. Even the horrors of the war did not prepare the soldiers for such shocking scenes. Although Hanna was alive on that April day when the liberators reached the camp, she could not grasp the fantastic news. She was too far gone; no spoken word could reach her.

Though the military mounted a valiant effort to help the many dying inmates, they could save but a few. The Herculean task was beyond even the best of human efforts of the time. Many died before any help could reach them and Hanna was one of them. She passed away in a fitful feverish sleep on April 17, two days after freedom reached the tortured inmates of Bergen-Belsen.

What Hanna never knew, and what mercifully remained concealed from her, was that her valiant search for the man she loved was doomed almost from the start. The Almighty spared her the knowledge that George did not live beyond the day of his arrival in Auschwitz. He did not pass selection performed by Dr. Mengele, who was displeased with the fact that George wore spectacles. While the Nazis hated all the Jews, the notorious "Angel of Death" especially targeted those wearing spectacles. They personified the prototype of the Jewish intelligentsia, the cultured, well-bred and often brilliant European Jew, the absolute anathema to all the Nazis held dear. George not only symbolized intelligence, kindness and handsome youthfulness, he was also unafraid. He stood ramrod straight, looking into the eyes of Mengele, who most likely interpreted it as defiance and Jewish arrogance.

To this peculiar mixture of hatred, contempt and jealousy, there was added a substantial inferiority complex of the "knights of Valhalla," which resulted in a potent and poisonous brew. While the Nazis demonized all Jews, they were simultaneously afraid of Jewish talent and capabilities. They genuinely believed that they would never rule the world as long as even one Jew was alive.

Talk about insanity!

Had Hanna remained in Prague curbing her own hastiness, she could have saved her life. She would have been deported much later. The other parents of the same mixed children arrived in January 1945. She would, in all likelihood, have remained in Theresienstadt until the end of the war, as Auschwitz no longer existed by January 1945, the Nazis having destroyed the camp by that time, fleeing like rats abandoning their sinking ship, attempting to escape the advancing Russian armies. There in Theresienstadt, with some luck she could have lived to see better days.

There is no doubt about the extent of her heartbreak. Not only did she lose the man she loved but her entire family perished during the cataclysmic years. Perhaps with time she would have acquiesced to the unalterable and could have rebuilt her life. But all that is pure speculation. Perhaps she is better off in her eternal rest, for her tempestuous disposition did not serve her well. While her peaks might have reached heights unattainable to more sedate individuals, her valleys were bottomless pits of dark sorrow and despondency.

None of the other members of the family pulled through the Jewish apocalypse. Hanna's parents, like George, died in the gas chambers in Auschwitz and Hanna's sister succumbed to malnutrition in one of the forced labor camps. Jeannie, Hanna's daughter, grew up in the only family she could remember: her father's. She was raised by her paternal grandparents.

Following the tradition of the Czech working class she was not afforded higher education, so, following the compulsory eight years, she went into trade school and learned to become a seamstress. She could not remember her mother or her other two grandparents. When anyone mentioned that she was part Jewish, Jeannie felt deeply embarrassed and vehemently denied such insolence. She was indoctrinated by her grandparents and her very own father in virulent anti-Semitism and had nothing but contempt for her mother, her grandparents, and Jewish tradition and heritage.

QUESTIONS AND ANSWERS

Should what is typically seen as a positive emotion such as love always come second to reason?

I would suggest that in such abnormal situations—as under the Nazi rule, full of lies, deception and terror—people should use cool reasoning to see if their actions lead them into perhaps a better outcome or into disaster. In the case of Hanna, she was almost pathologically overcome with love for a man that she overlooked the possibility that she might never see him again, Instead she was going to a place where she would likely die. That was her personal disposition: she always invested more into emotions than into cool intellectual reasoning. And that was really a luxury she was not able to afford. But in spite of all she did, she of course lost her own life. She not only gave up her own future, she also deprived her child of a mother because of her passionate love for a man she could not stay with. This was one of the many tragedies that unfolded during the Nazi times: people were separated and hectically searching for one another only to fall into the trap of the Nazis. They died while looking for somebody who had disappeared into one of the camps. There was no way to reconnect with somebody once people were deported. There was nowhere to go to inquire.

Can love for another be too strong?

Yes, indeed, if it is irrational and if we set aside the possibility that we may pay with our life without having a chance to reconnect or help the other one. Perhaps it can be too strong and perhaps people should revise what they are doing by rational consideration. But it is a tall order for a young woman who passionately loves a man—one who is all she really cares—about to exercise this type of self-discipline and judgment. Perhaps if she had remained in Theresienstadt she might have had a very strong chance to survive. But this is how she was and passionate people who are guided by their feelings more than their brain are often in a situation detrimental to their future well-being.

Why should love of a person and acting from love be viewed as wrong if it leads to tragedy? Is love not inherently good?

Love is inherently good in normal times, but we are talking about the times of the Nazis, when there were no normal motivations and normal values were topsy-turvy and upside-down. Certainly normal people would respect one person's love for another and would try to facilitate their unification and life together, but not under the Nazi system, which used emotion to promote faith that a person could be reunited with a loved one and stay with that person, which of course was an open lie. The Nazis used this type of false information and they would tell people if they loved someone going on a transport to volunteer to go with the person. This is because normally, from Theresienstadt, people were deported as couples. But a lot of people were not officially married, so the Nazis were saying, "Do volunteer! Go with your loved one, you will be able to stay with him. You will reunite with him and stay together!" So people believed this and jumped at this promise and they volunteered to go and of course they ended up in the gas chambers. So it was an infamous, dark, ugly, face of humanity's history and many fell victim to it. Hanna is just another example. I wrote these stories of those who did not survive to demonstrate that every day naïve people guided by positive emotions end up losing their lives because there is a criminal government that plans their demise.

This chapter seems to be about making bad choices, and Hanna chose to do all the wrong things, even though she seemed aware of the options.

We cannot understand a person so emotionally predisposed. Had she lived in normal circumstances I think she would have always made decisions guided by her heart and not by her brain. In normal times these decisions are not life-threatening. But under the Nazi terror it was a life-threatening inclination to go by your heart and avoid consideration of what was rational and what was really in store for you. Perhaps you can't say she was all that bright or maybe she was an indulged, high-tempered child from a comfortable family where she was never forced to look at the stark reality of the movement of an ugly law. Had she really been forced to see life as it was then, perhaps she would have sobered up and realized she was not helping the man she loved but essentially harming herself and, even more so, her young daughter. So I think where she went wrong, maybe, was all of her past upbringing as an indulged, pretty girl who went from one mistake to another, always guided by what she saw as being so important, namely her love for a man.

Did Hanna have a greater moral responsibility to provide better for her daughter and put her daughter before her own interest?

I would suggest that, yes, she did. I would suggest if you do have a child, irrespective of time and situation in life, you have to put the young life you brought into this world at the front and yours on the back burner. People who are not willing, or capable, of doing so should not really have children because an innocent child brought into this world deserves to receive care and optimal guidance into maturity. Hanna did not live up to her duty. Perhaps she thought that by passing her daughter on to the Gentile side of the family the daughter would have a better or easier entry into life. In a way, that might have been true, but she stripped Jeannie of the help of her mother, who should help her grow up and insert into her life the proper values. So I think Hanna did fall short of expectations in her role as a mother.

Was marrying a non–Jew considered an acceptable way to try to escape (like a marriage of convenience)? If not, why was this not an alternative to be considered?

Few Gentiles would be willing to marry a Jew aware there would be consequences brought about if they did so. With ongoing mixed marriages the Gentile was often encouraged, or pushed, into divorcing their Jewish counterpart. So a new Jew-Gentile union would have been officially not permitted because it was considered an unacceptable choice. It was considered soiling the Aryan blood by mixing with Jewish blood, so the Germans would not allow any new marriages between Gentiles and Jews. But with the existing ones, those that preceded the time of the occupation, the Gentiles were always very much encouraged to kick the Jew out of the habitat and eventually strip him of everything. As you know, there were laws that referred to mixed blood: first, second and third classes. So to protect themselves from persecution, many a Gentile woman married to a Jew divorced the husband and swore the children were sired by an Aryan lover. This way the children were declared to be Gentile and the curse of the Jewish persecution was lifted.

The intermarriages that preceded the 1939 Nazi occupation of Bohemia and Moravia were mainly where Jewish men married Gentile women. I don't know why, whether it was the fact that a lesser number of women intermarried because of an awareness of religion or societal taboos, where intermarriages were not really welcome by either side. Neither side was happy when people married out of faith. This, of course, is the sort of values expressed at the beginning and the middle of the twentieth century. During the Nazi years, some of them—a very small number of them— remained faithful to their vows, remained with their Jewish husband and shared his fate.

Strangely enough, these marriages really were not affected by the persecution. The first deportees of Jews who were married to Gentiles didn't occur until in January 1945, a few months before the end of the war. The children of these mixed marriages were evaluated to see if they were raised as Jews or if they were raised without religion or as Gentiles, etc., and this would qualify them as *Mischling* (mixed). First, Second, or Third class, according to the Nazi racial laws. The children, when perceived as Jews, were often deported to concentration camps. Those who were classified as non-Jewish cultured were often left in Prague.

So the phenomenon of mixed marriages in the years preceding the Nazi occupation was usually the case of a man marrying a Gentile woman and quite often she would convert. But after the Nazi occupation she would be encouraged to divorce and many made use of this very fast administrative procedure and got rid of the Jew, thereby retaining all the marital possessions. And it could affect the children's lives, making it easier for them by declaring them a product of sexual union with a lover who was not a Jew. So after the Nazis occupied the country there were no more Aryan-Jewish marriages possible, because the German considered that to be a criminal transgression. Intermarriages were not perceived as something that would be allowed.

Was there strong disagreement between those who sought assimilation and those who wished to maintain their overt Jewishness? What arguments were put forward on either side?

From 1918 and after the Czech republic was proclaimed, there was a great deal of assimilation by Jews into the mainstream Czechoslovakian society. Meanwhile, the Austro-Hungarian empire, although perhaps not violently promoting anti–Semitism, set restrictions and limitations on Jews if they remained in the fold, including the prohibition that they could not reach certain levels of government and military positions. The Czechoslovakian government lifted that and the Jews perceived that they had a chance to integrate. So there was a great deal of assimilation and with this came perhaps the loosening of ties with traditional Judaism and with perceived traditional observances of Jewish holidays, then sooner than later a drifting into the mainstream.

Of course there were elements who were vehemently and passionately objecting to the drift. They perceived it as a loss if the Jews were to assimilate into the mainstream and abandon Jewish values they considered eminently important. And of course these two factions were not only in Czechoslovakia but also in many European countries where there was attrition in the numbers of religious Jews to the less-religious, assimilated society.

Regarding the arguments on both sides, the person in favor of assimilation would try to convince you that the Czech society was tolerant and that Czech Jews could develop and live their full Jewish destiny. For a Czech of the Jewish religion there was an emphasis that their nationality would be Czech and the first loyalty would go to the Czechoslovak state, and their religious affiliation and devotion could be unencumbered and perused within that framework. Then, of course, the religious Jews perceived it as not really historically an option, because sooner or later in intermarriages the devotion to the religious commandments and traditions will be loosened and then eventually abandoned and the offspring from such unions will likely turn to the mainstream, because young people mostly like to be included in the mainstream and not necessarily belong to some minority. More than that, a minority was not always accepted with open arms and was often hated and resented for being Jewish. So, yes, there was the ongoing argument not only in the Czechoslovak Republic but also in Germany and, less so, in Poland, where the Jews retained their traditional faithfulness to religious observance. I think the arguments very much affected the relationship of these two factions within the state in that they really tried to convince one another that their position for the future was the correct one.

Is Hanna's daughter wrong to deny her heritage on the basis that she (probably felt that she) was abandoned by her young mother?

Hanna's daughter would have been right to feel that way, because her mother volunteered to put her into the custody of her non-Jewish relatives. She should have understood what her mother was thinking, namely as benefiting the daughter in that she would not suffer the restrictions imposed on Jews. But she might have also known there was another man her mother wanted to follow and did follow to her last day. So there might have this consideration that her mother was not really fully devoted to her.

There is also the possibility that her judgment was affected by her environment. While there was latent ongoing anti-Semitism in the Czechoslovak Republic this became greatly exacerbated by the day-in, day-out blast of Nazi propaganda concerning the Jews. The Nazis demonized the Jews every step of the way and, while the Czech initiatives were not perhaps about death and violent anti-Semitism, years of this seeding of anti-Semitism brought about a harvest of much worse anti-Semitism than before the occupation. For example, when we returned in 1945 I remember I was astounded by the cold, almost hostile acceptance of the Czech nationals to the Czech Jewish minority that remained.

Eight

Portrait of the Blue Polka-dot Dress

Frances and Lotte were daughters of a well-to-do, some would even venture to say rich, family. Their father was an owner of several jewelry stores in different districts of Prague, but most of their assets came from his considerable and brilliant investments in the stock market, called the "bursa" in those days.

The girls grew up in the lap of luxury, hardly ever denied a thing they fancied putting their well-manicured hands upon. Their home was not really a happy one, though, for their parents' marriage left much to be desired. It was not that Edmund and Rena were miserable—far from it! They had decided long before that it was in their best interest to go their separate ways but still stay married, for a divorce in those days was a major social calamity and an embarrassment to the entire clan. Therefore, many couples, and definitely Edmund and Rena, opted to remain together in a polite, detached way. They followed their own destinies, in parallel, but hardly ever on the same track.

The home atmosphere was gracious but lacked warmth; the adults spoke in respectful but impersonal tones to one another. The girls didn't fully understand what was amiss but the cool, detached, almost business-like interaction of their parents was markedly different from the climate they experienced in their many friends' households.

Though Edmund and Rena played their roles rather well, their near-frigid behavior towards each other prompted the two girls to ever-greater attachment. As Rena lost her passion for her husband, she tried to build closer ties with her daughters and before long the pattern was firmly established.

Moreover, Rena watched Edmund's parade of mistresses with jaundiced eyes, particularly the last one, whom he seemed to love dearly. Belatedly, she regretted settling for a marriage of convenience, but there was no backtracking. It was too late to make any changes. Their relationship was firmly set and deeply rooted. While Edmund relished his professional successes and unencumbered romantic life, Rena turned into a serious matron who occupied her days with multiple philanthropic activities and social functions. Nevertheless, most of her undertakings left her unfulfilled. The games of bridge and tennis were only time fillers that failed to offer her satisfaction. Against this cool backdrop both girls were developing into charming and attractive teenagers.

Frances was three years older than the effervescent Lotte and more serious, conscientious and diligent. She was also gifted with a unique razor-sharp intelligence. Lotte was perhaps a tad prettier, but Frances's darker complexion made her exceptionally alluring. Both girls were considered very beautiful by any standard and a full and productive life was predicted for each of them. Lotte, the younger sister, was more of a social butterfly, extroverted, with a ready smile and laugh; life for her was a never-ending party. It would be simplistic to suggest that Frances showed great intellectual promise whereas Lotte was a party girl, but on the face of it many thought so. It is impossible to know how their lives would have unfolded if they hadn't been overrun by the waves of sweeping fury of the Nazis.

The girls had a professional governess/teacher who designed an enhanced educational curriculum beyond their regular schooling. Both girls attended private lyceum, a preparatory equivalent of a middle school that would ready them for admission to a finishing school in Switzerland when they turned fifteen.

Fate, however, had its own design for the family as well as for all the Jews of Europe. The soil of Europe began to burn under the feet of the millions of Jews whose ancestors had lived there for thousands of years. While in many parts of Europe the Jews experienced ongoing brutal persecution through the generations, these two sisters had never experienced raw brutality until the Nazis arrived.

Initially, most Jews did not take the threat of the emerging Nazi Party seriously. They tried to laugh it off, albeit somewhat nervously. After all, it was the twentieth century and people were outgrowing their old prejudices and were more tolerant and free-minded. Had the world really matured or was it the Jews' wishful thinking? Many were dismissive of the writing on the wall, which spelled out the horrors to come.

Though the family gathered for the evening meals, little of substance

Eight. Portrait of the Blue Polka-dot Dress

was discussed. The conversation revolved around the girls' interests and their many upcoming activities: dances, socializing with the right crowd, visits to seamstresses and milliners and all that seemed so significant to the lives of the budding socialites. Indeed, it was not only this family but also many others who preferred to shut their eyes or gaze elsewhere.

Sometime in the late 1930s Edmund and Rena awoke to the new realities. They began to grasp that their very lives might be in jeopardy. Belatedly they realized that they couldn't stop or ignore the rapidly approaching disaster: the Nazi nemesis. Edmund contacted his Western European business associates and acquaintances in the U.S., Australia, and anywhere else he had connections. He was very confident that one of his many associates would come through for him and arrange an entry visa for emigration by his family. All his prior business partners answered in the affirmative, promising politely to try their level best for Edmund and his family. Sadly, with time, no tangible offers for a safe haven ever came forward. It seemed that the M. family was hectically running in circles, getting nowhere. And then the day came when the curtain came crashing down, ending all efforts of escaping Europe. On March 15, 1939, the German armies overran and occupied Czechoslovakia, tearing the state into two separate entities.

The curtain rose on the final act of the drama. Impoverished, isolated and abandoned by most of their friends, the M. family came together and developed new cohesion and loyalty. Frances and Lotte had always been close-knit but now Edmund and Rena, facing the unprecedented peril, also closed ranks, sharing their fears and searching for an escape. It is perhaps a bizarre irony that in the darkest, last days of their marriage, they became a caring, supportive and loving couple, a feat they failed to accomplish before, in the good old days.

Edmund, now stripped of his role as a business tycoon, was not only humbled but also completely lost. He knew how to function only in the mercantile world of business where he was most capable of interacting with his peers and associates. It was a rude awakening for a rich, middle-aged man. Also gone were his assorted mistresses and romantic flings. Belatedly, Edmund understood that most of his mistresses had been nothing more than opportunists—gold diggers—who stayed with him only as long as he was able to offer the luxuries they craved. It began to dawn on him that Rena, after all, was a very pleasant, understanding woman and that in her he had a true and loyal friend.

Rena also did her level best, trying to understand her Lothario, all the while trying to compensate for the new practical realities. There were no funds to pay the housekeeping staff and the racial laws prohibited Aryans working for Jews; so Rena took over the domestic chores and the girls pitched in. Even the chastised Edmund would offer to lend a hand at diverse household tasks, most of which he had hardly noticed in the past, like fetching buckets of coal from the cellar.

Frances made a few coins helping out in a millinery salon nearby. She was dexterous, had excellent taste, and worked for much less than would any qualified Gentile. Lotte helped her mother too, but the tough times turned the easygoing, cheerful girl into a fretful, often moody teenager. Though Rena was kind and patient with her, inevitably they ran afoul of one another and collided, for Lotte tried to get away with as little work as possible, still searching for a little fun time. Unlike Frances, the industrious, serious teenager, Lotte still hoped that her beauty and charm would provide an out for her predicament. It was not to be.

Edmund and Rena felt guilt and sadness, for they realized all they had squandered in their past. But their newfound cohesiveness had inspired their daughters. However, there is truth in the ancient Jewish adage that "the insight that comes too late should preferably stay away."

Their harmony, forged under the barrel of the gun, did not last for long. The M. family, along with many thousands of the Jews of Prague, were being deported to concentration camps. In mid-summer of 1942 there was a knock on their door that brought the long-awaited and much-dreaded summons, ordering them out of Prague. They were to be deported to an unknown destination for "resettlement."

All four of them spent three days in the Veletrzni Hall, being screened and processed for their new lives as inmates of a concentration camp. Their identity cards and food ration cards were confiscated. They had to surrender the key to their apartment, from which they were evicted. Eventually they were ordered to board an awaiting train. Two hours into the journey, the anxious deportees breathed a sigh of relief. When the chugging train slowed and came to a halt in a relatively short time, they realized they couldn't be in a distant camp somewhere in Poland. The caravan of unfortunates was ordered to dismount the cattle cars and march towards the fortress of Theresienstadt. It had been expropriated and expanded to function as a transit camp to hold Czech Jews on their way to dark places in the East, until they could be "accommodated." All things considered, the M. family was relieved, as this transit camp was perceived as a lesser evil. They sensed that they had received a respite, perhaps a short lease on life, and hoped to be spared the worst. These dangerous and tough

Eight. Portrait of the Blue Polka-dot Dress

times almost overnight matured all youngsters, and these two sisters in particular, into resolute and goal-oriented young adults.

On arriving in Theresienstadt, Frances, the firstborn, immediately searched to find lucrative work. In the camp's parlance that meant work dealing with food. The inmates' rations were so abysmally inadequate that without some augmentation inmates could not last more than a month or two. Frances was determined to find a way to supplement their starvation rations with much-needed nutrition. As for Lotte, she took it upon herself to establish contact with the Powers-That-Be, namely the inner circle of men in charge of the camp who were answerable to the Nazis. Fully aware that Theresienstadt was a transit camp, all inmates scrambled to find a loophole that would permit them a longer stay in this dark, foreboding, fortress and avoid the certainty of death. It was Theresienstadt's Nazi commandant who issued deportation orders specifying the number of people, age range and type of inmate to be sent to the East. For as long as the Council of the Elders adhered to Nazi stipulations, the Germans were satisfied. As it was, they knew that it was only a matter of time before every single Jew met his fate in the death camps. Therefore the council had some latitude in choosing who was to be consigned to any transport. It would be their decision who would temporarily stay and who would be pushed towards a quicker demise—clearly an unpleasant task indeed.

Frances secured a coveted position via an influential member of the Council of the Elders. She tended to the Nazis' vegetable and fruit crops. Jewish inmates worked plots of land for the benefit of the Nazi commandant and his cohorts. Not only was Frances able to surreptitiously supplement her measly rations by filching something edible on the job, with time she also became a master at hiding and smuggling fruits and vegetables, slipping them under her blouse and skirt with great speed and dexterity. It goes without saying that she had to be on constant high alert, keeping the overseeing Nazi officer in charge, the SS men, and the Czech gendarmes simultaneously in her field of vision. There were strict orders forbidding the workers from eating or taking any produce at the pain of death. Frances became lightning quick at squirrelling some tomatoes or lettuce into her blouse or in her loosely fitting skirt. In the camp all this bounty was pure gold, tradable for bread, medication or whatever was desperately needed.

Meanwhile Lotte reconnoitered the "Who's Who" of the camp's hierarchy. She zeroed in on a middle-aged German man—Harry G.—who was a lawyer and in Theresienstadt was a member of the powerful Judenrat, which had the task of organizing workers for German industrial projects. This post was of utmost importance since most able-bodied men were conscripted to serve in the German army, which led to serious labor shortages for their war effort. The Nazis used the inmates of the many concentration camps as slave laborers, essentially working them to death.

Few doubted that Harry G.'s work was of vital impact to the Jews. The Nazis oversaw the war production with tenacious severity, demanding quality work and quantities of output and their dissatisfaction resulted in serious consequences to the Jews. In return for his role, Harry G. and his family were granted protection. They were exempt from deportation to the East—but this could be revoked in a heartbeat if he was removed from his position or the Nazis decided to replace the camp's Jewish administrative leadership.

Now in her early twenties, Lotte began a serious relationship with Harry G., hoping to secure her family's exemption from deportation to Auschwitz.

The girls did all they could to ensure the family's survival but Rena and Edmund still struggled in the subhuman conditions, having great difficulty adapting. The crowded, dirty, vermin-infested barracks and the lack of food, hygiene and privacy all took their grave toll on them both, Edmund in particular. Unable to adjust to such primitive circumstances, separated from his wife and daughters (as the men were housed in separate barracks), ravenously hungry and in need of a cigarette, he began to decline. He exhibited the typical signs of a fading inmate, no longer paying any attention to his appearance, his clothes now always soiled. He suffered with prostate problems and his poor urinary control and long waiting at the men's barrack's latrines made yellowish spots of dried urine visible all over his pants. Those stains bothered him a great deal more than the yellow star he had to wear on his chest. He looked pathetic and it was very degrading for him, eroding the last traces of his self-esteem. He hated his own appearance and the stench of aged urine that suffused him. Such humiliations were hard on the once elegant Casanova. Soon he was shuffling around the camp, a broken man.

Rena, for her part, did relatively better, trying to keep her own and her daughters' clothes neat and forever hoping to prop up Edmund, who lived separately from them. Belatedly she understood that she had once projected an image of a cold, selfish socialite, a woman wrapped up in her bridge games and party circuit. Perhaps her posturing had been one of the reasons she was alienated from Edmund. She knew all too well that

Eight. Portrait of the Blue Polka-dot Dress

she could not turn the clock back, but in her own way she tried to make it up to him by showing him more affection and care. Only the cards were stacked against her because Edmund was already far too gone to notice. Fate has a cynical and bizarre sense of humor. What might have made him happy in the past no longer resonated with him. He wished to die. He found the life of a concentration camp inmate exceeded all his coping mechanisms. And he was not alone. A number of middle-aged male inmates, particularly men who were in positions of power before the war, these captains of industry, fell apart faster and more completely than the average, non-privileged men.

No matter how frequently Frances and Lotte attempted to lift their father's spirits he barely noticed their efforts. He didn't know what it took for the young, once carefree and frivolous Lotte to find that way to protect her family. Nor could he grasp the risks Frances took by stealing food from under their captors' noses, nor Rena's efforts to prepare these contraband foodstuffs on the cooker they kept hidden. They would offer him a few spoonfuls of soup or a turnip, but he hardly noticed what his family did to ease his starvation. Although the family had unquestionably fallen on hard times, they had no idea of what was in store for them next.

Sometime in the winter of 1943 Frances came down with what seemed to be tonsillitis or the flu. Initially she denied being unwell but eventually couldn't conceal her swollen knees, wrists and other joints or the fact that she was running very high fevers. Frances, who was the most energetic, indefatigable girl, was now incapacitated, helpless and in pain and the family was at a loss at how to deal with the new disaster. There were excellent physicians in Theresienstadt, and as a matter of fact some were among the best in their fields; but in the camp all their knowledge came to naught, as they had almost no supplies or medications to work with. The camp's hospital was more a hospice and a pre-mortuary station.

Rena was on the verge of a nervous breakdown. Her daughter, her staunch supporter and the self-appointed leader and organizer of the family's vagaries, was ill and unable to fill that role any longer. Rena had no idea how to supplement their meager rations through illicit means or how to spot signs of looming danger in the constantly fluctuating conditions of the camp. All this had been taken care of by the highly intelligent Frances. Rena needed to orient herself in the labyrinth of the camp's intricacies because Edmund was all but lost, loitering and sauntering about like a vagabond without a place to rest his head. By now he was a skinny, smelly, filthy old man, avoided by almost everyone.

What was Rena to do now?

Although she was not the most likely candidate to take charge, Lotte felt the call and tried to rise to the new challenge. While she couldn't hold a candle to Frances, she realized that the fate of her family now rested on her rather unsteady and inadequate shoulders. First things first: Frances's declining health required immediate attention. Luckily, one of Lotte's friends was a physician who nurtured some convoluted connections and was able to pull a few strings. Frances was transferred from the crowded barracks, where she bunked on the upper tier of a wooden bed, to the "Revier," the sick bay, where patients could sleep on narrow cots. Frances was no longer able to clamber up the narrow, rough-hewn wooden rungs to her bunk.

Lotte then scrambled to acquire additional food supplies and hustled for some medicines for Frances while navigating through the dangerous, ever-shifting currents in the camp. All these trials were ongoing for Lotte and no inmate could avert their eyes from the dreadfully repetitive and steadily departing transports to the East. All that was a tall order for anyone and, yes, Lotte did rise up, to a point, to meet what was a mammoth challenge.

Tragically, Lotte could not overcome all of the challenges. She could not find a way to save Frances, as her sister was beyond help due to her grave illness and her run-down condition. In spite of Lotte's valiant efforts, nothing made a difference and day by day Frances grew thinner, becoming almost translucent; her dark eyes shone with a strange, feverish sheen. The few drugs Lotte managed to obtain on the camp's black market failed to improve Frances's condition. Meanwhile, Edmund stumbled in and out of the sick bay, his bloodshot eyes revealing his anguish as he focused on Frances. He felt like such a failure; his dearest child was ill and he couldn't summon help. He couldn't summon a doctor or buy drugs or have her admitted into a decent hospital—all normal duties of a parent for an ill offspring.

Rena hovered over Frances all hours of the day and night, ignoring the medical staff's orders to clear the premises since she was constantly under foot in the crowded sick bay, where one cot was set immediately against the other. On occasion Rena would sit on the cot and cradle Frances in her arms. Frances was no longer slim and elegant; her torso had shriveled, resembling a withering doll. Rena could only hold her child in her arms, whisper a lullaby and words of love, trying anything to bring some comfort to the ailing girl.

Lotte also visited her sister but she had a somewhat strange reaction

Eight. Portrait of the Blue Polka-dot Dress

to her sister's deteriorating health. Every fiber in her body rebelled against seeing Frances when she was so gravely ill. She couldn't sit calmly, even for a moment, in the crowded, smelly sickroom. It was not the decrepitude of the sick bay that was the problem; she was unable to confront the thought that her sister might soon die. She tried to fight the angst of losing Frances, the solid rock of her life, the one person who never failed her and who always seemed to overcome life's hurdles.

Lotte embarked upon feverish activities, jostling for many deals aimed at accumulating food and cigarettes, which she exchanged for medication. With her beauty she easily seduced some gendarmes who gave her better food for barter in the camp. Lotte did not lose the slimmest of chances to help her sister. But nothing seemed to help her improve. Then one afternoon in early April, Lotte felt particularly depressed and miserable. Frances had faded to a mere shadow and even Lotte had to admit that without a miracle her sister would soon die. In her despondency she became so depressed she reached a depth where she felt unable to carry on.

Then she thought of a way to lift her downcast spirit. For the longest time she had nothing decent to wear and trying on clothes always lifted her spirits. What if she was to put on Frances's nice dress, the one she always liked, so elegant and classy when worn by Frances? Frances would never know and she would take extra care not to crease it. She would wear it for a brief moment and then place it back among the few treasured items that Frances secretly stashed away. Frances always placed that particular pale blue dress with tiny polka dots under the straw mattress, a treasure guarded with hawk-eyed attention, a reminder of better days.

Lotte took the pale blue dress out from its hiding place and put it on with great care. She liked the feel of it and, even better, she was pleased with what she saw. The princess-style regalia accentuated her slim figure. For a moment she strutted around the bunks in the barracks, and then she decided to go onto the staircase. Without apparent premeditation she ran down the stairs and all of a sudden, probably on an impulse, she found herself standing in front of the sick bay where Frances was fighting for her life. Perhaps it was force of habit, as her first steps every day led to visit Frances. Within a second or two she forgot her playfulness and stepped in to say hello to her sister. Frances's appearance gave her a hard jolt, for her sister's face bore no resemblance to the girl she was even a few weeks ago. Lotte bent down, kissed the burning cheeks of her ailing sister, and straightened a few loose strands of her dark, matted hair that were falling in waves down around her drawn face.

Suddenly Lotte noticed two large tears rolling down Frances's cheeks. Did Frances notice Lotte's horrified reaction to her appearance? Lotte was unsure and whispered a few endearing words and ran hurriedly away. It was only when she was standing outside that Lotte realized she was still wearing Frances's favorite dress. For a moment or two she stopped, frozen in dread. Did Frances notice? Was she upset about her sister's apparent indiscretion? She stood there paralyzed like Lot's wife, almost becoming a pillar of salt like that biblical sinner. Lotte dismissed the notion that Frances in her delirium even noticed what her whimsical, undisciplined sister was wearing. She was way too ill to pay attention to clothing, wasn't she? This rationale calmed her somewhat, and Lotte made a beeline back to the barracks. She took off her sister's dress gingerly, putting the polka-dot garment carefully back under the mattress after straightening every seam, and changed back into her own smock. But for the rest of the day she couldn't find her peace, becoming obsessed with the notion that Frances noticed her wearing the dress.

Evening came and Lotte sat on her bunk next to her mother, both sipping the watery soup that was their only meal of the day. For the longest time they sat in silence. But Lotte could no longer stand the quiet. "Did you visit Frances today, Mom?" The tired Rena nodded yes. "Of course I did, I am there every free moment of my day." "How was Frances? Did she speak to you?" "Hardly. She only whispered, 'Today I saw my dress flash by my bed.'" Lotte was stunned. Frances had noticed and was pained by her sister's stupidity and vanity. Mother and daughter exchanged horrified looks. "How could you have done this, Lotte?"

Lotte began to weep inconsolably, putting her head on her mother's shoulder. "I don't know what possessed me to put the dress on. I did not want to go visit Frances wearing it, only somehow I forgot what I had on and ran down to find out how was Frances was doing. You have to believe me, Mom, please, you have to!" Lotte was sobbing, gasping for air, clearly in emotional pain, staring at Rena with imploring eyes. Rena nodded wearily. "It matters little what I believe. The problem is how Frances interpreted you wearing her dress. She probably believes that you consider her to be dead already. She is well aware that the likelihood of her recovery is almost zero and she is in pain and tragically we cannot help. I know, my child, that you were just thoughtless and of late, perhaps understandably, you are often bitter and acrimonious, but I also know that you love Frances with all your heart and would never do something so horrendously cruel if you had given it serious consideration. I know you, my

Eight. Portrait of the Blue Polka-dot Dress

child, but Frances is well aware that she is in dire straits. Your stupid prancing in her dress could not have come at a worse time." Having said that, Rena began to weep too, in silent, heaving sobs of a brokenhearted woman fearing for her daughter's survival in the most barbarous place under the sun.

The fates proved Rena right. Not only did Frances perish a few weeks after that sordid mishap, but Edmund followed her in rapid sequence. The day the hearse carted off Frances's corpse was the saddest day of Lotte's entire existence and, although she lived many long years thereafter, she mourned her sister all her life. The sorrow Lotte experienced as a result of Frances's passing was different from the grief she felt when her parents died. Frances was Lotte's greatest supporter, who kept her on the straight and narrow. Lotte retained her childish faith in her sister until Frances drew her last breath. Little could go wrong when Frances was around and if there was a fly in the ointment Frances would know a way to fix any and all problems. Frances's passing left Lotte feeling like a rudderless ship.

Rena met her Maker only a few months after Edmund passed away. She was released from her earthly suffering while asleep; God gave her a smooth and painless final exit. Lotte took comfort in the fact that her mom was spared the awareness that she was leaving behind a young woman having to cope with the Nazis all alone.

Unlike the rest of her family, Lotte survived the war but her orphaned existence was not a happy one. Until her dying day she never forgave herself for having worn the blue polka-dot dress and Frances's words continued to ring in her ears. Every time she recalled her sister, in her mind she heard, "Today I saw my dress flash by my bed." These words tormented Lotte. Her silly vanity and desire for excitement and beauty cost her dearly, for, rightly or not, then and there she lost her peace of mind. Lotte remained convulsed with shame, believing that Frances died disappointed in her, perceiving her to be a selfish brat who could hardly wait for her sister to die so she could appropriate her favorite blue polka-dot dress. Lotte would never buy anything pale blue or with a dotted pattern for the remainder of her life.

This poignant episode was unfortunately not the only one Lotte could never forget from her time as an inmate. There was another fleeting moment from her life in the camp that was seared into her heart and mind.

This moment occurred when Frances was already ill and Lotte was the sole provider for the family. Hearsay circulating actively in the camp suggested that within days thousands of Theresienstadt's inmates would be deported to the East. Lotte recognized the looming danger and set out to find someone, anyone, who could provide a ruse and pretext to keep them in the camp. In the invariably changing tides of the powerful in the camp, Lotte maintained a vigilant lookout for those in positions who could shelter them at a moment's notice. With her ingenuity, she soon zeroed in on a member of the Judenrat who was rumored to have a roving eye and fondness for pretty girls.

With the instinct of a fox, Lotte found her prey and began to work on him. She realized she would be an even more alluring conquest if she emphasized her privileged background. Lotte chatted with him amicably, embellishing her upper-class past. He seemed captivated by her as they talked in front of the Magdeburg barrack. Lotte was fully absorbed by her bid to charm the man who could prevent their deportation and failed to notice Rena standing nearby, watching her with a sad expression on her face. It was her companion who observed Rena's intense gaze in Lotte's direction and asked, "Look, Lotte, that old woman over there seems to know you. Is she an acquaintance?" Lotte saw her mother all right, but felt that her pathetic appearance and worn, dirty clothes would diminish Lotte's standing in the eyes of the man she needed to impress. So she nonchalantly quipped, "That woman over there is just a pathetic Sieche I sometimes give a piece of bread."

Having called Rena in camp parlance a "bag lady," she turned abruptly, hoping to send a message to her mother that this was a bad time to acknowledge her. Rena understood implicitly and slowly dragged herself away, one small, despondent step at a time, occasionally turning to see if Lotte had changed her mind. She understood all too well that she was an embarrassment to her daughter. The once elegant black coat, a creation of one of Prague's famous fashion houses, hung so loosely around her withering torso she could have wrapped it twice around herself now. Smudges and smears defaced the garment, for she no longer took care or pride in her looks and hadn't for a very long time. Rena gave herself an honest check and agreed with Lotte. She looked and acted the part of a "Sieche," a run-down inmate who had lost their self-respect. Rena was not angry with Lotte, who so obviously felt the need to deny their tie; she was only saddened by the truth of her expression. If she still had a spark that could ignite anger it would have been directed at God and destiny rather than her one surviving daughter. What did she do to anyone that left her to this fate? She did not deserve to suffer such pain, a mother's pain, the loss of her magnificent firstborn, the creeping, slow murder of her husband, and her own obvious decline. She had become a starving beggar, slinking about the camp obsessed with only one drive in mind: to find or steal a bread crumb or a potato peel, to calm the incessant hunger. Most certainly her only surviving child had the right to deny her and be deeply ashamed of her. Rena accepted that she had fallen to arguably one of the lowest forms of humanity and therefore Lotte's rejection was appropriate and fully justified.

Not long thereafter Rena, too, joined her Maker.

Matters were not quite as simple for Lotte. Once she ended the desperate conversation trying to impress the powerful man, she began to feel a rising disgust within herself. Why did she pretend not to know her own mother? Why was she convinced that he had to act like just another selfish jerk who automatically condemned her mom to be one of the many starving, slowly dying, elderly inmates? Yet because she was overtaken by the urgent need to handle the peril of upcoming deportation she suppressed all these questions and doubts, trying to focus on the task at hand and remain pragmatic and energetic. She could ill afford self-doubt or the luxury of caving in under the enormity of guilt in denying one's own mother. This justification and rationalization worked for the duration of her incarceration.

Later in life she couldn't erase the image of the emaciated, unkempt Rena, her mother, whom she rebuffed, even momentarily, because she looked like a lost soul who would jeopardize her plan. All her life Lotte suffered profound guilt for having worn the blue polka-dot dress and for having rejected her own mother. The nights were worse yet for Lotte. In her dreams Lotte met Frances and tried to explain to her that she didn't grab her favorite dress, that she only tried it on to chase away depressing thoughts and then forgot to take it off as she ran to visit her. The Frances of Lotte's nightmare was nothing like the kind and understanding sibling she remembered, though. The Frances Lotte met during her long nightmares was stern, tough, unforgiving and scrutinized Lotte with reproachful eyes. If Frances could not forgive her, surely Lotte could not hope for absolution of her wartime indiscretions in her postwar life. Things were somewhat easier when she saw Rena in their frequent night encounters, for although her mother's eyes were always brimming with tears, she looked at Lotte with love.

Even though the war ended officially in 1945, for Lotte these events lived on within her, clouding the remainder of her life. During her days she drifted from place to place and person to person unable to find a home. In the privacy of her nights, she met, talked and lived with the two closest and dearest people of her life and continued to believe that she had wronged and hurt them during the lowest point of all their lives.

QUESTIONS AND ANSWERS

It is tragic that an action that was not meant to hurt seemed to have the same effect as if it was intended to cause pain. Even more, Lotte was hurt herself by the realization of her mistake. Yet is there any moral difference given that the outcome (namely her sister's being upset) was the same?

We first have to understand the state of mind of the two sisters and the duress where they saw a gradual decline of their father and mother unfolding in front of their eyes that they couldn't full well help. The older one, Frances, was usually in the leadership position, but eventually with her illness that too would be taken away from the family. So the state of mind of the ailing older sister lying in a place where sick people would be brought because they could no longer climb the ladders to the three tier bunks was very bitter for her because she knew as an intelligent young woman there was no help for her. To be convinced one is dying at such an inappropriate age, leaving two helpless aging parents behind and a sister whom she certainly perceived as perhaps less competent to fill in for her must have been upsetting Frances a great deal. Of course, in addition to this was the fact that she was in pain and there were no means to diminish the pain since there were no painkillers or any medications given to people who came down with whatever aliment. So when suddenly she noticed her rather flighty, easygoing sister had taken the one possession she left behind, this favorite blue polka-dotted dress, it upset her and brought her misery at the end of her life, more so than perhaps under normal circumstances when she wouldn't care—if she had been healthy. This misery was that her sister had deliberately or inadvertently taken the dress and walked with it. Perhaps Frances wanted a moment from her own past, when she was able to dress nicely and look after herself. Surely she would have understood her sister's act if things had been normal. But at that point her life was almost being taken away from her and so she interpreted this inadvertent step by Lotte as reflecting that Frances was already dead and gone and no longer had any influence in life. That must have been very bitter for a young woman. So the hurt she felt due to her sister's taking for a short time her dress was only accentuated by her terrible condition, and that

Eight. Portrait of the Blue Polka-dot Dress

was kind of hurt she interpreted herself—that even her own loving sister no longer believed in her recovery.

There is no real moral judgment here. Lotte did not do this to her sister to hurt her sister; she was distracted and perhaps poorly concentrated and not as serious as her older sister. But there was no intent, so there wasn't any moral failing of Lotte although her sister perceived it as such. And perhaps sometimes we do inadvertently hurt people by our thoughtlessness or by being distracted—we say thing or do things people interpret in a different way. And there was no way for Lotte to explain to Frances that it wasn't that she perceived her as already gone, but that only for a fleeting moment she wanted to put on something nice, wanted again to feel like a girl, not like the inmate she was, fighting for a bread crumb or a little bit of soup, and that it was just a mishap, not to be morally judged. But all of this happened because of the context of Frances dying in a hopeless situation.

Given this hell that inmates found themselves in, is it appropriate for people who were not there to make any comments or judgments about what was morally right and morally wrong?

I believe that people who were never in a similar predicament cannot really understand and therefore cannot pass judgment on things have transpired in situations of that abnormality in Nazi concentration camps. I think that unless you were there and understand how life in this antechamber of death was unfolding you have real difficulties grasping it and therefore you cannot judge or comment on anybody's deeds. For example, of course taking food away from a child is wrong and it is wrong in any situation, even in the darkest days of depravity in a Nazi concentration camp. And helping others of course was right, but I think people had very limited strength and possibilities to help others. We were moving in the pressure cooker lifestyle of running to and fro because the Germans never left us any time to relax, trying to figure out our next step and how next to prevent deportation to a death camp and how next perhaps to find someone who can barter a piece of bread for fixing their shoes that were falling apart. It was an abnormal life very few people can imagine.

How might your answer to question two inform us about the moral quality of, and our assessment of, the actions of those directly or indirectly responsible for the camps and who put people such as those described in this book in these types of situations?

Well, you know this is a multilayered reply. First of all, the crime, by way of the groundwork of the Nazi party, was of devaluing Jewish life and the decision to eliminate Jews from all walks of life in Europe and eventually all over the world. This is the first and heaviest guilt any man can inflict on another man. There were of course those people who put the anti-Semitic ways or anti-Jewish laws into reality and they were guilty as charged of the murder of millions. There's no reprieve, no explanation, no pardon for those who legislated and eventually helped to put into actuality or reality the Nazi policy against Jews. Then, of course, as this policy came into reality and began to be organized, there was the guilt of participation and cooperation coming through the ranks as the Nazis established the concentration camps. In some of those situations it was for Jews only; in others, there were other prisoners as well. But, of course, for the non-Jewish prisoner, that is, the criminal, habitual criminal, or for whatever reason they were there, they were superior to, and had better treatment than, the Jew.

In the ranks of people who were appointed to run these camps, the commandants who always had entourages of people around them who not only guarded us but also implemented the orders, these people all were guilty of the violation of human rights. There were witnesses to the mass genocide, there were witnesses to the brutality and cruelty inflicted on people, which in any civilized society is prohibited, and they were partaking in it. And some of them were even tormenting inmates because they had sadistic inclinations. But it was the only place where they could have discharged them and they did that frequently with no consequences.

The guilt repeated through their ranks. The commandant had his entourage, then these had appointed people who were Kapo, which is an abbreviation of the German words *comrade* and *polizei*. The Kapo were men, usually habitual felons, who were given supervisory positions for different barracks. All these people were responsible for a certain part of the camp's functioning, be it for an entire block or being responsible for going with people, bringing inmates for factories or mines or quarries where they worked. These were the people appointed by the block elders or the administrative hierarchy of the camp. So slowly we are coming from the people who signed on to the destruction of Jewish life in the Wannsee conference of 1942 down to a felon, a brutal murderer, who now is in charge and can at his will and liberty murder any inmate or any number of inmates, as pleases him. Then, of course, eventually the guilt would be brought down even further. You can think of people who were perhaps employed

Eight. Portrait of the Blue Polka-dot Dress

around food and appropriated more than what was their share in exchange for some other items they would have liked to have. So any single person in a camp who had some function in charge of inmates and was misusing this power was guilty of a capital crime because the inmates were defenseless; they had no recourse; they could not complain anywhere and if they had said any word they would have been killed on the spot.

So the guilt is multilayered and applies to a vast number of people who were employed in this tragic murder industry Hitler had created. And they were all guilty in the way I believe. It doesn't matter if you torment many or you torment one. You are guilty. You are sadistic. And you are liable to be punished and you are supposed to be prosecuted. But of course in the German universe, in Auschwitz and other camps, these were the people who ruled.

Was there a feeling of moral guilt common amongst survivors?

With the case of Frances and Lotte we have an individual case of an inadvertent omission of thinking and what she was doing with the only possession her ailing sister had: the polka-dot dress. But I think there were, of course, individual cases where people may have had situations in which they felt they could have perhaps helped a little more or tried to do something for the relative who obviously didn't make it and didn't survive the Nazi concentration camps. But this is very difficult.

People are talking about survivor's guilt—perhaps people felt "everybody died so why did I survive?" I think this: I never quite understood why this would be the overwhelming sentiment of a survivor. Those of us who survived by the skin of our teeth really did so and were liberated at virtually the last moment. So I think that, talking from my own personal experience, I always looked back at the tragedy and the fifty family members I lost with a deep pain and sorrow but I didn't feel guilt. I knew I tried to do my best with the very limited possibilities I had, to ease their pain, to facilitate the dying so it was somehow less painful or less terrible. But I don't think I could have done more as a teenager in a camp in which death was the only outcome of whatever you had done. And I think survivor's guilt many times was debated after the war that must be rooted in some different level, that perhaps they were not meritorious to have survived and somehow better people had died. And this is, of course, a very common sentiment amongst survivors because so many wonderful people who had so much to offer and could do so much for humanity perished in those dark places. And those of us who survived, sadly we didn't feel we were better qualified or had any better right or didn't quite compare to any other for this type of privilege. I think eventually every survivor did realize that survival was just a matter of luck; there was nothing we might have thought or could have done.

People did many things to survive and needed to do lots of things to survive—yet few report doing what we would call horrible or immoral. What happened here was not "horrible" in the grand scheme of things but clearly weighed heavily on Lotte. Did others who did worse things justify or rationalize their behavior and what should we make of those arguments?

How people behaved under duress of course very much depends on their character and moral fiber from their past. The pressure of the overpowering guilt Lotte felt was mainly based on the fact that she perceived one of the last things or interactions she had was negative and must have appeared to her sister as selfish, vain, and superficial at a time when her life was on the line and she knew that she likely would not live. That guilt was perhaps accentuated by the fact that she did little or could have done very little for her sister and what had transpired was of a negative nature and added to the pain of her sister, who already was in the last stage of her life. But now, getting into the general observation of behavior in camps, the brutal conditions sometimes bring out the worst in people and a lot has been reported of people's brutality, especially the German officers and the Kapo who were in charge of the fences and helpless prisoners. A lot of very low things were done and some people who were having sadistic inclinations were entrusted with positions to oversee the inmates and they of course often let go with their pathological inclination to inflict pain, out of which they drew their personal satisfaction. So in dark situations like this the scum is kind of flushed up and regain power and regain positions that they should never in normal life be afforded. But it is known in jails and many other institutions that sometimes people who are powerful are power hungry and sometimes they enjoy the possibility.

Edmund's business associates did not help even though money did not seem to be a problem. Can we generalize from this example, namely that it was hard for anyone who was Jewish to get out from under the Nazi shadow even before the war? What does this tell us?

This is another painful and shameful chapter in world history, because even before the Nazis occupied Czechoslovakia it was obvious not only to the Czechoslovakian Jews but also Jews in most parts of Europe that

Eight. Portrait of the Blue Polka-dot Dress

there was no future for Jewish life in Europe and the wisest thing to do was to leave. And it wasn't only a question of money. People who had astronomical amounts of money found it easier to get or buy visas to some countries or to certain parts or the world; for example, the Dominican Republic had accepted people with a certain amount of assets. But for the most part, Europe, and not only Europe but the world in those days, had a hardened attitude toward immigrants. Unfortunately, nobody was willing to open the gates and offer some haven to the beleaguered Jew of Europe. This is a shameful chapter that spreads the guilt of the annihilation of the six million to a very wide population, as nobody deemed it imperative to, at for least some, widen the quarters of who was taken in.

One might argue that Lotte's dismissal of her mother as a "bag lady" was not so wrong in that she was trying to assist the family by being appealing to someone from a higher class. What if she had succeeded in getting extra food? Would that have made right the apparent wrong done?

Again I think it was a subjective feeling of having let down, or being ashamed of, her parent. I think this is always very difficult on a son or daughter to have to deny or be embarrassed by the appearance of a parent and in that case, of course, the parent was totally not responsible for her rundown condition. It was not her personal neglect; it was what the circumstances did to her, this one-time elegant lady, someone who really looked like a vagrant roaming in the streets. Lotte was trying desperately to establish contact with people who had power. There was of course a hierarchy of different classes, and those people who were entrusted by the Nazis to be in power for some time were most of them the Judenrat (and different camps had different names for their functionaries). These people for the time being had a better life. They had larger rations of food. They had the least crowded and less horrendous living quarters. And of course for the time of their functioning they were sheltered from deportation to the East. All of this was enormously attractive to everyone because people didn't think in terms of long life survival; people were thinking just in terms of easing that one day.

Of course, if she had been successful in achieving her goal, maybe protecting her family from deportation or getting extra food, that would have made the "wrong" right. Well, you know a lot of it is the idea that the end justified the means, and in camps people were quite aware of this. This is because, food or additional food was a matter of life and death; so was deportation to the death camps. So if we think life is sacrosanct and if we are to fight for ours and those we love dearest, then, yes, it would have made it right, and any sacrifice would have been right.

One wonders what sort of physical and mental state people would be in, starving under such horrible conditions, and how one could be physically able to use sex as a commodity. How different or changed were people in Theresienstadt than what we would normally think of in everyday life? In other words, did the Nazis ever succeed in dehumanizing persons—other than themselves?

I certainly would confess that they did succeed at dehumanizing some, but again you have to consider the circumstances people were living in, not for days or weeks but for months and years. If you live for years in conditions of physical deterioration and fear for your own life and are fully aware a nearly all-powerful state machine is dead-set on killing you, this changes a lot of your personality and of course your priorities and values. So I think that the Nazis had succeed in some cases to affect people's character, but I don't think there was a generalized dehumanization, particularly in Theresienstadt, where people so desperately tried to hang on to their past and the world they once believed they belonged to. Later, further down in those death camps, I think our humanity bit the dust. I think that you see, day in and day out, coming and going and being forced into gas chambers and then the bodies being cremated and the ashes thrown around—that has got to affect anyone. And even short exposure to it would perhaps cause great changes, at least for the duration that the person is exposed to it.

Afterword
by Vera Schiff

> I hope after reading this work you can see how the Holocaust should not be characterized as being the same for every victim and survivor. It may have been a monolithic event involving many actors and actions but it reveals (among other things) not just the loss of those who loved and were loved but also of morally significant resistance.—*Jeff McLaughlin*

How do we remember?

What we know to be history is only as complete as the stories of the men and women who lived it. I watch with concern that the narrative of the Holocaust has been limited by stereotypes that reduce the chronicle to the fates of the famous few whose stories only reveal part of the truth.

This is at the expense of accuracy and compromises the scope of history.

The Holocaust is a one of a kind misfortune that should remain a watershed in human evolution.

Early after the end of World War II there came into public domain a diary of a young girl, Anne Frank, who penned her impressions while in place of hiding in an attic in Amsterdam. As it was the first such document, written by an innocent victim, it became an instant symbol of the Holocaust and remains such. The house in which she and her family took cover became a shrine, visited by many year after year. Many latched onto Anne's script as she professes faith in goodness of man. Yet her personal narrative does not reveal the full tragedy that ensued. Few stop to ponder if she would have had made similar observations while she was an inmate in Bergen-Belsen, where and when she drew her last breath.

Her diary, translated into many languages, is read by students all over the world. We must remember that her diary discloses only a small and selected fraction of the Holocaust.

Similarly another icon of the Holocaust, Elie Wiesel, published *Night* in 1956, while most survivors were trying to eke out a meager living and were not ready or able to write down their experiences.

I am not an iconoclast and I do admire Anne Frank and Elie Wiesel very much. My objection is that their accounts are only a tiny part of the whole, but somehow have become the symbolic representation of the period. I would like to offer some other notable and perhaps more typical reactions of inmates to their unlawful persecution.

The concentration camp Auschwitz-Birkenau became internationally known as a place that connotes hell on earth. It surely was a dreadful site, but believe it not, there were much worse camps in the Nazi fiefdom. Every student of history knows of Auschwitz but few were ever told about the death camps like those at Treblinka, Chelmno, and Belzec, where the gassing upon arrival was preceded by beatings, and torture of those who had just dismounted the trains. In Auschwitz there was at least some chance to have death briefly delayed by selection for hard labor that gave to some deferment of death for a short time.

But only Auschwitz is widely known and so it became a symbol of the Devil's workshop on earth. Many more were murdered by the Einsatzgruppen than in Auschwitz, yet the world chooses to see the Holocaust through the prism of Auschwitz.

What is missing in the public's narrow historiography of the Holocaust is a compilation of reports about resistance to the violence inflicted on Jews by the perpetrators.

1. Attempted uprisings in ghettos and camps including Ghetto Warsaw, Bialystok, the concentration camp Treblinka and the Sonderkommando uprising in Auschwitz. All were unsuccessful, shut down by the Nazis, but valiantly fought by the rebels.
2. Escapees attempting to inform the world: 1944 Auschwitz: Rudolf Vrba and Alfred Wetzler were sponsored by the underground of the camp, and charged with the duty to deliver accurate information about the genocide in Auschwitz to President Roosevelt, Prime Minister Churchill and the Pope. Their mission was accomplished, but there was no response by the free world, in part because the leaders couldn't, or wouldn't, believe it.
3. The 1944 escape by Viteslav Lederer from Auschwitz, who had a

message to Red Cross about the genocide. Successfully accomplished, but no response or help to the inmates.
4. Women inmates in Auschwitz who were assigned to work in munitions factories smuggled in small amounts of dynamite daily with which they hoped to stage explosions of the gas chambers. The explosion took place but the women were caught, tortured and already near-death were dragged into the camp for public hanging.
5. Inmates assigned to factories manufacturing ammunition routinely sabotaged the work flow by slowing it down, and producing defective goods.
6. The world does not appreciate or perhaps does not know about the artistic gesture of defiance by inmates of Majdanek, the most terrible hellhole on earth. The inmates' morale was sinking dangerously low when some alert men concluded that there was a need for an inspirational symbol. A graphic designer created a cast image of a bird and filled the hollow space within with the ash of murdered inmates. The underground of the camp advised the inmates on their the daily marching by commandos to salute the statuette, and in that way to honor the fallen comrades and at the same time to draw hope that one day they will soar just as the bird will, whose image they daily greeted. While free people may not quite understand the enormous boost such an act can offer, long term inmates would testify how much this kind of symbol would lift their spirits.
7. Perhaps these measures of rebelliousness seem insignificant but if you battle an overwhelming superiority without a fighting chance *any* act is weighty and meaningful.

Events of sabotage in Theresienstadt, a showcase camp, were more elaborate.

There were several attempts to flee the camp. Most failed abysmally until one inmate hit upon an idea to use a pipe attached to the outside of a barrack. It was a cosmetic feature planned to impress the Red Cross visitors, supposed to imply that there was a water supply. In reality it was just a fake pipe, not a water carrying conduit. One man succeeded in climbing down the pipe, and another one followed suit. The Nazis decided to sabotage other potential copycats. They did not remove the pipe, but cut it in the middle, so that anyone descending it to apparent freedom instead fell down a deep pothole to his death.

There were many high profile inmates in this transit camp. Many artists were kept for a while in Theresienstadt, just in case the world were to inquire about their whereabouts.

There were musicians, eminent before their deportation like Rafael Schaechter, Karel Schwenk, Viktor Ullman Gideon Klein, and many others.

Schaechter pushed for use of music in a chorus he established by teaching the group by rote the words of Verdi's composition *Requiem*. The words promise justice delivered by the Eternal God. The inmates were greatly stimulated by the prospect that their suffering would be avenged. Also it was Schaechter's initiative to involve children by bringing into their days the children's opera *Brundibár*.

All compositions were chosen to instill hope and bolster the sagging morale of the starving, deathbound inmates.

Ullman wrote the music to the theme of Emperor of Atlanta, in which we find a ruler so cruel that even Death, refuses to do her job, repelled by the savagery of this inhuman emperor. Schwenk composed another allegory titled "The Last Cyclist." A work implying that a crazy ruler aspires to kill all the cyclists bar one for placing blame for all the shortcomings on them.

Schwenk also penned an anthem of the camp that was full of promise for a better tomorrow. We the inmates drew strength from the words suggesting that the day will come when we will laugh on the wreck of the camp.

Few can understand the power of music that brings back the world of yesteryear, emboldening the disheartened inmates.

Then there was the bold sabotage of Nazi orders not to teach the children. There were quite a few educators, onetime teachers who took it upon themselves to defy the Nazi ban, to teach the poor kids who were prisoners in this dark, one time fortress. The handful of men and women charged with the duty to look after the children were the unsung heroes of this tragic era. They disguised lessons as play that the Nazis overlooked.

These educators transformed the bleak day of children who were hungry, cold and sickly into a meaningful time of creativity and learning.

Not only did the kids enthusiastically perform in the opera *Brundibár*, they took joy in acting in another play *The Fireflies*. The older youth were guided to concentrate on serious topics and participate in discussions of challenging issues. Their poems, stories, drawings show the bottled up talent of those kids, most of whom later died. Long after they perished their work was found stored in luggage and today it is on display at the Theresienstadt Museum, prompting tears over the talent that was not allowed to develop.

All these acts of resistance to the brutal rule were inspirational and encouraging to those who had no fighting chance.

I cannot conclude this brief essay without a mention of the painters of Theresienstadt, the brave men and women who risked their lives to preserve the image of the camp.

Among the celebrities imprisoned in Theresienstadt were some great painters whom the Nazis forced to produce propaganda posters for glorification of the Third Reich. These men had to comply but they used their assignments to pilfer some canvases to depict the true face of the camp. Leo Haas, Peter Kien, Bedrich Fritta, Otto Ungar, Karel Fleischman, and others used the canvases to draw the real unadorned faces of the camps, revealing the hunger, the dying and misery and abysmal wretchedness. These works were meant to document the reality of camp for posterity, and were hidden and buried deep in the grounds. Somehow the Nazis got wind of it, and unearthed the clandestinely hidden drawings. What followed was an unimaginable retribution. The artists were rounded up, brought into the high security prison and tortured. Their hands were mutilated; their fingernails were ripped out, their hands beaten with mallets. Only Leo Haas survived; all the others were murdered. Their courage to resist should be honored and remembered.

We must recall and record the acts of defiance that characterized the stance of the victims. It would be immoral to forget their courage and bravery.

Auschwitz was not a killing field that could be sanitized and decades later pointed to, with its manicured green grasses and silent trees, as if to announce "there, there is where it happened." There were not only a few bad Nazis, rather the world was filled with many who were complicit. Humanity constantly struggles with its base instincts that can only be reversed by moral fortitude and strong character, and a willingness to remember.

Jews should be seen as victims but not just as victims. They fought to maintain their humanity and morality in the most dire circumstances, none of their making.

Vera Schiff 3/01/2017

Appendix:
Theresienstadt Timeline

In 1780 the Austro-Hungarian Emperor Joseph II built a walled military garrison in the province of Bohemia near the Sudeten mountain range. He named it "Theresienstadt," after his mother, Empress Maria Theresa.

October 1–10, 1938   Nazi Germany occupies and annexes the Sudetenland in accordance with the provisions of the Munich Agreement of September 29, 1938. The Sudetenland consisted of the border regions of the Czechoslovak provinces of Bohemia and Moravia, directly adjacent to the territory of the Greater German Reich. The Bohemian city of Leitmeritz (Litomerice), on the new border between the Greater German Reich and the Czecho-Slovak state, lay within the Sudeten lands.

March 15, 1939   Nazi Germany occupies the remainder of the Czech provinces and establishes the Protectorate of Bohemia and Moravia as part of the Greater German Reich. The Czech garrison town of Theresienstadt (Terezín), less than a mile southeast of Litomerice, is located within the protectorate near the extended German border.

October 10, 1941   RSHA (Reich Main Security Office) chief Reinhard Heydrich expresses his preference for Theresienstadt as the site for a Jewish "settlement" for those German, Austrian, and Czech Jews who were:
1. over 65 years of age;
2. disabled or highly decorated World War I veterans; or
3. of sufficient regional, national or international celebrity to encourage domestic and foreign inquiry.

Heydrich tasks the Gestapo office IV B 4, under Adolf Eichmann, and the Prague Office for Jewish Emigration, under Rolf Günther, with the establishment and management of the Theresienstadt camp-ghetto.

October 17, 1941 The SS and police send the first transport of Czech Jews to the East, from Prague to the Lodz ghetto.

October 30, 1941 Heydrich appoints (SS) First Lieutenant Siegfried Seidl as commandant of the camp-ghetto.

November 16, 1941 The SS and police deport the sixth transport of Czech Jews to the East, from Brno to Minsk, Belorussia: 5,997 or 5,998 persons are on the six transports.

November 24, 1941 The first Jewish construction detachment arrives in Theresienstadt.

November 24, 1941–April 15, 1945 The SS and police deport to Theresienstadt between 73,608 and 75,958 Czech Jews residing in the Protectorate of Bohemia and Moravia.

December 4, 1941 Eichmann appoints Prague Zionist leader Jakob Edelstein chairperson of the Council of Jewish Elders, responsible for the "self-administration" of Theresienstadt. Edelstein arrives in Theresienstadt.

January 9, 1942 SS authorities send the first transport of Protectorate Jews, carrying 1,005 people, from Theresienstadt to the East, specifically to Riga, Latvia.

January 9, 1942–October 22, 1942 The SS and police deport approximately 42,005 people, most of them Jews residing in the Protectorate, from Theresienstadt to killing sites, killing centers, concentration camps, and forced-labor camps in the Baltic States, Belorussia, and the General government. Two hundred twenty-four are known to have survived the Holocaust (one-half of 1 percent of those deported).

January 20, 1942 RSHA chief Heydrich announces the existence and propaganda purpose of Theresienstadt to officials of the SS, the Nazi Party, and the German state gathered to discuss the implementation of the "Final Solution" policy—the annihilation of the European Jews—at the Wannsee Conference at a villa just outside Berlin.

June 2, 1942 The first transport of German Jews—50 from Berlin—arrives at Theresienstadt.

June 20, 1942 The first transport of Austrian Jews—between 996 and 1,000 from Vienna—arrives at Theresienstadt.

June 2, 1942–April 15, 1945   SS and police authorities deport approximately 58,087 Jews from the Greater German Reich (excluding Protectorate Jews) to Theresienstadt (Germany: 41,783; Austria: 15,266; Sudetenland: 611; German-annexed Luxembourg: 310; Danzig: 117)

July 14, 1942   The SS and police send the first transport containing German Jews from Theresienstadt to the East, specifically to Minsk.

October 26, 1942–October 28, 1944   German SS and police deport approximately 46,750 Jews from Theresienstadt to Auschwitz-Birkenau in 27 transports. Approximately 23,670 had been residents of the so-called Greater German Reich and 18,500 residents of the Protectorate of Bohemia and Moravia. Perhaps 3,450 survived.

January 1943   Eichmann appoints Paul Eppstein from Berlin and Benjamin Murmelstein from Vienna as co-chairpersons with Edelstein of the Council of Jewish Elders in Theresienstadt.

1943–1944   A total of 4,897 Jews arrive in Theresienstadt from The Netherlands via Westerbork or Bergen-Belsen. Those transported include a minority of German Jews who had emigrated to The Netherlands in the 1930s and three French Jews.

August 24, 1943   Polish Jewish children totaling 1,260, seized by the SS and police during the liquidation of the Bialystok ghetto, arrive in Theresienstadt. The SS management selects 53 ghetto residents to act as caregivers. On October 5, 1943, the SS authorities responsible for the camp-ghetto deported 1,196 surviving children and their 53 caregivers to Auschwitz. None survive.

October 1943   Approximately 456 Danish Jews rounded up in Denmark the previous month arrive in Theresienstadt. Twenty more Danish Jews will join them in Theresienstadt in 1944 via the Oranienburg and Ravensbrück concentration camps.

December 15, 1943   The SS sends Jakob Edelstein, co-chairperson of the Council of Jewish Elders, to Auschwitz on the deportation train leaving Theresienstadt on this day. Auschwitz camp authorities murder Edelstein on December 20, 1943.

May 15–18, 1944   The SS and police deport approximately 7,503 prisoners from Theresienstadt to Auschwitz to lessen crowding in the camp-ghetto in preparation for a visit by the Red Cross.

June 23, 1944 Two representatives of the International Red Cross and one representative of the Danish Red Cross visit Theresienstadt. The International Red Cross later issues a bland report about the visit, indicating that the two representatives were taken in by the elaborate fiction.

August–October 1944 Slovak underground organizations rise up against the Germans and the puppet Slovak regime. The Germans use the opportunity to deport most of the remaining Slovak Jews to Auschwitz via the Sered transit camp.

September 27, 1944 The SS shoots Paul Eppstein, the representative leader of the German Jews and co-chairperson of the Council of Jewish Elders in Theresienstadt.

September 28, 1944–October 28, 1944 The SS deports approximately 18,402 Theresienstadt prisoners to Auschwitz. Approximately 1,574 survive the war. By the end of October, approximately 11,077 Jews remain in the camp-ghetto.

December 1944–January 1945 Approximately 416 Slovak Jews arrive in Theresienstadt from Sered.

December 1944 Murmelstein becomes chairperson of the Council of Jewish Elders in Theresienstadt, with the German-Jewish theologian and philosopher Leo Baeck as deputy chairperson.

February 5, 1945 The RSHA transports approximately 1,200 Jews from Theresienstadt to Switzerland.

March 8, 1945 Between 1,070 and 1,150 Hungarian Jews deported to the Austrian border in 1944 arrive in Theresienstadt.

March 1945 International Red Cross representatives visit Theresienstadt to negotiate authority to provide food and other necessities for the prisoners of the camp-ghetto and the release of some prisoners.

April 1945 With the evacuation of the Sered transit camp, the SS transports the remaining (approximately 1,031) Slovak Jewish prisoners to Theresienstadt.

April 6 and 21, 1945 International Red Cross representatives visit Theresienstadt.

April 14–15, 1945 Trucks hired by the Swedish Red Cross pick up approximately 423 surviving Danish Jews in Theresienstadt and transport them back to Denmark.

April 20–May 11, 1945 Between 13,500 and 15,000 concentration camp prisoners evacuated from Buchenwald and Gross-Rosen subcamps arrive in Theresienstadt, increasing the camp population to approximately 30,000. Most, but not all, of the prisoners are Jewish.

April 30, 1945 Nazi dictator Adolf Hitler commits suicide in Berlin.

May 2, 1945 German troops in Berlin surrender to Soviet forces.

May 2, 1945 SS commandant Rahm relinquishes the administration of the camp to the International Red Cross.

May 5, 1945 The Council of Jewish Elders dissolves and Murmelstein ceases his activity after a last meeting with Rahm. Leo Baeck takes over.

May 5–6, 1945 Commandant Rahm, the SS staff, and Czech gendarmes abandon the camp-ghetto, though the inhabitants remain in danger from radical remnants of the Wehrmacht and Waffen SS as Soviet troops advance on Prague and Leitmeritz.

May 7, 1945 Nazi Germany surrenders to the Allies and the Soviets, but individual units continue to fight on the Eastern Front until May 9.

May 9–10, 1945 Soviet troops enter the camp on May 9 and take responsibility for caring for the prisoners from the International Red Cross on May 10. Around 30,000 prisoners are in the camp at the time of liberation.

Source: United States Holocaust Memorial Museum. "Theresienstadt Timeline." *Holocaust Encyclopedia.* https://www.ushmm.org/wlc/en/article.php?ModuleId=10007460. *Accessed on June 21, 2016.*

Index

Aachen 51, 68
abandoned 20, 45, 89, 95, 161, 173, 177, 205
abortion/abortionists 42, 43, 48, 127, 131, 132, 146, 147, 149
academia 74, 76, 99, 103, 105, 140
Adlerstein 99
admirers 44, 62, 72, 74, 77, 88, 94, 95, 156, 164
adolescence 73, 140
aggression 20, 33, 34, 103, 153
allies 19, 20, 33, 58, 92, 105, 129, 131, 205
allotments 159
alps, Bavarian 19
Altmann 3
altruism 52, 118
America 3, 115
ammunitions 62
Amsterdam 195
anesthetics 147
animals in camp 130
annexes 19, 83, 91, 93, 201
anthem 66, 198
antifascism 105
anti-Judaism 80, 190
anti-Nazism 20
anti-Semitism 19, 23, 50, 51, 78–80, 87, 125, 130, 137, 151, 169, 173, 174, 190
apartment 74, 150, 152, 154, 155, 160, 178
appeasement 20, 32, 33, 103, 117
April 25, 28, 167, 183, 204, 205
arguments 79, 137, 172, 173, 192
arms-gaining 117
army/army-in-exile 11, 18–21, 26, 27, 33, 46, 73, 91, 103–105, 110, 120, 133, 180
Arthur 11, 12, 18, 21, 29, 93, 102–117, 119, 121
artisan 29
artists 197–199

artwork 3
Aryans 171, 172, 178
ashes 62, 66, 73, 79, 194
assassination 92, 93, 111, 112
assimilation 102, 137, 151, 172, 173
attic 126, 195
attorney 3
August 40, 66, 95, 203
Auschwitz 11, 12, 18, 22–24, 26–31, 34, 35, 46, 55–57, 59, 62–64, 66, 68, 70, 113, 119, 120, 128, 133, 168, 180, 191, 196, 197, 199, 203, 204
Australia 177
Austria 3, 73, 88, 124, 201–204
Austro-Hungarians 37, 73, 75, 173, 201
authority 109, 146, 147, 157, 202–204
Avraham 37–40, 44–48

baby 40, 73, 124, 126–128, 133, 134, 149, 155–157
bachelor 87, 94
barbiturates 64, 68
barracks 54, 55, 61, 63–66, 71, 93, 112, 113, 124, 131, 163, 164, 166, 180, 182–184, 186, 190, 197
bathing 42, 147
battle 73, 104, 197
battlefield 26, 46, 57, 73, 129
beatings 21, 38, 65, 68, 153–157, 165, 196, 199
beauty 23, 70, 74, 77, 100, 101, 131, 163, 178, 183, 185
Bebouf 101
Beck 29, 30, 34, 99
bedbugs 130
Bedrich 199
beggar 187
begging 61, 63, 64, 95, 126, 144, 149, 153
Belarus 95, 96

207

Index

beliefs (believers) 5, 17, 25, 26, 31, 33, 35, 36, 41, 48, 50–52, 54, 59, 61, 62, 64, 65, 69, 76, 82, 87, 92, 100, 112, 114–117, 119, 122–127, 131–134, 137, 138, 141, 144, 151, 164, 167, 168, 170, 184, 185, 188, 189, 191, 194, 196
Belorussia 202
Belzec 35, 196
benefits 47, 48, 161
Berchtesgaden 19
Bergen-Belsen 166, 167, 195, 203
Berlin 99, 113, 202, 203, 205
Bialystok 54, 55, 66, 196, 203
biases 67, 79
bicycle (bike) 28, 110–112
bird, statue 197
birth (birthday) 140, 146, 155, 156
blacklisted 105
Blahovstina 95
blame 94, 138, 152, 157, 158, 198
blankets 156, 157, 165
bleeding 31, 43
Blockaelteste 64
blocks, camp 24, 31, 57, 61, 64, 68, 112, 133, 190
boasts 39, 102, 116, 141, 142, 145
body 40, 44, 46, 51–53, 63, 65, 66, 69, 70, 87, 95, 96, 145, 148, 153–157, 159, 166, 183, 194
Bohemia 19, 20, 67, 83, 91, 120, 132, 159, 172, 201–203
bookkeeping 62, 74
bordellos 145
boxcar 165, 166
boyfriend 11, 17, 18, 21, 29, 79, 115, 147, 148, 158, 159
boys 41, 52, 63–65, 74, 86, 102, 127, 128, 138, 140, 141, 145
bravery 18, 20, 26, 27, 31, 35, 55, 64, 70, 91, 151, 199
bread 83, 118, 179, 186, 187, 189
breakdown, nervous 181
bribes 46, 126
bride 72, 151
brigade 22, 26, 29
Brno 23, 202
Brundibár 135, 198
brutality 5, 68, 101, 116, 120, 121, 153, 156, 157, 167, 176, 190, 192
Buchenwald 205
buckets 95, 110
bullies 19, 33
bunk 23, 163, 164, 167, 182–184, 188
burghers 142
burns 56, 59, 63, 77, 114, 176

Bursa 175
businesses 40, 41, 74, 77, 79, 81, 88, 138, 147, 177, 192
businessman 150
butchery 42
butterflies 57
bystanders 80

calisthenics 61
camp-ghetto 201–205
camps 21, 22, 24, 32, 35, 45, 49, 59, 61, 67, 70, 84, 92, 94, 95, 99, 112, 120, 122–124, 126, 127, 129, 130, 132–134, 159, 163–165, 167–169, 172, 178–182, 189–194, 196, 199, 202, 203
captain 90
captors 181
capture 13, 55, 105, 111
car 18, 56, 79, 95, 96, 128
carbon monoxide 95
cards 21, 90, 94, 105–107, 178
careers 18, 19, 32, 41, 45, 51, 74, 77, 82, 98, 140
caregiver 125, 160, 203
Carpathian 38
Carpe Diem 40, 48
carriage 127, 128
cars 31, 55, 95, 96, 110, 114, 120, 133, 178
catacombs 28, 29, 115
Catholic 20, 151
cattle 18, 55, 95, 110, 114, 128, 133, 178
celebrities 199
cells 21, 105, 110, 113
cemetery 107
censorship 25, 59
census 23, 110
ceremony, wedding 43, 151
chairperson 202, 204
Chamberlain, Prime Minister 19, 20
chambers 22, 24, 46, 57, 60, 62, 63, 66, 68, 114, 115, 128, 168, 170, 194, 197
chance 3, 20, 27, 46, 48, 53, 69, 70, 80, 82, 88, 89, 93, 95, 97, 98, 115, 118, 119, 127, 128, 133, 162, 164, 169, 170, 173, 183, 196, 197, 199
Charles 72–74
chastity 147
Chelmno 35, 196
chemicals 17, 110
children 2, 7, 10, 13, 22, 24, 29, 40, 43, 51, 52, 54, 55, 57, 63, 66–71, 73, 78, 79, 87, 98–100, 102, 112, 118, 119, 123–136, 139, 140, 141, 143, 146, 147, 149, 154–157, 161, 164, 166, 168, 169–171, 172, 182, 184, 185, 187, 189, 198, 203

Index

chimneys 24, 56, 65–67
cholera 115
chorus 198
Christianity 78
cigarettes 81, 180, 183
citizens 33, 97, 103, 106, 108
city 19, 39, 40, 44, 51, 102, 115, 116, 120, 123, 201
civilian 83, 93, 120
co-chairperson 203, 204
coat 85, 110, 147, 186
cobbler, practical skill of 122
coconspirator 90
colonel 27, 28
commandant 21, 55, 60, 65, 115, 125, 179, 190, 202, 205
commandments 32, 173
commandos 22, 163, 166, 197
communist 21, 87, 88, 105, 116
community 39, 41, 44, 45, 47, 84, 85, 88, 90, 99, 102, 105, 107, 123, 124, 130, 138, 151, 159, 161
compassion 24, 130, 135
comrade 190
concentration camp 12, 21, 35, 45, 49, 54, 67, 68, 70, 84, 88, 89, 99, 108, 109, 112, 135, 159, 162, 164, 167, 172, 178, 180, 181, 189–191, 196, 202, 203, 205
condemnation 187
conferences 19, 20, 190, 202
confiscation 98, 107, 163, 178
conscience 6, 92, 119, 158
conspirators 29, 64, 105, 112
Constance, Switzerland 30
contagion 114, 120
coping 6, 7, 83, 90, 93, 118, 121, 125, 132, 145, 185
coreligionists 28, 34, 66, 110
corpses 60, 95, 167, 185
country 5, 19–21, 33, 38, 47, 73, 83, 103, 105, 117, 130, 138, 145, 159, 172, 173, 193
courage 2, 7, 10, 14, 35, 45, 52, 65, 70, 88, 104, 107, 108, 113, 120, 153, 199
courier 61, 62, 64
cousin 12, 72–74, 76, 77, 81, 85, 91, 93, 94, 96
cowardice 33, 82, 117
crematories 6, 57, 60–62, 66, 69, 194
crime 22, 26, 42, 51, 98, 116, 128, 129, 146, 147, 155, 170, 172, 190, 191
currency 26, 84, 127
Czech 10, 11, 18–21, 23, 24, 27, 31, 33, 54, 57–60, 62, 64, 66, 69, 79, 80, 85, 91–93, 102, 104, 107, 108, 111, 112, 117, 124, 137, 138, 151, 162, 169, 172–174, 178, 179, 201, 202, 205
Czechoslovakia 19, 20, 33, 39, 50, 52, 75, 76, 81–83, 86, 103, 105, 116, 123, 137, 138, 173, 177, 192
Czechoslovakian 19, 20, 102–105, 110, 111, 117, 118, 132, 172, 173, 192

dad 80–82, 150, 152
daladier 19
daughter 41, 73–75, 90, 97, 137, 138, 140, 142, 143, 145, 148–151, 155–157, 161, 168, 171, 173–175, 178, 180, 181, 184–186, 193
decency 3, 31, 48, 116, 119, 120, 159, 182, 183
dehumanization 101, 194
democracy 20, 21, 103, 116
deportations/deportees 1, 12, 18, 22–26, 29, 39, 40, 44, 46, 54, 56, 67, 82, 84, 88–91, 93, 97, 99, 100, 107, 110, 112–114, 120, 127–130, 132–134, 159–162, 164, 168–170, 172, 178–180, 186, 187, 189, 193, 198, 202–204
destiny 6, 24, 37, 55, 57, 62, 64, 80, 143, 161, 166, 173, 175, 186
diary 11, 125–127, 130, 133, 195, 196
dictator 20, 34, 36, 205
disease 43, 112, 114, 120, 147
divorce 171
doctor 24, 29, 34, 43, 59, 64, 94, 99, 100, 109, 114, 127, 146, 148, 154, 168, 182
document 12, 21, 28, 30, 46, 58, 88, 106, 107, 109, 195, 199
Dominican 193
double-cross 111
drawings 135, 198, 199
dress, blue polka-dot 12, 183–185, 187, 188, 191
duty 12, 23, 46, 62, 66, 74, 90, 96, 104, 108, 116, 120, 138–140, 161, 171, 182, 196, 198
dying 30, 43, 55, 63, 64, 97, 108, 110, 115, 118, 127, 165, 167, 185, 187–189, 191, 199

East 11, 12, 17, 18, 20, 22, 24, 34, 38, 40, 44, 45, 55, 70, 73, 86, 91–93, 104, 112, 113, 116, 124, 129, 132, 159, 164, 178–180, 182, 186, 193, 202, 203, 205
Edelstein 22, 113, 124, 125, 202, 203
Edmund 175–178, 180–182, 185, 192
education 38, 48, 51, 71, 77, 85, 98, 122, 125, 134, 145, 146, 151, 152, 161, 169, 176
educator 10, 11, 22, 52, 66, 69, 125, 128, 131, 134, 135, 198
Egon 12, 54, 69, 70, 123, 126

209

Index

Eichmann 201–203
Einsatz-gruppen 196
elderly 96, 126, 140, 155, 187
elders, Jewish 22, 30, 31, 34, 77, 94, 99, 100, 113, 119, 124, 125, 128, 147, 163, 179, 190, 202–205
emigration 39, 177, 201
Emperor 73, 198, 201
Empress 201
England 20, 33, 104
enlistment 91, 104
epidemic 114, 115, 120, 166
Eppstein 113, 203, 204
escapes/escapees 1–3, 11, 18, 24, 26–30, 34, 35, 38, 44, 48, 52, 54, 62, 63, 86, 89–92, 95, 101, 113–115, 146, 148, 168, 171, 177, 196
ethics 13, 32, 70, 79, 117–119, 121, 134
eugenics 126
Europeans 5, 6, 11, 58, 103, 116, 117, 137, 168, 173, 177, 202
Eva 72, 80, 82
evacuated 205
evil 9, 27, 104, 140, 155, 178
excrement 43, 95, 120, 166
execution 2, 25, 27, 31, 47, 54, 65, 91, 93, 96
experiments 126
extermination 25, 85, 126
extinction 64

factory 60, 66, 110, 166, 190, 197
family-like unit 57
father 20, 38, 40, 73–77, 80–83, 102–104, 123, 124, 138–140, 146, 148–150, 152, 153, 156, 159, 168, 169, 175, 181, 188
fatherland 23, 108, 114
fear 30, 43, 56, 83, 108, 109, 114, 120, 129, 130, 142, 151–154, 157, 159, 194
February 116, 204
felons 28, 190
female 108, 126, 140
femininity 23, 88
femme fatale 53, 85
fever 43, 93, 114, 167, 181, 182
fiancée 81, 89, 94
fighters 52, 59, 111
fighting 30, 31, 49, 104, 105, 113, 120, 126, 127, 167, 183, 189, 197, 199
finances 27, 74, 89, 138, 139, 150, 152, 157
firearms 18, 31, 56, 113
Fleischman, Karel 199
force 49, 60, 83, 104, 111, 121, 157, 183
forgiveness 63
fortress 18, 21, 29, 31, 115, 178, 179, 198

fortune 27, 90, 114, 162
France 33
Frances 175–179, 181–185, 187–189, 191
Frank 141–145, 149, 150, 152–155, 157, 161, 195, 196
Fredy 11–12, 22–25, 51–57, 59–71, 128
freedom 35, 41, 59, 82, 85, 104, 105, 125, 152, 153, 159, 167, 197
friends 10–12, 18, 25, 26, 28, 29, 32, 40, 51, 52, 54, 58, 66, 68, 70, 79, 93, 100, 102, 111, 114, 116, 120, 124, 138, 143, 153, 156, 158, 175, 177, 182

garrison 201
gassing 1, 24, 26, 28–30, 32, 34, 35, 46, 59–61, 66, 69, 115, 196
gate 28, 162
Geheime 84, 123
Gehenna 95
gendarme 112, 118, 135, 179, 183, 205
generation 6, 41, 73, 121, 137, 147
genocide 9, 14, 30, 190, 196, 197
gentile 25, 30, 50, 78, 81, 85, 89, 93, 124, 137, 159–161, 171, 172, 178
George 158, 160–163, 165–168
Germans 19, 20, 25, 33, 35, 39, 44, 47, 59, 60, 62, 65, 68, 69, 83–85, 89, 92, 94, 98–101, 112, 119, 120, 126, 127, 129, 130, 132, 134, 135, 159, 171, 179, 189, 204
Germany 5, 19, 23, 30, 33, 51–53, 67–69, 76, 80, 82, 103, 108, 121, 124, 125, 134, 158, 173, 201, 203, 205
Gestapo 27, 84, 90, 95, 123, 124, 160, 201
ghetto 1, 2, 10, 12, 159, 196, 202, 203
girlfriend 30, 81, 85
girls 41, 42, 52, 53, 74, 76, 77, 88, 102, 138, 140–144, 149, 158, 175–178, 180, 186
God 38, 48, 57, 64, 65, 79, 104, 114, 126, 164, 185, 186, 198
Gonda 12, 71, 123–131, 133–135
goods 80, 84, 110, 197
government 3, 20, 21, 50, 75, 92, 103, 159, 170, 173, 202
grand Mufti 66
grandchildren 44, 150, 156
granddaughter 73, 75, 97
grandmother 73–75, 77, 83, 88, 89, 91–93, 97, 158
grandparents 157, 161, 168, 169
Greta 126–128
groom 41, 72, 150, 151
Gross-rosen 205
guardian 74
guards 96, 113

Index

Haas, Leo 199
Hachscharot 123
half-breed 81, 160
half-Jews 159
Hamburg 113
Hanna 12, 137–145, 147–171, 173, 174
happiness 37, 45, 46, 48, 51, 65, 72, 73, 77, 81, 98, 102, 127, 140, 144, 151, 154–157, 162, 172, 175, 181, 185
Hapsburg 37
Hatikvah 66
hatred 6, 7, 18, 36, 38, 52, 54, 79, 80, 92, 108, 122, 129, 132, 141, 158, 164, 168, 173, 180
headquarters 27, 84, 109
heads, shaved 57, 166
health 25, 29, 48, 51, 112, 114, 150, 155, 166, 182, 183, 188
heartbreak 73, 78, 90, 91, 164
Heidebreck 65, 66
heim 124, 125, 127
heroes 2, 52, 71, 92, 117, 118, 121, 135, 144, 198
Heydrich 92, 111, 112, 201, 202
hiding 11, 18, 27, 29, 31, 94, 115, 179, 183, 195
Hilda 37, 40–46, 48
Hirsh 22, 52, 128
Hitler 19, 20, 68, 103, 111, 112, 114, 117, 125, 128, 191, 205
hoarding 60
Holocaust 1, 2, 5–7, 9–11, 13, 46, 48, 102, 116, 195, 196, 202, 205
Holzer 26, 29
homosexuality 53, 67
hopefulness 125, 134
hopelessness 44
hospital 12, 18, 43, 48, 93, 115, 154–157, 181, 182
Hudal 115
humanity 3, 6, 13, 32, 36, 51, 66, 68, 87, 128, 130, 170, 187, 191, 194, 199
humiliation 20, 33, 38, 73, 105, 151, 153, 180
Hundertschaft 112
Hungarian 204
hunger 23, 54, 57, 71, 75, 83, 126, 131, 163, 164, 180, 187, 198, 199
husband 11, 17, 46, 72, 73, 139, 143, 150, 152–154, 156, 171, 172, 175, 186
hygiene 101, 130, 180

identification 89, 90, 106, 107, 110, 114
identity cards, counterfeit 105, 106
immigration 31, 66, 124
in-laws 43, 150, 151, 162

incarceration 12, 17, 21, 24, 54, 105, 147, 187
infection 114, 120, 147, 167
infestation 130, 159
inmate 18, 22–25, 28, 31, 55–60, 62, 63, 65, 66, 88, 93, 95, 96, 101, 110, 113–115, 120, 124–128, 130, 133, 160, 162–165, 167, 178–182, 185–187, 189–192, 195–198
innocents 14, 52, 59, 63, 73, 128–131, 133, 134, 143, 171, 195
insecticide 115
inspiration 22, 51, 67, 68, 123, 131, 134, 178, 197, 199
instinct 146, 199
institutions 48, 146, 192
intellectual/intelligentsia 36, 51, 67, 70, 75, 80, 85, 100, 122, 132, 134, 168, 169, 176
intentions 13, 58, 158
intermarriages 78–81, 151, 172, 173
interrogation 21, 27, 31, 106
intimate 14, 76, 143, 149
israel 11, 31, 78

Jacob 22, 99, 124, 125, 202, 203
jail 21, 52, 54, 56, 90
January 1, 22, 46, 97, 113, 168, 172, 202, 203
Jeannie 157–162, 168, 169, 171
jeopardy 21, 45, 93, 177
Jeremiah, Prophet 63
Jerusalem 66
Jew-baiting 137
Jew-Gentile 171
"Jewish Ramp" 24, 29, 56, 114
Jewishness 5, 6, 25, 79, 81, 153, 172
Joseph 201
Judaism 54, 78, 87, 102, 137, 173
Judenaelteste 113
Judenrat 34, 100, 110, 112, 113, 118, 179, 186, 193
July 1, 93, 203
June 26, 110–113, 202–205
justice 10, 111, 115, 151, 198
justification 108, 187, 192

Kaddish 66
Kapo 56, 190, 192
Karel 41–46, 198, 199
Kashrut 102
Katowitz 27
Kavalirka 97
kids 25, 52, 53, 55, 57, 66, 76, 78, 119, 124, 126, 131, 139, 198

INDEX

Kien, Peter 199
kill/killers/killings 30, 38, 56, 58, 60, 62, 70, 84, 95, 97, 108, 111, 114, 125, 127, 134, 147, 153, 155, 156, 158, 191, 194, 198, 199, 202
kindness 74, 168
King David 52
kitchen 43, 147, 150
Klein 198
knowledge 10, 13, 41, 42, 97, 99, 115, 119, 123, 125, 128, 131, 133, 142, 145, 168, 181
Kovner, Abba 2
Kraemer, Salo 110
Kraus, Bella 107
Kreta 55, 66

labor 24, 32, 54, 57, 60, 87, 92, 107, 110, 112, 124, 154, 165, 166, 168, 180, 196
Latvia 202
laughter 74, 76, 77, 160, 176, 198
laws 25, 39, 80, 102, 128, 147, 159, 170–172, 178, 190
leader 12, 23, 29, 60, 61, 64, 68, 69, 89, 99, 103, 107, 123, 181, 196, 202, 204
leadership 7, 19, 20, 51, 61, 67, 68, 99, 100, 127, 180, 188
Lederer 11, 17–23, 25–29, 31–35, 49, 113, 196
Leitmeritz 201, 205
Leo 29, 30, 99, 113, 199, 204, 205
letters 30, 58, 59
Ležáky 93, 112
liberation 31, 49, 104, 115, 116, 119, 167, 191, 205
lice 166
Lidice 93, 112
lifestyle 34, 54, 67–70, 79, 101, 189
Lithuanian 95
Litomerice 201
Lotte 175–189, 191–193
lovers 25, 37, 39, 41, 43, 45, 47, 49, 80, 87, 141–144, 148, 150, 161, 164, 172
loyalty 78, 104, 173, 177
Lublin 44
luck 21, 35, 55, 83, 100, 112, 129, 155, 157, 164, 168, 182, 192
luggage 96, 161–163, 198

Magdeburg 112, 163, 186
Majdanek 35, 197
male 72, 74, 104, 108, 145, 163, 181
malnutrition 57, 126, 129, 131, 134, 168
Maly 12, 95, 100
marriage 1, 10, 12, 18, 32, 40–44, 48, 72–74, 77–82, 88, 97, 98, 138, 139, 142, 143, 145, 146, 149, 151, 152, 155, 157, 158, 170–172, 175–177
massacre 61, 63, 113
matrimony 146
Mclaughlin, Jeff 9–14, 195
meaning (significance) 10, 20, 40, 58, 113, 134, 167, 197, 198
medications 103, 107–110, 118, 119, 179, 181–183, 188
memory 2, 6, 7, 39, 126
Mengele 29, 59, 114, 168
menstruation 126
mercilessness 63, 111
midwife 154–156
Milada 12, 72–77, 79–101
minister 19, 20, 196
ministry 21, 105, 106
minority 19, 44, 78, 80, 83, 92, 99, 138, 159, 173, 174, 203
Minsk 95, 202, 203
miracle 6, 21, 26, 29, 40, 57, 113, 114, 129, 167, 183
Miriam 72, 73, 75, 89–91, 93, 95, 97
Mischling 172
Mislovitz 26
mistress 101, 139, 175, 177
money 38, 42, 47, 111, 145–147, 159, 161, 192, 193
Monsignor Hudal 115
morale 22, 197, 198
morality 13, 20, 42, 68, 99, 100, 116, 143, 148, 171, 188, 189, 191, 192, 199
Moravia 20, 23, 40, 67, 83, 102, 120, 123, 132, 159, 172, 201–203
Moravska 40, 102
morganatic 80
mother 2, 17, 18, 23, 24, 27, 30, 31, 35, 41, 48, 73–77, 81, 83, 87–92, 94, 95, 98–100, 104, 124, 127, 134, 138–143, 148, 149, 154, 159–161, 169, 171, 173, 174, 178, 184, 186–188, 193, 201
motivation 13, 32, 34, 47, 51, 111, 117, 118, 126, 170
motorbike 31, 39, 45, 47, 84, 85, 90
mountain 31, 33, 103, 201
mourning 46, 78, 79, 97, 128, 185
Mufti 66
Munich 20, 201
munitions 60, 66, 166, 197
Munkacs 38
Muntz 12
murder 1, 2, 6, 9, 10, 14, 17, 23, 29, 30, 32, 35, 50, 56, 60, 69, 70, 92, 96, 100, 101, 111, 112, 115, 129, 131, 133, 135, 154, 186, 190, 191, 196, 197, 199, 203

Index

Murmelstein 203–205
museum 125, 134, 199, 205
musicians 198
Musselmen 167
mutiny 64, 66

naïveté 106, 117, 124, 125, 137, 142, 143, 170
nationalism 79, 117
nationality 19, 34, 92, 137, 173, 174
necessities 103, 106, 107, 204
negotiations 19, 58, 59, 204
Netherlands 203
Neumann, Renée 23
newlyweds 44, 78, 150
news 42, 57–59, 73, 77, 93, 127, 148, 149, 156, 167
newspapers 2
Nisko camp 44
non-Jews 102, 171, 172, 174, 190
normality 32, 44, 49, 65, 70, 77, 116, 122, 125, 129, 132, 134, 135, 165, 170, 182, 188, 192, 194
Normandy 129
Nuremberg racial laws 80, 159
nurse 18, 66
nurseries 98, 156

objectification 101
obligations 157
observances 79, 151, 173
obstacles 91
obstetricians 132
occupation/occupiers 12, 19–21, 39, 44, 47, 67, 84, 92, 100, 105–107, 111, 130, 132, 159, 161, 171, 172, 174, 177, 192
October 44, 46, 66, 113, 127, 128, 201–204
officers 11, 18–21, 23–28, 54, 70, 73, 88–90, 103, 104, 108, 109, 113, 130, 138, 162, 165, 166, 179, 192
offices 39, 44, 45, 74, 81, 84, 85, 90, 99, 105, 106, 109, 112, 123, 148, 151, 161, 201
official/official-appearing 20, 21, 74, 84, 92, 105–107, 115, 139, 161, 163, 202
offspring 41, 53, 81, 127, 145, 147, 159, 173, 182
opiates 118
opportunists 3, 85, 121, 177
oppressors/oppression 3, 7, 111, 116, 120
optimism/optimist 17, 51, 53, 57, 74, 127, 130, 131, 133
Oranienburg 203
ordinances 12, 87
orphanages/orphans 54, 66, 124, 146, 149, 185

Oskar 49
Ostrava 40, 42, 44, 102
ovulation 126
owners 1, 40, 47, 50, 79, 91, 98, 106, 108–111, 123, 130, 133, 142, 161, 175

packages 108–110
pail 55, 95
pain 21, 33, 43, 49, 50, 58, 60, 63–65, 67, 73, 79, 82, 85, 118, 121, 128, 132, 145, 148, 151, 154, 156–158, 160, 161, 179, 181, 184, 186, 188, 191, 192
painkillers 188
painlessness 57, 68, 132, 185
painters/paintings 84, 199
Palestine 39, 66, 68, 70, 89, 91, 124
panic 31, 82, 89, 92, 93, 115, 153, 157
partisans 2, 31
passages 18, 28, 31, 113
password 27
patients 18, 182
patriot 104, 106
penalties 81, 128
perpetrators 120, 196
persecution 35, 45, 76, 80, 81, 98, 101, 104, 171, 172, 176, 196
personality 72, 84, 106, 152, 194
Pestek 23, 25–28, 30–32, 34–36, 49
pharmacy 103, 105, 109
philosophy/philosopher 5, 9, 13, 41, 79, 99, 101, 113, 119, 120, 204
physician 24, 42, 43, 63, 64, 66, 114, 120, 146, 148, 149, 181, 182
Pilsen 19, 28, 30
pogroms 78, 138
poison 17, 63, 92, 95, 97, 108, 168
Poland/Polish 26, 40, 44, 66, 91, 93, 124, 173, 178, 203
police 84, 123, 162, 202, 203
politics/politicians 19, 20, 21, 38, 79, 103, 105, 158, 159
polizei 190
possession 50, 106, 127, 188, 191
possessions 39, 159, 172
postcards 25, 58, 59, 160, 162
postdating 25, 59
Prague 12, 20, 21, 25, 28, 30, 38, 39, 44–46, 50, 52–54, 67, 74, 75, 79, 81, 83–85, 88, 89, 91–93, 95, 97, 99, 103, 109–112, 115, 123, 124, 132, 134, 141, 142, 145, 151, 155, 160–162, 165, 168, 172, 175, 178, 186, 201, 202, 205
pram 127, 128, 133
prayer 28, 57, 73, 94, 95, 154, 165
Prchala 104

pregnancy/pregnant 42, 43, 48, 73, 87, 126, 127, 131–134, 146, 147, 149, 152, 153, 155
prejudices 6, 19, 67, 79, 176
president 92, 196
priest 20, 83
principles 32, 70, 143
prisoners 21, 25, 28, 30, 32, 54, 58, 59, 66, 69, 95, 125, 163, 190, 192, 198, 203–205
privations 38, 87
privileges 24, 25, 39, 47, 48, 61, 65, 84, 85, 119, 159, 161, 186, 192
prohibition 55, 80, 114, 135, 146, 173, 178, 190
promiscuity 142, 146, 148, 149
propaganda 174, 199, 202
protectorate 20, 31, 39, 67, 83, 84, 107, 108, 120, 132, 159, 160, 201–203
protocols 21, 34, 146
punishment 22, 28, 31, 35, 54, 55, 68, 77, 96, 101, 113, 116, 120, 128, 153, 191

qualities 51, 67, 68, 80, 81, 86, 129, 131, 146, 180, 189
quarantines 115
quarters 54, 124, 166, 193
quasi-independent 20
quasi-mayor 124

Rabbi 29, 30, 34, 43, 99, 113
race 5, 36, 128
racism 5, 151
Rahm, Karl 115, 205
railway/railroads 28, 30, 31, 91, 120
rationalization 161, 187
rations 23, 45, 54, 62, 119, 125, 126, 159, 160, 166, 179, 181, 193
Ravensbrück 203
recklessness 107, 143, 150, 161, 164
Redlich 12, 54, 69, 123, 126
registrar 61, 63, 64
registration 94, 110, 111
Reinhard 92, 93, 111, 201
relocation 65, 84, 162
Rena 181, 186
Renée 23–27, 30, 31, 34, 35, 49
republic 10, 19, 20, 40, 75, 107, 116, 132, 159, 172–174, 193
resettlement 18, 45, 123, 124, 178
resistance 1–3, 12, 20–22, 25, 28, 30, 31, 58–61, 63, 64, 92, 100, 104–106, 110, 112, 113, 116, 117, 140, 143, 195, 196, 199
responsibility 13, 18, 23, 73, 75, 83, 88, 89, 98, 99, 104–106, 149, 150, 152, 157, 158, 171, 189, 190, 193, 202, 203, 205

restrictions 12, 25, 84, 103, 159, 161, 173, 174
reunification 19, 25, 46, 160–162, 164, 165, 170
revolt 60, 66
rights 80, 157, 159, 190
rituals 78, 79, 96
Romania 23, 89
roomette 22, 23, 25, 26
Roosevelt, President 196
Rottenfuehrer 25
rumors 18, 24, 25, 31, 54, 55, 57–59, 65, 66, 76, 85, 92, 115, 162, 186
Russia/Russian 23, 30, 84, 95, 104, 114, 115, 129, 133, 168
Ruthenia 20, 37, 38, 85, 88

sabotage 11, 12, 21–23, 104, 105, 107, 108, 110, 113, 197, 198
Schaechter 198
scheme 30, 46, 64, 88, 106, 109, 115, 161, 192
Schiff, Vera 1–3, 5–7, 9–11, 195–199
Schindler, Oskar 49
Schoenberg, E. Randol 1–3
school 38, 40, 41, 51, 52, 74, 103, 124, 125, 134, 140, 141, 145, 169, 176
Schwenk, Karel 198
secrets/secrecy 12, 22, 28, 29, 39, 53, 61, 66, 105, 107, 108, 110, 114, 116, 123, 143–145, 147, 183
selection 22, 24, 29, 57, 59, 93, 114, 168, 196
self-confidence 37, 44, 141
self-denial 78
self-discipline 54, 69, 170
self-esteem 180
self-interest 34, 47
self-preservation 34
self-respect 142, 186
selfishness 3, 161, 180, 185, 187, 192
selflessness 51, 71, 127
sewing 75, 83, 118
sex/sexual 25, 41, 48, 53, 67, 76, 80, 86, 88, 106, 124, 138, 140, 142–147, 150, 172, 194
Shiva 79
Shoah 21
shooting/shootout 56, 63, 111
shortages 23, 86, 125, 180
showers 22, 69, 166
siblings 45, 71, 187
sick/sickness/sickroom 24, 42, 57, 71, 110, 112, 114, 118, 119, 129, 131, 144, 182, 183, 188, 198

Index

Sieche 186
Siegfried 202
Siegmund 1
Sigi 84–92, 95, 97, 98
sisters 1, 2, 12, 72, 74, 75, 102, 104, 118, 140, 153, 160, 162, 168, 176, 179, 182–185, 188, 189, 191, 192
Slavek 11, 18–23, 26–32, 34, 35, 49, 113; *see also* Lederer
Slovakia/Slovak-Hungarians 20, 31, 33, 62, 64, 83, 89–91, 204
smoke 24, 56, 57
smoking 22, 26
smuggling 12, 21, 22, 60, 62, 66, 84, 96, 100, 101, 112, 118, 179, 197
Sobibor 35
socialites 143, 177, 180
soldiers 22, 33, 60, 63, 108, 111, 167
son-in-law 150, 152, 157
Sonder-Behandlung 24, 59
Sonderkommando 60–64, 66, 196
Soviets 26, 46, 116, 120, 205
Sperre 65
sports 52, 102, 138, 140
SS 23, 25, 26, 30, 31, 46, 55, 56, 61–63, 65, 70, 88–91, 93, 95, 96, 108–110, 112, 130, 162, 165, 166, 179, 202–205
Staatspolizei (Gestapo) 84, 123
starvation 10, 23, 88, 95, 118, 159, 166, 187, 194, 198
stench 42, 56, 95, 165, 180
sterilizer 115
Stresovice 109
students 6, 38, 40, 74, 76, 77, 79, 85, 103, 138, 195, 196
studies 38, 67, 70, 88, 103, 123, 135
Sub-Carpathian 20, 37
subhuman 17, 35, 101, 107, 129, 180
Sudetenland 19, 20, 33, 103, 117, 201, 203
suffering 17, 21, 23, 25, 26, 30, 49, 52, 63, 65, 73, 93, 96, 97, 110, 112, 116, 120, 127, 128, 132, 141, 148, 153, 154, 156, 157, 174, 180, 185–187, 198
suffocation 30, 63, 97
suicide 39, 132, 205
superstitions 38, 108
supervision 27, 56, 93, 95, 109, 124, 141, 162, 190
supplies 107, 108, 115, 119, 126, 181, 182, 197
survival 1, 3, 6, 10, 12, 17, 18, 21, 31, 32, 34, 43, 46, 48, 54, 70, 87, 88, 94, 97, 98, 107, 113, 116, 117, 118, 119, 125–127, 129–131, 133, 147, 165, 167, 170, 180, 185–187, 191, 192, 193, 199, 202–204

survivor 2, 6, 9, 10, 12, 13, 48, 49, 191, 192, 195, 196
suspicion 59, 62, 105, 164
Švejk, Good Soldier 33
Switzerland 176, 204
symbols 39, 133, 168
synagogue 107–109, 112

taboos 41, 139, 145, 172
Tarjan 94, 100
teacher 29, 32, 52, 54, 57, 61, 67, 71, 111, 123–126, 129, 131, 134, 135, 140, 152, 176, 198
teenager 9, 74–76, 102, 124, 125, 141, 144, 158, 176, 178, 191
Terezin 107, 201
terror 3, 6, 55, 89, 105, 107, 117, 153, 169, 170
theologian 204
Tiso, Father 20, 83
Torah 32
torment/tormentor 50, 63, 64, 68, 69, 87, 91, 92, 126, 132, 154, 156, 185, 190, 191
torture 10, 21, 31, 50, 68, 105, 167, 196, 197, 199
trains 12, 17, 28, 30, 31, 34, 55, 56, 90, 91, 93, 110, 120, 128, 162, 165, 178, 196, 203; boarding 1, 17, 89, 90, 107, 114, 128, 146, 155, 178
transport 1, 21–24, 26, 28, 30, 34, 46, 55, 57, 58, 60, 66, 69, 90, 91, 93–97, 107, 110, 114, 119, 120, 124, 128, 162, 164, 166, 170, 179, 182, 202–204
treatment 24, 43, 59, 190
Treblinka 1, 196
trimester 127, 132, 152
Tucholsky, Kurt 97
Turek 102
typhus 115, 166, 167

Ukrainian 93
underground 12, 18, 20–22, 24, 28, 29, 31, 58, 59, 61, 62, 68, 105, 107, 110, 111, 113, 116, 118, 196, 197, 204
Ungar 199
university 18, 74, 76, 81, 85, 103
uprising 2, 60, 68, 121, 196

valuables 84, 87, 91, 95, 96, 100, 101, 118, 127
values 41, 116, 131, 138, 151, 170–173, 194
Vatican 115
Veletrzni Hall 178
vermin 54, 130, 166, 180

victims 1–3, 7, 10, 14, 34, 35, 56, 96, 111, 116, 128, 147, 170, 195, 199
Victor 23, 26–28, 31
Vienna 1, 202, 203
Vilna 2
virgin 65, 76, 149
Viteslav 11, 18, 19, 196
volunteer 25, 160, 163, 164, 170, 174
Von 101
Vrba, Rudolf 61, 196

Waffen 205
Wannsee 190, 202
warehouse 75, 107, 108, 111, 112
Warsaw 2, 196
wartime 25, 46, 59, 187
weakness 24, 33, 52, 57, 64, 71, 85, 86, 90, 100, 101, 149, 167
weapons 22, 30, 60
wedding 41, 42, 72, 73, 94, 143, 146, 149–151
wedlock 143, 149
Wehrmacht 23, 26, 27, 205
Westerbork 203

widow 1, 74, 75, 90
Wiesel 196
wife 1, 12, 44, 73, 79, 81, 126, 134, 139, 155, 156, 180, 184
willingness 13, 18, 42, 45, 78, 79, 89, 92, 94, 106, 120, 121, 139, 158, 171, 193, 199
wisdom 11, 55, 138, 145
witnesses 7, 11, 60, 76, 95, 96, 190
workers 12, 88, 111, 179, 180
worry 26, 42, 43, 52, 55, 77, 78, 93, 113, 114, 130, 148, 159, 166
wounds 86, 92
writing 5, 6, 9, 11, 13, 25, 54, 58, 59, 69, 71, 108, 109, 125, 131, 134, 135, 157, 176, 195, 196

youngsters 52–55, 57, 145, 179
youth 12, 41, 48, 51–53, 123–126, 146, 147, 198

Zeisl, Kamilla, and Siegmund 1
Zentralstelle 39, 45
Zionism 38, 68, 70, 99, 102, 123, 124, 202
Zyklon 63, 115, 128

www.ingramcontent.com/pod-product-compliance
Ingram Content Group UK Ltd.
Pitfield, Milton Keynes, MK11 3LW, UK
UKHW041956140426
5217IPUK00015B/824